THE CHINESE PATH AND PHILOSOPHY

THE CHINESE PATH AND PHILOSOPHY

YAN YILONG

UNICORN

Published in association with CNPIEC by Unicorn
an imprint of Unicorn Publishing Group, 2022
Charleston Studio
Meadow Business Centre
Lewes BN8 5RW

www.unicornpublishing.org

All rights reserved. No part of this publication may be reproduced, stored in or introduced into a retrieval system, or transmitted, in any form or by any means (electronic, mechanical, photocopying, recording or otherwise), without the prior written permission of the copyright holder and the above publisher of this book.

Every effort has been made to trace copyright holders and to obtain their permission for the use of copyrighted material. The publisher apologises for any errors or omissions and would be grateful to be notified of any corrections that should be incorporated in future reprints or editions of this book.

© Yan Yilong

Translators: Joshua Gong, Mengdie Sun
Editor: Katrina Jia
Proofreaders: Dmitry Kuleshov, Tong Xiaohua
Typesetting: Vivian Head

Originally published by China Fangzheng Press

10 9 8 7 6 5 4 3 2 1

ISBN 978-1-914414-93-0

Printed in the UK

TABLE OF CONTENTS

INTRODUCTION:
The Chinese Philosophy of the Chinese Path ... 9
1. Unprecedented miracle of development ... 9
2. China's practical innovation calls for theoretical innovation ... 10
3. A new economic road that integrates socialism and market economy ... 12
4. A new political path that is concentrated, efficient and lively ... 17
5. A new way of 'The World is Equally Shared by All' ... 20
6. A new approach to globalisation with 'communism' ... 23
7. New order of human society ... 27

PART 1   THE METHODOLOGY OF CHINESE DISCOURSE

CHAPTER 1   China's Great Rejuvenation Calls for the Chinese School ... 32

CHAPTER 2   'One Base and Three Uses' Construction of the Chinese Discourse System ... 39
1. From theory as base to practice as base ... 41
2. What is 'unify the three traditions'? ... 45
3. Practice-ism research methodology ... 47
4. Some extended discussions ... 51

PART 2   CHINA'S ECONOMIC MODEL

CHAPTER 3   Overall Knowledge Application Mechanisms: Understand the Five-Year Plan Under the Market Economy ... 58
1. Has the national planning system failed? ... 58
2. A new type of national planning: a five-year plan using holistic knowledge ... 62
3. Challenges facing national planning ... 71

CHAPTER 4   Five-Year Plan: A National-Target Governance System ... 75
1. Promise must be kept and action must be fruitful ... 75
2. Institutional safeguard for management by objectives ... 78
3. Three mechanisms of governance-by-objectives system ... 82
4. Challenges of the governance-by-objectives system ... 89

CHAPTER 5 Construction of a Minsheng State in the New Era 95
    1. Building a Minsheng state 95
    2. Minsheng state versus welfare state 99
    3. Imbalance between people's well-being and economic development 107
    4. Promoting the construction of an all-round and all-cycle Minsheng state 110

CHAPTER 6 Dealing with Insufficient Effective Demand with New Demand Management 114
    1. The fundamental challenge to China's economic development lies in the lack of effective demand 114
    2. The 'six carriages' on the demand side and new demand management 118
    3. Dealing with the lack of effective demand with new demand management 121

PART 3 CHINESE POLITICAL SYSTEM

CHAPTER 7 Comparison of Chinese and American Political Systems: 'Seven divisions of power' versus 'Separation of three powers' 130
    1. China's 'Seven divisions of power' political system 132
    2. Division of labour and coordination versus division of power and checks and balances 137
    3. Competitive selection versus competitive election 141
    4. Cumulative adjustment versus swing adjustment 144

CHAPTER 8 Collective Wisdom Decision-Making System 149
    1. Collective wisdom decision-making model 149
    2. Historical evolution of decision-making 151
    3. Decision-making process 152
    4. Characteristics of collective wisdom decision-making model . 155

PART 4 CHINESE GOVERNANCE MODEL

CHAPTER 9 The World is Equally Shared by All – Traditional Concept of Good Governance 160
    1. The paradigm of 'The World is Equally Shared by All' 161
    2. The world is the master, the ruler is the guest 166
    3. Integrate feudalism in the system of prefectures and counties 171

    4. Selecting and appointing the talented 175
    5. Morality is the mainstay, while punishment is auxiliary; Ruling with rituals and laws combined 181
    6. Regarding the central area as the foundation for taking care of the world 186
    7. 'The World is Equally Shared by All' and contemporary good governance 189

CHAPTER 10 The Leadership of the Communist Party of China and the Chinese Version of Good Governance 195
    1. The diamond model of the Chinese version of good governance 195
    2. The Avant-Garde Party 197
    3. Party leadership and the well-functioning government 201
    4. The Party's leadership and the beneficial market 206
    5. Party leadership and organic society 210

PART 5 CHINA AND THE WORLD

CHAPTER 11 Where the World Is Going: The New Order of 'contact of two extremes' 218
    1. The debate on the changing trend of the international pattern after the Cold War 219
    2. Introduction of the concept of 'contact of two extremes' . . . 222
    3. The long-term weakening of U.S. hegemony and the formation of the international pattern of 'two poles and multiple powers' 225
    4. China's dual role in the existing global order 233
    5. The long-term grand strategic competition between China and the United States 235
    6. 'Connected two poles': The new global order 239

CHAPTER 12 China's 'Three Circle Theory' and the New Strategic Opportunity Period 247
    1. Framework: China's 'Three Circles Theory' of strategic management 247
    2. Review: Three periods of strategic opportunities since the founding of New China 252
    3. Changes: The third strategic opportunity period closes 258
    4. The right time: The general trend of the world in the new era 260

     5. Geographical advantage: domestic conditions in the new era 264
     6. Risks: New Age strategic traps 266
     7. Harmony among the people: grand strategy to create the fourth strategic opportunity period 268

CHAPTER 13 **Communitism: A New Paradigm for International Relations in the 21st Century** 273
     1. Universal security concept versus the balance of power security concept, collective security concept 274
     2. The concept of common development versus zero-sum game, the concept of free development 278
     3. Views on the theory of blending of civilisations versus theory on clash of civilisations in multiculturalism 280
     4. Partnership versus alliance 281

CHAPTER 14 **'One Belt One Road' and Geo-Development Political Economy Exploration** 286
     1. Building a big platform for geopolitical development 287
     2. Building a new order of geopolitical development 293

Postscript 300

INTRODUCTION
The Chinese Philosophy of the Chinese Path

We should move faster to establish our own discourse and narrative, interpret China's practice with China's theory, and enrich China's theory with China's practice. We should create new concepts, domains and expressions that are accessible to an international audience, and present panoramic and distinctive stories of China and its culture.

– Xi Jinping made these remarks when addressing the 30th group study session of the Political Bureau of the 19th CPC Central Committee (31 May, 2021)

1. Unprecedented miracle of development

The rise of modern China is a miracle that mankind has never seen before. China has created a miracle of rapid development with the largest scale, fastest speed, and the longest duration in the history of human development.

China has grown from a 'poor student' in the world-class to an out-and-out 'super scholar' in just a few decades. In 1949, China had one of the lowest GDP per capita in the world, with an average life expectancy of only 35 years, lower than France's in 1820. But today, we have become the second-largest economy in the world, with a per capita GDP exceeding $10,000, and will soon cross the threshold of a high-income country.[1] China's average life expectancy has reached 77.3 years, increasing to 78.3 years during the '14th Five-Year Plan' period, while the US had an average life expectancy of 78.8 years. In 2020, due to the Covid-19 pandemic, the US life expectancy dropped by one year to 77.8 years old. This means that although China's per capita GDP calculated by the exchange rate method is only about one-sixth of that of the United States, China's per capita life expectancy is already close to that of the United States and may surpass the United States shortly.

More importantly, from a global perspective, China's rise has broken three major development myths.

Firstly, it breaks the 'glass ceiling' of developing countries. Developing countries have long been included in a global development system with a Western centre/non-Western fringe, and can gain a certain space for development, but are not allowed to break through the 'glass ceiling' of development. Developing countries can only develop in a dependent or semi-dependent manner, but cannot truly develop independently; they can only develop within the division of labour allowed by the hegemonic countries, and cannot touch their 'cheese'. Many countries have thus fallen into the 'middle-income trap'. China has not only achieved endogenous and independent development, but has also continuously climbed a new ladder of development. It has overcome the 'poverty trap' and 'middle-income trap', and in the future will also overcome the 'high-income trap', that Japan and other countries have fallen into, and move towards the highest level of development.

Secondly, it breaks the myth that only the capitalist system can develop quickly. The countries that achieved modernisation in the past were all capitalist countries. The Soviet Union's highest per capita GDP was estimated to be only seven or eight thousand dollars at its peak. As a socialist country, China has achieved much faster development than that of a capitalist country, built a moderately prosperous society in all respects in just a few decades, and will have achieved socialist modernisation by the 100th anniversary of the founding of the People's Republic of China.

Thirdly, it breaks the paradox of Western powers that 'A strong nation is bound to seek hegemony', 'The city's rulers keep changing, you step down, and I come on stage'. The protagonists on the stage of world history are constantly changing, but the theme of the battle for hegemony has never changed. Only the rise of China has truly broken this spell. It is not the rise of a new hegemony, but the return of the king of a new type of world power. Unlike hegemony in Western history, China did not get rich by colonising and plundering all over the world, but by the hard work and innovative revolution of more than a billion people. What China pursues is not hegemony, but harmonious way (王道). It is not 'A strong nation is bound to seek hegemony', but 'a strong nation loves benevolence'; China does not export wars, turmoil and suffering, but creates huge development opportunities for the world, allowing countries in the world to ride on China Development Express; China is not trying to be the king and hegemon in the world, but to firmly uphold genuine multilateralism and promote the building of a community of human destiny.

2. China's practical innovation calls for theoretical innovation
(百年大道责人开生面)

For human beings in the 21st century, the rise of China is not only a new reality, but also a new meaning. It is not only Chinese power, but also 'Chinese-ism' and 'Chinese Path'. In the Western knowledge system, a country like China will either follow the Western model step by step, or sooner or later collapse, unable to rise. The unexpected rise of China, however, will make Western political theories disguised as 'universal theories' face an overall challenge. People will truly disenchant themselves from centuries of Western-centric knowledge systems and realise the so-called 'universality' is Westernness, the so-called 'universal values' are just Western values, and the so-called 'end of history' is just a moment in history.

The rise of China can only be described in Chinese words, and the Chinese Path can only be explained in terms of Chinese philosophy. The paradox of history is that the transformation from traditional China to modern China was mainly driven by the integration of the Western system, but it cannot be completely Westernised after all. Because China is too big, the tents of the West are too small, the bones of China are too hard, and the digestion capacity of the West is too weak. China undertakes the historic mission of not only absorbing the Western system but also breaking the Western system, creating a new system for mankind.

Just as Chinese experience has contributed Chinese solutions to the world, Chinese philosophy will also contribute Chinese wisdom to the world. Chinese philosophy will re-interpret the whole world and re-write the system of human knowledge. At the same time, this does not mean changing from 'Western-centric theory' to 'Sino-centric theory'. Rather, it means a liberation of a knowledge system that has been suppressed and marginalised in the Western-centric knowledge system, and a redemption of the progress of human thought that has been imprisoned by Western ideology.

The great revival of China calls for the Chinese School (Chapter 1). In other words, the so-called Chinese school is based on the genes of China's own civilisation and borrows from Western theories to construct a theoretical system for modern China's revolution, construction, reform and revival, in order to achieve the unity of theory and practice, the unity of consciousness and existence, to propose new explanations and new expressions for the universal problems of human society, to explain human development with

Chinese philosophies, and to tell world stories with Chinese discourse. This will be a knowledge revolution that spans multiple disciplines, lasts for generations, and involves countless scholars. The Chinese school is not a supplement to the Western knowledge system, but a fundamental change of thought that moves the heart of the world.

The paradigm revolution of knowledge construction needs to transcend the century-old 'dispute of body and use' (体用之争) between China and the West, shift from the Western theory-centred paradigm to the Chinese practice-centered paradigm, and promote the construction of Chinese discourse of 'one body and three uses' (一体三用) (Chapter 2), with practice as the body and three theoretical resources (Marx-China-West[2] 马中西) as uses to promote the innovation of theoretical discourse. Practice as the body means to change from 'learning from the West' to 'learning from practice', get rid of the shackles of Western theoretical dogma, break the myth of blindly pursuing formal scientificity, and advocate practicalism in methodology, rather than deductivism, falsificationism, and positivism. It means to base the scientific demarcation of theory on originating from practice, conforming to practice, and being able to stand the test of practice, not just on the metaphysical 'scientific methodology', let alone on the logical deduction of a specific theory, and obtain the sideness (此岸性), the truthfulness and the innovation of the theory in the continuous cycle of 'practice-theory-practice'.

China's practical innovation calls for theoretical innovation. Chinese principles cannot use Western doctrines to 'annotate me in the six classics' (我注六经), but have to use 'the six classics being my footnote' (六经注我). The fundamental reason is that the Chinese Path is the holistic and fundamental transcendence of the West, rather than a partial difference. The economic, political, social, governance, international relations and other aspects have formed an innovative Chinese Path.

3. A new economic road that integrates socialism and market economy

On the economic way, China has embarked on a new way of socialist market economy that surpasses both the Soviet-style planned economy and the capitalist market economy. Can socialism be combined with a market economy? Mainstream Western theories hold that, just like a rabbit can't have horns, a horse can't have wings, the market economy and socialism are incompatible, and the socialist market economy is doomed to fail. China's socialist market economy has broken this 'curse' and realised the organic combination of socialism with market economy.

China's practice has proved that the market economy cannot only be used as a tool by capitalism, but also by socialism, where it can be used to great success. The fundamental reason is that market logic cannot be confused with capital logic. Capital logic is capital proliferation, whereas market logic is equal trading; capitalism is the jungle law, whereas market economy is the principle of equivalent exchange. In order to achieve self-proliferation of capital, of course, it needs an unfettered market. However, in most modern product and factor markets, capitalism does not maintain market logic, but distorts it. It is not an exchange of equal value, but an exchange of unequal value. It is not who contributes more and who has more return, but who is stronger and who pays the most.

Socialism and the market economy are not incompatible, but in harmony with each other. Socialism and the market economy are more logically self-consistent, and socialism can better maintain and enhance the logic of the market, and can create a market economy of a higher level than capitalism. The logic of socialism is the logic of the community. Socialism is people-centred and pursues the continuous increase of people's well-being. Therefore, realising the division of labour and cooperation through the market equivalent exchange is necessary. It needs an incentive mechanism that is consistent with individual contributions and returns. And it requires the mutual promotion of 'making the cake bigger' and 'dividing the cake well'. At the same time, socialism can make up for market failures at multiple levels and enhance market effectiveness. The practice has proved that the superiority of the socialist market economy lies precisely in the qualifier of socialism and in the combined advantages formed by socialism and the market economy.

First, public ownership of land provides a common foundation for national development, and land becomes the greatest public wealth that guarantees the common well-being of the people. Collective ownership of land is the foundation of rural development and stability, providing a foundation for hundreds of millions of farmers to settle down and avoid 'proletarianisation' in the process of urbanisation. Under the conditions of market economy, public ownership of urban land provides a financing tool for urbanisation and industrialisation, and creates conditions for promoting large-scale infrastructure construction. In contrast, many other developing countries, due to land privatisation, are constrained by the lack of public financing tools and fragmentation of land ownership in the development process, making it difficult to break through the development investment bottleneck and promote large-scale infrastructure construction.

Second, the state-owned economy and the private economy can play to their respective advantages and go hand in hand to enhance the competitiveness and vitality of the Chinese economy. State-owned enterprises not only play a major role in the process of national industrialisation, but also play a major role in the process of Chinese enterprises going global. The proportion of China's public assets to total social assets is much higher than that of most countries in the world. The larger proportion of the public economy enables China to protect public interests better and provide better public infrastructure for economic development. For example, the rapid growth of high-speed rail and the popularisation of 4G and even 5G signals have greatly reduced the cost of economic activities and enabled people to enjoy a higher level of public welfare.

Third, national planning can make up for market failures and lead and promote economic and social development. Neoliberal economics believes that the market economy and state planning are incompatible. With the disintegration of the Soviet Union and the drastic changes in Eastern Europe, state planning as an institutional experiment seems to have failed. However, China has shattered the myth of the 'failure of state planning'. National plan (planning) has achieved great success in China, and has become China's most important super public policy, an important means to promote China's development.

Neoliberal economics believes that the key information about the economy and society is scattered, so the national planning trying to promote 'social engineering' will face serious information asymmetry problems, but it is an 'arrogant conceit'. The defect of this view is that there is a type of key information for economic and social operation, which is not scattered, but exists in a holistic way. Even the so-called scattered and invisible information has been discovered in today's big data era, and can be efficiently integrated.

China's innovation lies in the use of the market as a mechanism for the use of 'scattered knowledge' and national planning as a mechanism for the use of 'holistic knowledge' (Chapter 3), realising the complementary advantages of the two. National planning makes up for the blindness of the market mechanism at the macro level, makes up for the failure of the market in the allocation of non-pure private goods resources, improves the direction and overall planning of national development, and improves the overall social resource allocation efficiency. In the real world, it is a myth that the market can spontaneously equilibrate. For example, short-term market rationality may not be rational in the long run. After adding time variables, the so-called market equilibrium often turns into an imbalance. China has a five-year plan, which enables China to plan development on a time scale of five, decades, and hundreds of years, and can do many things that seem uneconomical in the short term, but lay an important foundation for long-term development. National planning can promote development to achieve a higher level of balance, and promote supply and demand balance, time balance, space balance, ecological balance, and internal and external balance.

At the same time, the Governance-by-Objectives (Chapter 4) system enables China to have a strong ability to achieve national objectives. Western countries can implement management by objectives at the enterprise level, while China can implement Governance-by-Objectives at the national level. China's ability to make 'Promise be kept and action be resultful' when it comes to its national objectives, is in stark contrast to the countless beautiful visions that many Western countries have promised but failed to deliver. Once the five-year plan objectives are passed, they will be transformed into the will of the country. It is necessary to concentrate resources and mobilise all forces, to play a comprehensive role in various departments and fields to realise the integration of resources, so as to form a strong synergy, promote the realisation of common objectives, promote the development of the country to a big step every five years. After decades of accumulation, the whole country has undergone earth-shaking changes.

Fourth, China has taken a road that is different from both liberalism and the welfare state (Chapter 5). Liberalism assumes that the well-being of individuals depends entirely on their success in the market, but in a capitalist market system, atomised workers are extremely vulnerable. Welfare states provide individuals with state protection outside of the market, but most so-called welfare states provide low levels of welfare with strict conditions. A combination of privileged resources, small population, and a highly developed economy is necessary to consistently provide the kind of high-level welfare, widely available in some northern European countries. In fact, many countries are trapped in a fiscally overburdened 'welfare state trap'.

Different from the basic concepts of corporate nationalism, social risk protection, and social rights in the welfare state, the most fundamental concept of the Minsheng state (state that provides people with good livelihood) is the socialist community. That is, a big family built and shared together. This means that individual people's livelihood issues cannot be solely depended on by the individual, but must also be shared by the collective, society and the state. At the same time, it also means that each member is a builder of the community. For disadvantaged groups, the welfare state usually spends some money to raise them. Although they do not worry about food and drink, they will not make any contribution, and they will eventually become a burden to the whole society. What the Minsheng state does is to expand opportunities for vulnerable groups to participate in community building and enhance their capabilities, so that they can participate, develop, and will not stay behind in the process of social progress. In that case, the people's livelihood policy and economic development can form a virtuous circle.

The community logic also means that basic livelihood issues, such as medical care, elderly care, and housing, cannot be completely solved by the logic of the market. It cannot be that 'Only rich people can have access to medical care, elderly care, and housing.' Instead, it should be highly decommercialised and ensure the basic livelihood needs of all people through various means. The community logic also means that the financing channels of the Minsheng state are much more extensive than that of welfare countries, which mainly rely on tax revenue. A large proportion of public assets and the coordinated assistance of all social parties can provide resources for constructing the Minsheng state.

The Minsheng state has the dual functions of social protection and economic efficiency promotion and can achieve efficient fairness, which not only guarantees individual well-being, but also avoids falling into the 'welfare state trap'.

Fifth, since the reform and opening up, local governments have gradually withdrawn from direct involvement in economic activities, but they are still an important force in promoting development. Local governments in China are platform-type governments, important players in making the cake bigger, and key links in economic production activities. Although the government does not directly carry out production activities, it builds a platform for production and trading activities, optimises the market ecological environment, empowers market players, and promotes chemical reactions between market players, thereby creating huge value and promoting China's economic take-off. Platform-based local governments are in the process of upgrading. Local governments not only traditionally attract investment and develop industrial parks, but also actively cultivate new advantages in local industries through innovative incubation platforms, industrial funds, and the promotion of talent aggregation.

At the same time, a socialist market economy can create a more sustainable growth mechanism than a capitalist market economy. Due to the decline in return on capital and the lack of potential consumer demand, market economy countries will face the problem of insufficient effective demand at a certain stage of development. Even the new demand space created by innovation will be quickly filled by new production capacity. Capitalist countries solve the problem of insufficient effective demand in their own countries by launching wars, industrial transfer, and economic virtualisation. While capital gains high profits, it has brought many problems to their own countries and other countries in the world. China also encountered a 'ceiling' of insufficient effective demand, but instead of following the old path of developed capitalist countries, we gave full play to the advantages of socialism and promoted 'new demand management' (Chapter 6). Expand the 'troika' of demand into a 'six chariot' according to private investment and public investment, private consumption and public consumption, export and global potential demand. Under this new framework of total social demand, it is precisely by giving play to the advantages of socialism that we can promote public investment, public consumption and the common development of all countries in the world. This can tap potential demand, create a higher level and more sustainable growth, and help form a new development pattern in which the domestic cycle is the mainstay and the domestic and international economic cycles promote each other.

4. A new political path that is concentrated, efficient and lively

On the political road, China has also embarked on a new path that surpasses both the Soviet and Western political models.

From the perspective of Western political science, the Chinese political system is often labelled as a 'totalitarian', 'authoritarianism' and 'party-state system'. Under this label-type thinking, the Chinese system is regarded as a transitional system, and it is constantly predicted that with the growth of private capital, the expansion of the market economy, and the rise of the middle class, the Chinese political system will be unsustainable and will collapse sooner or later. This is an important premise in the US 'contact policy' towards China.

Facts have proved that there has been a serious strategic misjudgment in the West, and it is not China that collapses, but the 'China Collapse Theory' itself. China's political system is not a shortcoming of great power competition, but rather a strength that has shown great vitality and is China's invincible fundamental institutional advantage.

Although the concept of 'authoritarianism' is vague, it is increasingly difficult to explain the actual operation of Chinese politics, yet for decades, Western scholars have always adhered to this kind of thinking, adding dozens of different definitions to 'authoritarianism' to describe China's political system. This does not enhance its explanatory power, but only highlights the dilemma of its inability to justify itself.

An important reason why China's political system is labelled 'authoritarianism' is that Westerners believe that China's political power is too concentrated. In fact, the principle of separation of powers, which the West is proud of, has become the crux of the rigidity and inefficiency of political systems in the 21st century. The author believes that China's political system is not a system of division, but a 'system of division of labour'. China's political system is the 'Seven divisions of power' (Chapter 7), including: the leadership of the Party Central Committee, the legislative power of the National People's Congress, the executive power of the State Council, the consultation power of the CPPCC, the supervisory power of the State Supervisory Commission, the judicial power of the Supreme People's Court and the Supreme People's Procuratorate power and the military power of the Central Military Commission. It is precisely because of the unifying function of the leadership of the Party Central Committee that China's political system is a division of labour system, not a division system. The basic operating principle of China's political system is the division of labour and coordination, which is the structure of a 'well-functioning government'; In contrast, the basic operating principle of the American political system is the separation of powers and checks and balances, which is a 'limited government' structure. In comparison, the Chinese political system is more efficient and effective than that of the United States. An important reason in the United States choosing a separate system is to avoid the corruption of power, which prevents the abuse of power to a certain extent, but it comes at the cost of the system's inefficiency. At the same time, it has not been able to avoid some people taking advantage of loopholes in the system to carry out a lot of 'corruption under the sun'. China avoids the corruption of power through monitoring, not checks and balances, which ensures both efficiency and integrity.

China is often criticised for not having competitive elections. In fact, today's Western competitive elections have degenerated into a 'competitive talent show', which has become the root cause of national leaders' lack of professional competence, institutional shortsightedness, and capricious policies. The main method for the generation of Chinese government officials is through competitive selection, but elections, examinations, and other methods are also used. Competitive selection is based on actual performance rather than electoral ability. The selected leaders are practical, experienced, and supervised by the organisation, not politicians who are good at showing off. At the same time, the long-term rule of the Communist Party of China has also made China's policies more sustainable, avoiding the constant 'flipping' of policies brought about by different political parties taking turns 'taking positions' in the competitive electoral system.

Corresponding to the 'authoritarianism' label, the West often says that China has no democracy. In fact, if you understand the political operation of China, you will know that the saying that China has no democracy is as absurd as the saying that there is no sand in the Sahara Desert and that there is no love story in 'Dream of the Red Chamber'. Chinese-style democracy is different from Western-style democracy centred on elections, but is full-process democracy, multi-channel democracy, and substantive democracy. For example, a label often attached to China's decision-making process is 'fragmented authoritarianism', or some scholars simply call it the 'black-box model'. This kind of explanation is either misleading, or unclear. In fact, China's decision-making process is the embodiment of Chinese-style decision-making democracy. China has developed a 'Collective wisdom' decision-making model (Chapter 8), which can pool the wisdom of all parties to formulate high-quality policies through democratic mechanisms.

Taking the five-year plan as an example, in the process of compiling the plan for two or three years, countless people contributed their wisdom, and it took a great deal of in-depth research, subject study and repeated discussion, to finally form a text of just a few tens of thousands of words. Every word is precious. The participants in the 'Collective wisdom' process constitute China's 'policy circle', including the decision-making level, the drafting level, and the participation level. Party and state leaders guide the formulation of the plan, the decision-making meetings of the Party Central Committee, the State Council, and the National People's Congress serve as gatekeepers for the different stages of preparation, drafting groups are set up to draft the plan; other state organs such as the NPC and the CPPCC participate in research and provide suggestions; think tanks, experts and the public participate in planning research and put forward policy proposals through different channels.

'Collective wisdom' decision-making is democracy first and centralisation second, which is a new decision-making model that incorporates science into democracy. We consciously use traditional language to describe the five-stage model of 'Collective wisdom' decision-making. (1) Make everyone offer good ideas: Mobilise all parties to offer suggestions and recommendations in the early stage of compiling the policy text, which is the 'Collective wisdom' in the early stage of policy formulation. (2) Collecting ideas broadly: The drafting group implements the instructions of the state leaders, integrates the opinions of all parties, collects relevant information, and drafts phased policy texts. (3) Extensive consultation: After the phased policy text is formed, opinions are solicited from all parties and amendments are made to form a policy draft. (4) Collegial decision-making: The decision is discussed collectively in a formal meeting at different decision-making levels to form a formal policy document. (5) Informing the public: The policy document is communicated to all parties and implemented.

5. A new way of 'The World is Equally Shared by All' (公天下)

On the way of governance, China has also surpassed the Western 'good governance model' and embarked on a Chinese-style governance path.

The modernisation of Chinese governance is not Westernisation, nor is it to achieve the so-called 'good governance' introduced from the West in the 1990s. China's civilisation foundation, basic national conditions and social system are all different from those of the West. The modernisation of China's governance is the self-improvement of China's system and governance system.

When talking about good governance, it is absolutely unnecessary to mention the West, thinking that good governance is just an imported product. China is a country with the richest tradition of good governance in the world. The Tao Te Ching (《道德经》) has already put forward the concept of 'just and good governance'. The theories of various schools of thought are mainly about how to govern the country well. In the long history, countless great thoughts and practices of good governance have emerged.

'A public spirit will rule all under the heaven when the great way prevails.' Chinese traditional good governance can be summarised as the governance that 'The World is Equally Shared by All' (Chapter 9), Chinese traditional culture is 'citizen-oriented', not 'private right-oriented', and the political power is just the 'God' implements its public will and is the governance tool for the people of the world to govern the world. Good governance is governance that reflects the public will to the greatest extent and protects the public interest. The traditional 'The World is Equally Shared by All' governance includes the following specific connotations:

First, 'Put the people as the master, the monarch as the guest' ('天下为主，君为客'). 'Respect the monarch to prevent the bias of the individual, and focus on the people to prevent the selfishness of the monarch, through both ways to achieve fairness.' (尊君以克个体之偏，民本以克君主之私，二者并举以臻于公) The purpose of establishing a monarch is to govern the world. The monarch is the representative of the national community, but in order to respect the monarch, one must put the people first, take the will of the people as the will, listen to the people, and value the lives of the ordinary people, so that the monarch and the people get along well with each other and they can be like-minded. (上下交，其志同也)

Second, incorporate the meaning of feudalism into the county. The disputes between feudal prefectures and counties appear throughout Chinese history. When citing its major points, feudalism 'is mostly out of necessity, the prefecture-county system ensures long-term stability and is a system that ensures fairness. At the same time, prefectures and counties also have their own shortcomings that the authority is too centralised.' (多

出于势所不得不然，郡县制乃是长治久安，大公之制，同时郡县亦有其专在上之失') The 'integration of feudalism in the county' for Gu Yanwu is an effective mode of traditional Chinese governance.

The third is to choose meritocracy. The Chinese system of electing the meritocracy has a long history. The world cannot be ruled by the monarch alone, but must be ruled together with sages. It does not matter whether one's background is distinguished or low. Only virtue is the criteria for selection.

Fourth, morality dominates punishment, and rites and law govern together. The order of governance is to guide people with virtue, constraint people with rituals, regulate people with governance, and punish people with law. Virtue is the root of governance, while politics and law are the end of governance.(德礼为治本，而政法为治道之末)

Fifth, China as the foundation, thinking about the world. 'No matter how far or near the crowd is, how big or small the region is, the world is like a whole', (远近、小大若一). Good governance is not to govern an individual, one family, or one country, but to govern the world. Recognise the two directions of good and evil in the development of things, and then adopt the moderate ones. 'China as the foundation, thinking about the world' ('中国为本，天下为怀') should be precisely the meaning that 'the world is like a whole'.

The traditional good governance of 'The World is Equally Shared by All 'is still of great significance to the advancement of governance modernisation today. Contemporary Chinese good governance is to organically combine traditional governance with modern governance concepts, governance systems, governance capabilities, and governance techniques to create a higher level of good governance.

The modernisation of China's national governance is to achieve Chinese-style good governance. The fundamental is to realise the subjectivity of the people, to fully ensure that the people are the masters of the country, and to give full play to the enthusiasm, initiative and creativity of the people. Party leadership is the essential feature of China's national governance system. Good governance in China can be summarised as the 'diamond model' of Chinese-style good governance (Chapter 10), which consists of four elements: 'pioneering political parties', 'well-functioning government', 'beneficial market', and 'organic society', which together guarantee the realisation of people's subjectivity.

To understand Chinese-style good governance, we must first understand the nature of the Chinese Communist Party. To avoid the preconceived cognitive trap, we cannot view the Communist Party of China with Western electoral party thinking. The Communist Party of China is an organisational party that realises the national strategic mission by leading, organising and mobilising party members and the people. The vanguard of the Chinese Communist Party is a prerequisite for realising its organisational function, and it is also a key variable in realising Chinese-style good governance. The Communist Party of China is not an elite party, but a vanguard party. The elite party is above the people, but the vanguard party is among the people. It wants to be with the people, work together with the people, and charges ahead while enjoying afterwards.

The Chinese government is a 'promising government' rather than a limited government. The leadership of the party has enabled the effective integration of the power of the state and the more efficient operation of the system, enabling China to achieve the unity of high political concentration and administrative decentralisation. The party's mass line is embedded in the government system. This makes the Chinese government a responsible government rather than a limited liability government.

China implements a socialist market economy, not a capitalist market economy. It serves the maximisation of people's well-being, not the maximisation of capital interests.

China's modernisation of social governance is to build an 'organic society' rather than a so-called 'civil society'. In a modern society dominated by mobile strangers, the premise that China can build an 'organic society' lies in the role of the party's leadership as a social glue and catalyst. This makes society an organic whole that maintains a high degree of diversity as well as a high degree of cohesion.

6. A new approach to globalisation with 'communitism'

From the perspective of China's relationship with the world, China is embarking on a new path to redefine the global pattern and global order.

The rise of China will not repeat the history of hegemonic shifts of different countries since the 'long 16th century', but as a new type of global power, it will promote the evolution of the world order in a more just and rational direction. The world is undergoing major changes unseen in a century, highlighted by six major changes. First, the international pattern has undergone major changes: the Post-Cold War international pattern of 'one superpower with multiple powers', has changed to 'two poles and multiple powers'. As a stabilising and a transformative force in the existing global order, as a 'pole' of a global power, China also joins the global order structure as a 'pole' of opposition and unity with the United States, thus forming a 'connection of two poles' (Chapter 11) in the new global order. Second, major changes in globalisation: the continuous upward trend of globalisation since the end of World War II has reversed. Third, the global capitalist system has undergone major changes: the integration process of the global capitalist system since the end of the Second World War has broken down. Fourth, there is a major change in the power balance between the East and the West: world history has changed from a great diversion to a great reversal. The great diversion centred on the West for hundreds of years has turned into a great reversal of the collective rise of non-Western countries. The trend of 'rising in the east and falling in the west' is obvious. Fifth, the great changes in the industrial revolution: The fourth wave of the industrial revolution has emerged, and China has become one of the leaders of the emerging industrial revolution for the first time. Sixth, the major changes in Sino-US relations: The Trump administration has changed the United States 'contact policy' towards China since the establishment of diplomatic relations between China and the United States, and launched a 'grand strategic confrontation' with China. Sino-US relations have entered a 'new stage of fighting and cooperation'. The Covid-19 Pandemic has accelerated six major changes unseen in a century.

At the new historical juncture, there are major strategic challenges and major strategic opportunities, which require us to conduct a new strategic analysis. Different from the strategic analysis framework of 'value-capability-support' and 'three circles theory' proposed by Harvard professors, China's 'three circles theory' (Chapter 12) strategic analysis framework is 'favourable timing, geographical advantages, and human conditions'. (天时—地利—人和). The primary element of management is to adapt to the favourable timing, the basic element is to identify the geographical advantages, and the dynamic element is the people's support. The coupling of the three elements of favourable timing, geographical advantages, and human conditions constitutes a period of strategic opportunity. Since the founding of New China, China has experienced three periods of strategic opportunity: the first period of strategic opportunity happened in the early days of the founding of New China; the second period of strategic opportunity happened in the early stage of reform and opening up; After the end of the Cold War, China has ushered in the third strategic opportunity period through the transformation of the market economy and opening up to the outside world. The third strategic opportunity period was closed with the deterioration of Sino-US relations and the drastic changes in the international environment.

Opportunities vouchsafed by heaven are less important than terrestrial advantages, which in turn are less important than the unity among people' It is the combination of people and timing with geographical advantages that shapes the period of strategic opportunity. There has never been a period of strategic opportunities in the world where 'you can win while lying down', and all need to be won through great struggles, especially today. Since entering the new era, China has followed the changes in the right time and place, promoted high-quality development internally, gave full play to its leadership externally, and took the initiative to realise a series of strategic transformations. In particular, the 'Belt and Road' initiative and the concept of 'building a community with a shared future for mankind' were put forward. Hence, it gradually opened the fourth strategic opportunity period. Compared with the previous strategic opportunity periods, the connotation of the new strategic opportunity period has undergone profound changes. We need to further shift from the dividend of reform and opening up to the dividend of innovation and leadership, not only to promote peaceful rise, but also to promote inclusive rise.

At present, the liberal international order is facing unprecedented challenges, and human beings cannot return to the realist 'jungle world' in which they fight each other. Neither 'liberalism' nor 'realism' can effectively respond to two phenomena in the contemporary world: the unevenness of globalisation and the continuous expansion of the global public sphere. The concept of building a community with a shared future for mankind proposed by President Xi Jinping and the practice of China's exchanges with other countries in the world in recent years have actually put forward a new paradigm for international relations in the 21st century – communitism (Chapter 13). Communitism not only conforms to the reality of international politics in the 21st century, but also responds to the challenges of international politics. It is also idealistic, reflecting Chinese tradition, Chinese solutions and Chinese wisdom. Compared with 'realism' and 'liberalism', communitism mainly has the following characteristics:

In terms of security, communitism is a universal security concept, which goes beyond the concept of 'equilibrium security' and 'collective security'; in terms of development concepts, communitism is a common development concept, surpassing the 'zero-sum development concept' and 'liberal development concept'. In the concept of civilisation, communitism is a view of the convergence of civilisations, which goes beyond the 'clash of civilisations' and 'multiculturalism'; in terms of state relations, communitism emphasises partnership and goes beyond alliance and non-alignment.

'In this peaceful world, the whole earth will feel warm and cool.' Communitism represents the mighty world trend of the 21st century. Whether it is 'realism' which emphasises 'America First', or a 'small circle' of global governance centred on a few countries and demarcated by ideology, both are Cold War mentalities that are behind the times. The world's progressive forces represented by the 'Community with a Shared Future for Mankind', 'One Belt, One Road', and genuine multilateralism have brought light and hope to mankind and provided a new engine for a new type of globalisation.

Western countries are keen to use 'geopolitics' to explain China's 'Belt and Road' initiative. They believe that China is promoting geopolitical expansion, and it is the latest practice of mixing well-known geopolitical theories such as 'sea power', 'land power' and 'world island', which has shaken the world pattern and posed a new threat to the Western world. This interpretation not only reflects the arrogance and prejudice of centuries of Western centralism, but also reflects the inevitable misreading brought about by observing the new practice of the 21st century with the outdated theoretical thinking of the 20th century.

In fact, no geopolitical theory can explain the 'Belt and Road' initiative. The 'Belt and Road' is not a geopolitical expansion, but builds a political and economic platform for the common development of the world. Therefore, it is necessary to discuss the 'political economy of geo-development' based on the practice of the 'Belt and Road' (Chapter 14).

The 'Belt and Road' is a major political and economic platform for geopolitical development that shapes points, lines, surfaces, and trends. 'Clustering at the point' refers to the clustering effect of promoting local economic development through industrial layout, park construction, port construction, etc. 'Online smooth flow' refers to promoting large-scale infrastructure construction, promoting the interconnection of railways, highways, waterways, airways, pipelines, and information highways, and shortening the economic distance between different development nodes. 'Connecting on the surface' refers to reducing the cost of cross-border economic activities and promoting the cross-border flow of goods, personnel, information and capital through policy communication, financial integration, and unimpeded trade. 'Forming a trend' refers to connecting the scattered pearls to form a strong trend of common development. The six major international economic cooperation corridors across Europe and Asia constitute the main framework of the 'Belt and Road'.

At the same time, the 'Belt and Road' is a new model of common development, from unbalanced globalisation to a more balanced globalisation; It is a new model of international cooperation, from strategic competition to strategic cooperation; It is a new model of international exchanges, from unequal political order to equal political order. The 'Belt and Road' is the most magnificent geo-development initiative put forward by mankind at the beginning of the 21st century and a vivid practice of building a community of shared future for mankind. The 'Belt and Road' is the best gift given to the world by the rising China and the greatest opportunity for China.

7. New order of human society

The innovation of China's road is that it is a new order of human society and a new order centred on the people. It is fundamentally different from the traditional order centred on power or capital.

Modern western society is a capital-centred order, which constructs a complete set of western academic discourse systems around the meta concepts of freedom, democracy and human rights. On the contrary, Chinese society is a people-centred order. The people's subjectivity, the party's leadership and socialism constitute the 'iron triangle' of China's system and the meta concept of constructing China's academic discourse system.

Taking the people as the centre does not mean taking individual rights as the centre. The people not only refers to each individual, but also as a whole. Without common freedom and common rights, individual freedom and individual rights are out of the question. Taking the people as the centre means that this 'collective person' composed of more than one billion Chinese people obtains subjectivity and becomes the centre of the political and economic order. Taking the people as the centre is a set of political and economic order covering economy, politics, society and culture. Economically, there are public assets that protect the common interests of the people, rather than pure private ownership; Politically, the people are the masters of the country, and the political power serves the people, not plutocracy; Socially, we should build a social community jointly built and shared by all, rather than promoting 'civil society'; Culturally, it protects the dignity of workers, rather than using money as the highest yardstick to measure social value.

The leadership of the Communist Party of China defines the essential characteristics of the Chinese Path, and its political and economic meaning is that the leadership of the party represents the overall interests of the people. It is through the leadership of the party that more than one billion Chinese people have gained the subjectivity of collective objectives, collective will and collective action, and thus gained the initiative to control their own destiny. It is through the leadership of the party that China's socialist market economy has realised 'people-centred' rather than 'capital centred'. As an overall power, the party's leadership can control and manage capital power while protecting capital rights, avoid the disorderly expansion of capital, avoid the infiltration of capital logic into the superstructure, and guide the motivation of pursuing the maximisation of capital profit to the socialist direction of maximising people's well-being.

Socialism is the economic, political, social and cultural community of all people. Each member is the master of the community, which is different from the logic of capitalist capital proliferation. Socialism is the logic of the community, and all the people constitute a community of interests, a community of culture and a community of destiny. Socialism is actually a simple truth, that is, we work together, we eat together, we share difficulties, and we share the glory. Socialism is a new way of human society with a symbiotic economy, shared distribution, common prosperity and common ideals. Without taking the socialist road, the party will lose its direction and cannot win the love of the people. Without the leadership of the party and the will of the people, it is impossible to build a socialist community in any sense.

The Chinese Path is a new road for mankind, a right path for mankind and a new order for mankind; The Chinese philosophy is the principle of the Chinese Path, the principle of the right way and the philosophy of impartiality. It is a new knowledge system for mankind. In terms of its particularity, the Chinese principle is just the concept presentation and self-confirmation of the Chinese Path, and further establishes its subjectivity in exploring the distant future; As far as its universality is concerned, the Chinese philosophy means a great liberation of the bound new human knowledge system, which is long overdue. The Western principle is still strong, but it represents only the past. The Chinese philosophy is still on edge, but it is the coming future.

---

1 The current World Bank standard for high-income economies are those with a GNI per capita of $12,696 or more, <https://datahelpdesk.worldbank.org/knowledgebase/articles/906519-world-bank-country-and-lending-groups>, [4 May 2021]
2 Refers to Marxist theory, Chinese traditional culture, Western philosophy and social science

PART 1
THE METHODOLOGY OF CHINESE DISCOURSE

This is an era that needs theory and gives rise to theory, this is an era that needs thought and gives rise to thoughts.

– Speech by Xi Jinping at the Seminar on Philosophy and Social Sciences (17 May, 2016)

CHAPTER 1
China's Great Rejuvenation Calls for the Chinese School

[*The original text is Yan Yilong, 2017, 'Constructing the Chinese School Based on Revival Practice' (People's Watch), People's Daily, 24 Sept, p. 5, with abridged when published. 原文为鄢一龙：《基于复兴实践构建中国学派》（人民观察），《人民日报》2017年9月24日，第5版，发表时有删节。]

Throughout human history, the prosperity and development of any school is the product of the great practice of a specific era, and is a public declaration of the spiritual power of a specific era. It is an ideological response to the problems of the times, a theoretical summary of the practice of the times, and a precursor to lead and promote the changes of the times.

Since what historians call the 'long 16th century',[3] the knowledge system of modern Western philosophy and social sciences has gradually formed and developed, and has become increasingly refined. Western civilisation, centred on the Greco-Roman and Hebrew-Christian axes, prepared the placenta for its birth, and the evolving modern capitalist system has become its midwife. It is a spiritual reflection of the political and economic reality of the modern West, and a self-affirmation of the modern Western society. It is an authentic child of the Western world, bearing the pain, joy, and pride of centuries of Western transformation, yet proclaiming to legislate for the entire human race.

The global expansion of Western material power is accompanied by a global expansion of Western spiritual power. The Western world has become the centre of the new 'universal church,' the Western model has become the 'universal model,' and Western values have become 'universal values.' Under the pressure of the strong military, material, and spiritual superiority displayed by the West, all non-Western and Western differences in civilisation and reality are disciplined as the gap between premodern and modern, periphery and centre. This set of knowledge systems claims that only by fully accepting Western values and models can we obtain a ticket to enter the modern world and achieve salvation from barbarism to civilisation, from backwardness to advancement.

The Chinese civilisation occupies the eastern part of the world, and it has continued to this day. Since the Western Zhou Dynasty, it has maintained great unity for over 3,000 years. Thousands of years of splendid civilisations have never been suspended regardless of numerous chaotic periods. Tens of thousands of miles of beautiful rivers and mountains have been divided and merged several times but have never been broken apart. These two characteristics are unique in the world. For a long time, the Chinese civilisation has been one of the most advanced civilisations in the world.

Modern China 'suffered a major change, and a formidable enemy unprecedented in thousands of years'. Under the huge impact of the West, China has fallen into an unprecedented crisis. The main axis of China's historical development since modern times is to respond to this unprecedented crisis, explore how to save the nation and survive, and realise the great rejuvenation of the Chinese nation.

The Communist Party of China led the Chinese people in a great and unyielding struggle, saving the fate of the Chinese nation from falling into the abyss in modern times, and found a way out of the crisis. The great practice of China's revolution, construction, reform, and new era is an unprecedented exploration.

The great renaissance of China is a very different story from the rise of the Western world, a story that cannot be explained in a Western-centric knowledge system. The great practice of modern China has surpassed Western experience in terms of its civilisational foundation, development miracle and development path, and thus has entered waters uncharted by Western knowledge systems.

First, from the perspective of civilisational roots. Chinese civilisation is fundamentally different from Western civilisation. Chinese civilisation has continuously integrated and developed independently throughout history, and has reached a very high level of sophistication. In the process of modern transformation, Chinese civilisation has not disintegrated or broken up, but has maintained its subjectivity, continuity, and inclusiveness. While absorbing Western ideas, it has achieved revival and opened up to a new realm of civilisation.

The birth and development of modern China was based on a civilisational matrix fundamentally different from that of the modern West, which caused the difference in the overall framework between the two. Traditional Chinese culture flows in the blood of the Chinese people, shaping their personality, ideology, and unique way of thinking, and deeply influences the choice of paths, system construction and ideology in modern China. This not only makes the practices of contemporary China exhibit fundamental Chinese characteristics and forms, but also makes the contemporary Chinese knowledge system inevitably show Chinese style and Chinese manner.

Second, China's modernisation process surpassed that of Western countries and created a miracle of development. Since the founding of New China, in just a few decades, it has gone through the journey of more than 200 years of Western history. During the period of socialist construction, China built an independent and complete industrial system and national economic system in just 30 years of difficult exploration. Laying the foundation for industrial dividends, national defence dividends, human resources dividends and socialist system dividends for the development achievements of reform and opening up. After the reform and opening up, China has achieved sustained high-speed growth. Professor Spence, winner of the Nobel Prize in Economics, pointed out that among all the high-growth cases in the world, China has the largest and the fastest growth rate. The growth in speed and in scale is unprecedented.[2] At the same time, China is also the country with the greatest achievements in poverty reduction in the world. Based on the international poverty line of less than US$1.25 per person per day, more than 700 million people have been lifted out of poverty since 1980. In 2021, under the current standards, all people living in rural areas have been lifted out of poverty.

Third, Chinese socialism has surpassed the capitalist modernisation path. The process of Western modernisation is also the process of the formation of the capitalist system. The logic of capital surpasses everything and becomes the highest priority logic, and capitalism has become the basic paradigm of modernisation. The socialist movement that originated in Europe, itself was a counter-movement to the capitalist system. After World War II formed an evenly balanced pattern of mutual competition. With the disintegration of the socialist camps in the Soviet Union and Eastern Europe at the turn of the 1980s and 1990s, capitalism seemed to have finally won out in the institutional competition, so American scholar Fukuyama began to declare that 'history has come to an end'.

However, history will not end. Only the vain conceit of Western scholars will end. At the turn of the first and second decades of the 21st century, the pendulum of history seems to have moved to the other side. After the 2008 international financial crisis, the process of the global capitalist system, formed after the Cold War, was reversed. The confrontational contradictions between classes in developed Western countries intensified, ethnic conflicts intensified, and populism and extreme right forces rose. The former 'model students' of the global system have begun to expose the shortcomings of the economic, political and social systems which cannot be effectively corrected. It is as if the international 'boss' the West is beginning to lose his vitality. In 2020, the outbreak of the global Covid-19 pandemic was more like a 'monster-revealing mirror', exposing the crisis of the Western way model and institutional model.

At the same time, China's socialist cause has shown vigorous vitality. The path of socialism with Chinese characteristics is not only different from the capitalist modernisation path of the West, but also different from the Soviet-style socialist path, and has opened up a new chapter in the world socialist movement.

In 2010, China surpassed Japan to become the world's second largest economy. In 2014, it surpassed the United States to become the world's largest economy in terms of purchasing power parity. In exchange rate terms, it may surpass the United States to become the world's largest economy by 2030. An emerging global power is approaching the centre of the world stage with a confident attitude.

The great rejuvenation of China and the collective rise of non-Western countries have changed the basic trend of the great divergence between Western and non-Western countries, which had been present for hundreds of years, and the basic world pattern of the Western centre and the non-Western fringes. The history of the world has moved from divergence to reversal and convergence. The 'long 16th century' is coming to an end, and mankind will usher in the 21st century when the world will be 'one and the same'. (环球同此凉热)

With the disintegration of the gigantic material empire, the foundation on which the gigantic spiritual empire is built will be loosened, and the Western-centric way of constructing knowledge will eventually come to an end.

What is not commensurate with the great revival of China's material power is that China has not yet built its own ideological system, and the contribution of modern Chinese thought to the world is extremely limited.

Of course, there are reasons for the hegemony of Western discourse, but there are also factors of ideological self-restraint. The root cause is that we have formed a knowledge construction method centred on Western theories, and spent our main energy on preaching and providing footnotes for Western theories. For more than 100 years, we have been looking westward. It is time to change our posture and look at the practice under our feet. It is time to change from 'learning scriptures from the West' to 'learning scriptures by practice'.

The great renaissance of China will promote the revolution of China's knowledge construction paradigm, from the Western theory-centred paradigm to the Chinese practice-centred paradigm. This revolution will lead to the emergence of the 'Chinese School'. In other words, the so-called 'Chinese School' is the construction of a theoretical system for the entire revival process of modern China's revolution, construction, and reform, in order to achieve the unity of theory and practice, and the integration of consciousness and existence to make Chinese ideological contributions to the reinterpretation of human society, rewriting the human knowledge system.

The paradigm revolution centred on Chinese practice needs to realise the unification of name and reality. A theory that cannot explain practice is not qualified to guide practice. The confusion and separation of name and reality in the discourse system of philosophy and social sciences are rooted in the fact that theory lags behind practice and theory separates from practice. What we need is not to justify Chinese practice in terms of Western theories, but to innovate Chinese theories based on Chinese practices, and then use Chinese theories to guide Chinese practice. Taking Chinese practice as the body, and taking Marxism, traditional culture, and Western theory as the 'three traditions' (三统), to promote the construction of a Chinese discourse system of 'one base and three uses'.

A paradigmatic revolution centred Chinese practice needs to realise the unity of universality and particularity. Universality is contained in particularity. As long as successful practice has universal significance, it will have a demonstrative effect on other countries. China's practice as the centre not China's particular theory, but takes China's practice as the basis, responds to the general concerns of mankind, provides Chinese answers to the problems of common concern to mankind, and provides Chinese solutions to the challenges faced by mankind. China's practice as the centre is not a closed-door country to engage in epistemology, but to widely learn from and actively absorb the results of international theoretical research. Use it if it fits, don't use it if it does not fix. 'Understand the objective truth and use the understanding of predecessors to elucidate their own thoughts', (六经皆我注脚) which is not only independent originality, but also an international dialogue. It is not only a Chinese position, a Chinese viewpoint, but also a Chinese discourse system of universal significance.

China's practice as centre also requires a change in research methodology. From in-line research to independent research, advocating practicality instead of positivism, falsificationism and deductivism, from the research path of theoretical hypothesis-empirical testing to the research path of 'fact immersion'-theoretical dialogue-theoretical hypothesis-empirical testing. China's practice as a centre also needs to change the academic evaluation system, from formal evaluation to more emphasis on substantive contribution evaluation, to form an academic evaluation system more rooted in China, and to evaluate more theoretical originality, practical impact and practical contribution.

The great renaissance of China has provided an unprecedented scale of human experiments and incomparably rich practical soil for an unprecedented historic opportunity of theoretical innovation. As President Xi Jinping said: 'This is an era in which theories are needed and can certainly be produced, and an era in which ideas are required and can certainly be produced. We cannot fail this era.' The Chinese School is not a school of thought of a certain discipline or a certain group, but an all-round ideological revolution that involves the participation of scholars from different disciplines and generations. This will be a thought transformation of 'source', 'moving the heart of the world', and 'High tolerance'. It will be a fundamental paradigm shift in how to view the universe and life, and ideological changes in all fields of philosophy, economics, politics, law, sociology and management alongside other fields.

In this great ideological revolution involving countless people, China will form a Chinese knowledge system in various disciplines. China is not only an economic giant in the world, but also a spiritual giant in the world. Not only will it contribute Chinese products to the world, but it will also contribute Chinese thought to the world.

1 What historians call the 'long 16th century' is not the same as the 16th century in calendar terms, but rather the second half of the 15th century to the first half of the 17th century, when the capitalist world economic system began to take shape. See Immanuel Wallerstein, 2013, The Modern World-System, Vol. 1, Social Science Literature Press, p. 74. 历史学家所说的'漫长的16世纪'并不等同于历法上的16世纪, 而是指15世纪下半叶到17世纪上半叶, 这期间资本主义世界经济体系开始形成。参见沃伦斯坦：《现代世界体系》（第1卷），社会科学文献出版社2013年版，第74页。
2 Michael Spence, 2008, *Successful Experiences and New Challenges of China's Reform and Opening-up*, 30 Years of China's Economy Watched by 50 People: Review and Analysis, China Economic Press, p. 43. [迈克尔·斯彭斯：《中国改革开放的成功经验与新挑战》，见《中国经济50人看三十年：回顾与分析》，中国经济出版社2008年版，第43页]
3 For example, Zhu Xi: 'The essence has no place to be found, so it can only be seen in use.' 例如，朱熹："本体无著莫处，故只可于用处看。"

CHAPTER 2

'One Base and Three Uses' Construction of the Chinese Discourse System

[*The first draft of this article was delivered by the author on 30 March 2014 at a seminar on 'Institutional Civilisation, Chinese Perspectives' organised by the Centre for China and World Studies and the Centre for Rule of Law Studies of Peking University. The second draft is a speech delivered at the 16th Open Times Forum on 'Chinese Discourse' on 3–4 November 2018. The third draft was completed on 25 July 2020, with comments from scholars including Wen Tiejun, Ding Cai and He Xuefeng.]

In modern China, not only have the utensils experienced major changes unseen in thousands of years, but the spiritual level has also experienced major changes.

In just over a century, various theories have been surging, among which the three major schools of thought are the Chinese school, Western school and Marxism, and the most lasting and influential ones are Marxism, New Sinology, and Liberalism. The three ideological schools converged and merged, and the three ideological trends stirred and evolved with each other, jointly promoting the great revolution of Chinese thought.

Chinese thought has always tended to be inclusive. Although the three major trends of thought are quite different, they are also quite complementary. Although there are primary and secondary differences, it is not necessarily impossible to compromise comprehensively.

Zhang Zhidong advocated Chinese learning for the essence, western learning for practical use, which means compromising between Chinese and Western schools, keeping the old school while absorbing the new one.[1]

At the same time, the debate between Westernisation and conservatism was opened up, and various arguments emerged such as Western learning, Marxism or Confucianism for base.

Zhang Dainian advocated the 'three-in-one' of Chinese learning, Western learning, and Marxism, and put forward a comprehensive innovation theory of Chinese culture, which Fang Keli further summarised as a comprehensive innovative theory of 'Marxism soul, Chinese essence, and Western use'. Taking the ideological system of Marxism and socialism as the guiding principle, the Chinese national culture is the main body of life, the main body of creation and the main body of acceptance, and the object of learning and reference is Western culture.[2] Gan Yang has a saying of 'unifying the three traditions'. He believes that there are three traditions in contemporary Chinese society that are colliding with each other. One is the tradition that has been extended after the reform and opening up with the 'market' as the centre, and the other is the pursuit of equality and justice, formed in the Mao Zedong era. The last one is Chinese traditional culture or Confucian culture.[3]

Corresponding to this 'Three Traditions', many commentators also regard Neoliberalism, New Left, and New Confucianism as the divisions of contemporary Chinese ideology.

How can the 'combining three streams' and 'unifying the three traditions' be legible? Where do they merge? How can they fit together? 'Methods appear for solving the breaking world.' Neoliberalism, New Left, and New Confucianism not only have difficulty communicating with each other, but instead speak their own words, and social ideology is on the verge of tearing apart.

What is the reason for this? The 'three streams' and 'three unities', each with its own origin and direction, 'People of different moral convictions cannot get along.' but without the base, it is difficult for them to converge. 'Unifying the three traditions' often becomes 'Putting together the three traditions', and 'combining the three streams' often becomes 'Putting together the three streams'.

'Combining the three streams' is for comprehensive innovation, and 'unifying the three traditions' is for the creation of a new convention. More important than dealing with existing theoretical resources is to promote academic localisation and innovation in contemporary China. Since the 21st century, discussions such as the 'Beijing Consensus'[4] and 'China Model'[5] have emerged, which are all useful explorations, but these discussions are, after all, too general to penetrate deep into the discipline. In recent years, there have been discussions on the Chinese School, which has made the pursuit of academic autonomy go deep into different disciplines and enter a more refined stage. This is a response to the central government's call to build a system of philosophy and social sciences with Chinese characteristics. It also marks China's entry into an era of academic self-awareness and academic autonomy.

'The construction of the Chinese School is not the construction of a certain disciplinary school, but a paradigm change involving philosophy, history, economics, political science, law, sociology, ethnology and other disciplines.'[6] Some scholars have different opinions on this. They believe that this view is very bold, but it does not conform to the law of discipline development, because schools belong to specific disciplines or are premised on specific paradigms. They take Marxism as an example and believe that with the Marxist paradigm, many disciplines are in the Marxist school, because there is no paradigm of 'Chinese-ism', there is no so-called multidisciplinary Chinese school.[7]

The development of the 'Chinese School' fundamentally needs to deal with the relationship between modern Chinese practice and existing theoretical resources. This chapter believes that the methodology of Chinese academic discourse innovation is 'one base and three uses', with modern Chinese practice as the base, Marxism, traditional culture, Western theory as the uses. The past serves the present, the foreign serves the Chinese, and Marxism serves the Chinese. Only by establishing the practical status of practical and theoretical resources can we promote the innovation of Chinese academic discourse and truly integrate 'Marxism, Chinese learning and Western learning', 'Three Streams' and 'Three Traditions'.

1. From theory as base to practice as base

When it comes to the construction of Chinese discourse, we can refer to an important category of ancient philosophy – Body and Use (体和用). Although *Book of Changes* (易经) does not explicitly propose the category of base and use, it is embedded in it. The 'Shuogua' (说卦) says: 'Qian means sturdiness, Kun means suppleness, Zhen means turbulence, Xun means fit, Kan means pit, and Li means attachment. Gen means to stop, Dui means to speak.' (乾是刚健，坤是柔顺，震是动荡，巽是契合，坎是坑穴，离是依附。艮是停止，兑是讲说。) This shows that the Eight Trigrams are all useful.[8] According to scholars, the concept of body-use (体用) may have first come from Wang Bi, but later on the concept of body-use was applied in various ways, either as ontology-utility,[9] ontology-phenomenon,[10] spiritual substance-concrete use,[11] etc. Whatever the usage, the traditional philosophy is that body-use is one source and the two are inseparable; use is the use of body and body is the body of use.

Zhang Zhidong's point of view that 'Chinese learning for the essence, western learning for practical use' divides two things into the body and use, which is clearly different from the traditional meaning of body and use. Therefore, Yan Fu criticised that Chinese learning has its body and use, likewise, the Western learning also has its' body and use. Therefore, Chinese learning as the body and Western learning for practical use is not appropriate.[12]

However, Zhang Zhidong has created a widely accepted new connotation of body and use, which differs from the traditional use in that the body and use are used in parallel to illustrate their fundamental-secondary relationship, where the body is the fundamental, and the use is not the manifest use of the body, but the use for me. Later, the dispute over 'Marxism, Chinese learning and Western learning' style was also used in this sense. The concept of body and use in this paper is also based on the relationship between the fundamental and the auxiliary, which means that the innovation of the Chinese discourse system must be based on practice as the body and theory as the use.

Either the advocates of the Chinese school as a body or those of the Western school as a body in fact the advocates of theory as a body. The Chinese school as a body advocates a return to the basics and a renewal of Confucianism, hoping to revitalise it and use it to shape contemporary Chinese society. Contemporary Chinese practice provides an opportunity for the renewal of Confucianism, and the new Confucianism is known as the third phase of Confucianism. There are also advocates for restoring traditional Daoism culture and developing new Daoism.

Western learning as the body is hoping to implement the so-called 'knowledge enlightenment' in China, and use the Western knowledge system to discipline Chinese practice. They claim that Western learning has universal significance and that Chinese practice has no value of theoretical innovation but is merely the application and sample of this universal knowledge system, and the deviation from the Western value system is a deviation from 'universal values'. Whether it is Chinese learning or Western learning as the essence, they are all dogmatic, trying to use theory to discipline reality.

'One body and three uses' means that practice is the body, and the three theories of 'Marxism, Chinese learning and Western learning' are used. Practice as the body refers to the root and source, not the subject. The subject is an innovative Chinese discourse system, which is fundamentally derived from modern Chinese practice. Theory as use refers to a knowledge system that has been objectified. The use is not the manifestation of the body, but the application and reference. It means that the innovation of the Chinese discourse system requires the application and reference of the existing theoretical resources.

Why is practice as the body, not theory as the body? The concept of practice needs to be further explored. In the essay 'Theses on Feuerbach', Marx took the concept of practice as the key to distinguishing 'new materialism' from old materialism, arguing that practice cannot be 'understood only in its object or intuitive form', but is to be seen as 'sensual human activity'. He sees the 'conformity of environmental change and human activity or self-transformation' as 'revolutionary practice'.[13]

Marx saw practice as a 'living' historical process, or as Lukács expressed, it is a continuous, concrete 'generation' in which 'the true nature of the object is revealed in this generation, in this tendency, in this process'.[14] It cannot be regarded as a fixed object. Practice, therefore, is essentially a creative activity, but it is subject to a given economic and social condition. The creative process of practice, which is constantly self-generating, makes it impossible for us to discipline practice through the theory that has been objectified. On the contrary, the theory must enter into the concrete process of practice generation in order to gain vitality and prove its truthfulness and heritage in practice.

Theories and practices linked together in a specific historical process constitute a reflective relationship, in which practice reflects theory and, in turn, theory tries to dominate practice; Thought strives to become reality, and reality also strives to tend towards thought.[20] Whether this reflectivity tends to converge or diverge determines the evolution state of the generated sequence.

Convergence is the convergence between theory and practice in a reflexive evolutionary process, where theory is able to reflect practice and guide it effectively. Practice is the body, which enables people to adjust their belief system and cognitive system according to practice, and at the same time to transform the world according to the cognition that is in line with practice, and as practice goes further, theory grows an inch, and as theory grows an inch, practice goes further. This evolutionary process will result in the two leaps that Mao Zedong described as matter becoming spirit and spirit becoming matter again. When people have accumulated more material for their perceptual understanding of the objective world and grasped the laws of operation of objective things, they will make a leap and turn it into a theory. People's understanding has been tested by practice and has achieved success, which has produced another leap. The latter leap is greater than the former because it proves that the former is correct.[16]

Taking theory as the body will cause theory to become a thing-in-itself, and it will be separated from the concrete and practical historical generation process, which will bring about the reflective divergence of theory and practice, and theory and practice will become more and more disconnected. A theory that is divorced from practice cannot overcome its own rigidity, and can only achieve unity with practice through compulsory adaptation. Theoretical dogma either causes major setbacks in practice or becomes an obsolete and rigid system. There are many lessons to be learned from history, and there are many dogmatic traps in our research today.

The paradigm of constructing knowledge centred on 'universal' Western theories to explain Chinese practice and to conduct validation and case studies will face the problem of double disconnection.

First, Western theory is disconnected from Chinese practice. Although the modern system of social science is manifested as a universal interpretation system, it is generally constructed on the basis of hundreds of years of practice in the West. China has embarked on a path different from that of the West, and has built a unique political and economic system and its practice has actually sailed into the uncharted waters of the modern social science system.

Second, the Western theoretical system lags behind the development of the times. Human beings are in the early stage of the fourth industrial revolution. This great revolution will render many of the traditional Western philosophical and social science theories ineffective. Human beings need to rebuild new philosophical and social science theories based on new era conditions and practices. China and the West are on the same starting line, and there is absolutely no need to 'Talk about Greece'. (言必称希腊，which means blindly praise foreign things regardless of the actual situation).

In order to 'combine the three streams' and 'unify the three traditions', we must first turn the 'headstand' of theory and reality upside down again.

No matter which tradition we start from, we must first recognise that modern Chinese practice is the body, and take practice as the starting point and destination, combine the three uses into one, promote the innovation of Chinese discourse, and create new opportunities for the three traditions.

2. What is 'unify the three traditions'?

The evolution of the human knowledge system is cumulative, and knowledge innovation is inseparable from existing theoretical resources. At the same time, it is also necessary to conduct dialogue with existing knowledge systems to find the position of new discourses in the knowledge spectrum.

The innovation of China's academic discourse system should be based on 'Marxism, Chinese learning and Western learning' and 'Three Traditions': guided by Marxism, forming a mutually supportive relationship with Chinese Marxism; based on traditional culture, drawing on its useful ideological resources through creative transformation and innovative development; Take the Western academic discourse system as a reference to the dialogue object, forming a 'second-order continuous relationship' with the Western academic discourse system.

Marxism is a magnificent theoretical framework, which combines philosophy, economics, political science, history, and sociology into one pot, and is a 'great tool of knowledge'. The Marxist methodology emphasises that there should be not only a key theory, but also a two-point theory, seeing both trees and forests, analysing phenomena, revealing their essential characteristics, and providing guidance for academic innovation.

Sinicizing Marxism has pushed Marxism to a new level. Mao Zedong Thought is the first sinicisation of Marxism, and the socialist theoretical system with Chinese characteristics is the second sinicisation of Marxism. Sinicized Marxism is the product of practice and exploration in different periods of the Chinese revolution, construction, reform and new era. The Party and the government have already demonstrated a high degree of theoretical consciousness and confidence. It is also necessary for academics to be academically self-aware and academically self-confident to carry out the theoretical interpretation of Chinese Marxism, so as to get rid of the apprenticeship of 'learning from the West' for a century and build an independent academic discourse system.

In the process of constructing a Chinese discourse system, consciously conducting theoretical dialogues with Sinicized Marxism, and further academicising and refining some empirical and practical generalisations may be an effective way to construct a Chinese discourse system. For example, based on an empirical study of China's five-year plan, we summarise it as the 'Collective wisdom' decision-making model, which has gone through five stages: Make everyone offer good ideas, Collecting ideas broadly from the public, extensive consultation, Collegial decision-making, and Informing the public,[17] which can be regarded as an academic representation of the democratic centralist decision-making process.

Throughout its long history, China has developed a Chinese culture dominated by Confucianism, Buddhism and Daoism. We need a holistic understanding of Chinese culture in order to take its essence and remove its dross. We cannot simply judge Chinese civilisation with a westernised vision, and we must build up cultural confidence and civilised self-confidence. Chinese civilisation differs from Western civilisation in a number of fundamental ways. China is a civilisation path of 'seeking from inside', which is different from the Western civilisation path of 'seeking from outside'[18]; China is a holistic and coherent way of thinking, as opposed to a reductionist and analytical mode of thinking. China is a theoretical principle that emphasises practical results, which is different from a theoretical theory that advocates form; China is 'Recognise the two directions of good and evil in the development of things, and then adopt the moderate ones ' (执其两端而用其中), which is different from attacking heresy and standing on one end (不同于攻乎异端而立其一端). These characteristics of Chinese civilisation, which are very different from those of the West, make the construction of a modern Chinese discourse system inevitably represent Chinese style and Chinese manner.

Chinese discourse innovation should take traditional culture as an important ideological resource and promote the creative transformation and innovative development of traditional culture.[19] Not only should 'annotate me in the six classics' (我注六经), but more importantly, 'the six classics being my footnote'.[20] (六经注我). The innovation of Chinese discourse requires the 'creative transformation' of the traditional discourse system, so that the past can be used for the present and bring forth the new ideas, absorbing the reasonable elements of traditional civilisation, discarding the unreasonable ones, and giving it a new connotation in line with the times. This kind of creative transformation is not only the need for

Chinese civilisation to return to its roots and write a new chapter, but also a way for traditional discourse to influence contemporary Chinese practice and contribute to the contemporary Chinese discourse system.

'Ways run parallel without interfering with one another.' ('道并行而不悖'), the integration of traditional culture into the contemporary Chinese discourse system does not cancel the evolution of its own path, but instead provides an opportunity to 'open up new'. Confucianism, Daoism, Legalism, Buddhism and other time-honoured traditional concepts and forms will be inherited and innovated, and will further flourish, entering a new period of development.

The Western system of philosophical and social sciences has become increasingly mature and refined over the past two to three centuries. Although we cannot apply this system of theories to explain Chinese practice, at the same time, if we set aside Western theories and start anew, it will be detrimental to the development of Chinese social sciences, and will also cause a setback in Chinese social sciences. The use of Western theory is not an application, but a critical use, forming a 'second-order continuity' with Western theory rather than a 'first-order continuity'.[21]

'First-order continuity' regards Western theories as universal, directly applied to explain or criticise Chinese practice. 'Second-order continuity' means that the problems are universal, but the answers are diverse. Western theories are based on their own historical conditions to provide Western answers to common human problems, while China is perfectly capable of coming up with a different answer. For example, the theory of 'separation of powers' is often used to criticise China's lack of judicial independence from a first-order continuity perspective; but from the perspective of second-order continuity, we have made an attempt to believe that China's political system is not 'separation of three powers', but 'Seven divisions of power'. The two systems are fundamentally different, but they also need to answer the universal question in the political system. Different answers to questions such as operational efficiency, avoidance of corruption of power, selection of officials, and continuity of the political system can lead to different results and different advantages and disadvantages.

3. Practice-ism research methodology

One of the progresses brought about by the integration of social sciences with international standards in recent decades has been a greater emphasis on the use of empirical research methods and an increasingly scientific and normative approach to social science research, which has led to a paradigm shift away from metaphysics and towards positivism in Chinese social science.

But without the necessary reflection on the philosophical underpinnings of the methodology behind empirical research, much social science research has either been a rigid adaptation of Western theories tested against Chinese data or has become a formalistic game of pure presentation of data and methods.

Whether it is early positivism, logical positivism, or falsification-ism and operational positivism, they are all based on dissatisfaction with the scientific nature of social sciences and try to evolve social sciences into more scientific disciplines like natural sciences, which are able to formulate actionable hypotheses and test propositions based on objective observation and the collection of data.

The problem is that the practical nature of the humanities and social sciences differs from the objective nature of the natural sciences in that subjectivity cannot be separated from objectivity, and the researcher needs to be involved in the process of generating concrete practice. Without entering the process of generating concrete practice, not only is it impossible to understand the world, but it is also impossible to ask meaningful questions. The scientific division proposed by positivism is still essentially a metaphysical scientific division, while the scientific division of pragmatism requires the integration of theoretical research with concrete practice. The recognition of truth in practice and the testing of truth in practice make the theory acquire its sideness and scientific nature.

The methodological paradigm of pragmatism advocates the inductive testing in terms of research methodology, which is to further form a strong connection with facts based on Popper's test of deduction, emphasising that the formulation of hypotheses is primarily based on the induction of facts, and that the testing of hypotheses does not only lie in falsification or confirmation but needs to be further tested by practice.

The inductive test method assumes that the most important aspect of research is not the testing of hypotheses but the process of formulating them. A leap of theoretical intuition is formed through the induction of facts and a hypothesis is formulated by engaging in a theoretical dialogue, rather than by a literature review based on existing theory. The inductive test method divides the research process into four steps.

A. 'Fact immersion'

The inductive method, despite the problems raised by Hume, Popper and others, such as the 'inability to draw inferences from past experience', the inability to transition from the singular description to the universal description and that it cannot be used as a logic of scientific discovery,[22] however, the positivists' criticism of the scientific nature of the inductive method is not to the point. The fundamental significance of the inductive method is to establish theoretical hypotheses on the basis of practical experience, rather than establishing a formal 'scientific foundation' for the hypotheses, denying that the induction method actually collapses the most important factual basis of positivism itself.

Practical-ism not only does not deny the role of empiricism and induction, but also further believes that experience, rather than old theories, is the starting point of empirical research. The formulation of a good theoretical hypothesis is a cognitive leap based on fact immersion. The inductive method from the perspective of practical-ism refers to the formation of this cognitive leap, rather than the derivation process from individual judgment to holistic judgment.

The formation of hypotheses is based on theoretical intuition, which is the seed from which all theories can grow. A good intuition is much more valuable than a dozen mathematical models. But this intuition is not a mysterious psychological phenomenon, but a leap from objective cognition to subjective generalisation, and it is the formation of this theoretical intuition that makes the cognitive leap from the concrete to the abstract, from the individual to the general. This leap is only preliminary and its scientific validity still needs to be tested repeatedly.

To achieve this leap, we must have a full perceptual and rational understanding of the facts. Just like seeds need to be germinated in suitable soil nutrients, the generation of theoretical intuition comes from 'fact immersion'. This process is what Bacon called the wine of science that blesses mankind is made from the 'countless grapes' of rich human practice.[23] He Xuefeng calls this the Saturated Empirical Method,[24] just as a chemical solution must reach a certain concentration to crystallise, and a factual material must be saturated before an intuitive leap can occur. 'Fact immersion' is a process of immersing in practice, not just collecting materials and summarising them, but including participating in policy research, field research, in-depth interviews, and 'dissecting sparrows'.

B. Dialogue with theories

After forming a theoretical intuition, a dialogue with existing theories is required. After 'fact immersion', a theoretical immersion is required, with extensive reading and combing of the relevant theoretical literature. The dialogue with existing theories is mainly conducted at three levels: firstly, to compare the consistency between existing theoretical systems and the theoretical intuition, and whether existing theoretical systems have explanatory power for the observed phenomena, this inconsistency is where the room for innovation lies; secondly, to examine the position of the concept and theoretical hypothesis to be proposed in the existing knowledge spectrum, and to find the entry point to weave it into the knowledge system; finally, to form a direct dialogue with a particular theory, to find a starting point for describing where one's theory 'starts from', and to form a relationship with existing theories in terms of critique, inheritance, development and integration.

C. Hypotheses proposition

Theoretical hypotheses are formulated based on practical generalisation and dialogue with existing theories. Theoretical hypotheses are the refinement of theoretical intuitions, which are transformed from vague intuitions into theoretical concepts and propositions. Concepts are clearly defined, operational definitions and testable hypothesis propositions are formed, and a research design is proposed.

Theoretical hypotheses based on inductive methods can introduce methods such as grounded theory, big data induction and other methods.

D. Empirical test

This step is an empirical test of theoretical hypotheses. The empirical test can be carried out by various quantitative and qualitative methods. According to the research subject, methods such as econometrics and case analysis can be flexibly selected or comprehensively used.

Empirical testing has both the characteristics of falsifiability and verifiability. We should not seek to prove or confirm a theory thoroughly. However, theories that are falsified by more and more empirical tests become less and less tenable, and theories that are supported by more and more empirical tests become increasingly convincing.

The scientificity of practical research methodology is not based on the impeccable scientific method and logic, but on the strong connection between theory and practice. The method of proposing theoretical hypotheses through fact immersion is a process of mapping from practice to theory. In contrast, the empirical testing of theoretical hypotheses is a mapping process from theory to practice. This is because hypotheses must be formulated based on facts and at the same time, the hypotheses should be tested with facts, which makes the weakly linked relationship between theory and practice into a strongly linked relationship. The degree of refinement of this dual mapping depends on the soundness of each step and also on the iterative cycle that is performed.

Unlike the theory-centred test-deductive method 'theory-hypothesis-test-theory', which is a cycle of coming from theory to theory, the inductive test method of pragmatism is 'practice-theory-hypothesis-test', which is a cycle of coming from practice to practice. The scientific nature of pragmatism is based on this cyclical process. It is through the cyclical sequence of mutual mapping and mutual generation between theory and practice that the convergence of theory and practice has been achieved, and the theory has truly acquired its truthfulness and sideness.

4. Some extended discussions

One is the problem of vulgar justification. Theory is transcendental in relation to practice. The dogma-oriented research paradigm has a strong critical character, and dogmatism often exhibits a sharp critique of reality.

The practice-oriented research paradigm is often regarded as a vulgar justification, always hesitating before criticising the practice, arguing that theories that cannot explain the practice are not qualified to criticise the practice. Therefore, it is important to first understand the reality. Only after we fully recognise the reality will we have the right to criticise it, rather than starting to criticise as soon as we see a reality that is inconsistent with our own perception.

In fact, behind the strong critical spirit of the dogmatists is another kind of spiritual bondage, which is an unreflective adherence to an existing body of knowledge, a theoretical critique of reality, without ever reflecting on the theoretical system they hold in the light of reality.

The practice-based research paradigm essentially advocates a double critique: the first is the critique of practice against theory, and the theory remains open to practice; the second is the critique of theory against practice. which, on the basis of explaining practice, raises problems in practice and uses theory to guide the direction of practice. What we need is responsible thinking that sees theoretical perspectives as a link in the chain of mutual generation between practice and theory. Theoretical understanding needs to correctly reflect practice and promote better practice through constructive criticism.

The second is the question of universality and particularity. Taking practice as the body also means breaking the myth of abstract universalism. The dilemma of abstract universalism lies in the opposition between universality and pluralism. Just as dogmatism makes the mistake of detaching from practice, abstract universalism encounters the same difficulty of a disconnection between rigid theory and concrete and rich practice. The real universality lies precisely in the pluralism and particularity. The real universality is the commonality in the pluralism, and the real universal value is the common value of the plural subjects, or 'family resemblance' in Wittgenstein's words. In July 1973, when Mao Zedong and Yang Zhenning talked about philosophy, Mao said: 'The universality of contradiction does not exist alone, but exists in the particularity. Human beings cannot see it. They see John Doe, they see adults and children, but they do not see "people".'[25]

This does not mean that Chinese theory is a particular theory, but diversity means that there are multiple answers to the same general question. Western-centrism has chosen precisely one of these answers as the only one, leaving other possibilities either suppressed or marginalised. The universal significance of China Theory lies precisely in the process of constructing theories. It provides Chinese answers to questions of common concern to mankind, new answers different from the West for mankind to answer common problems, and new paths for mankind to solve common issues that are different from the West.

The third is the issue of interdisciplinary Chinese schools. From the perspective of theory as the body, it is true that there is no interdisciplinary Chinese school because there is no 'Sino-ism' theory. Precisely because we return to practice as the body and theory as the use, we must recognise the Chinese school is taking place in the overall sense. The transcendence of Chinese practice over Western-centric theoretical systems is a transcendence in a holistic sense, a fundamental paradigm change in how to view the world and life, and it will also bring about an interdisciplinary change in thought, and in the process will make a Chinese intellectual contribution to the world.

Looking back at history, the formation of any innovative school trend is a spiritual response to the practice of a great era. China is in such an unprecedented era, and each of us is situated in a Chinese aura where practical innovations are constantly emerging and ideological debates are unprecedentedly active.

As long as we take Chinese practice as the main body and absorb the nourishment of the 'Three Traditions', in the next few decades, we may be able to witness the formation and growth of the 'Chinese School', and gradually change the recent pattern of not only lagging behind the West in terms of artifacts, but also in terms of discourse. China will end the old era of borrowed language speaking and enter a new era of autonomous language speaking.

---

1 In 1896, Sun Jianai proposed in his submission for the establishment of the Imperial College in Beijing that 'make the Chinese learning as the base, and Western learning for practical use.' In 1898, Zhang Zhidong wrote *Encouraging Learning*. The inner part talks about the Chinese learning and the outer part talks about Western learning, which systematically expounds the idea of using Chinese learning as the base and Western learning as applications. Zhang Zhidong, 2010, *Encouraging Learning*, Jilin Publishing Group Co., Ltd

2 Zhang Dainian and Wang Dong, 1997, *Modern Revival and Comprehensive Innovation of Chinese Civilization*, Teaching and Research, No.5; Fang Keli, 2006, *About the Physical Use of Culture*, Social Science Front, No. 4; Li Yi et al., 2007, *Comprehensive Innovation Theory* and *Marxism Soul, Chinese Essence, and Western Use: A Discussion on the Construction of Contemporary Chinese Culture*, Journal of Shanghai Normal University, Nov. [张岱年、王东：《中华文明的现代复兴和综合创新》，《教学与研究》1997年第5期。方克立：《关于文化的体用问题》，《社会科学战线》2006 年第4期。李毅等：《综合创新论与'马魂、中体、西用'：关于当代中国文化建设的探讨》，《上海师范大学学报》2007 年11月]

3 Gan Yang, 2007, 'Understanding the Three Traditions', *Life·Reading·Xinzhi Sanlian Bookstore*, p. 3. [甘阳：《通三统》，生活·读书·新知三联书店2007年版，第3页]

4 See Huang Ping and Cui Zhiyuan, eds, 2005, *China and Globalization – The Washington Consensus or the Beijing Consensus*, Social Science Literature Press; Yu Keping, ed, 2006, The Chinese Model and the Beijing Consensus, Social Science Literature Press, 2006. [黄平、崔之元主编：《中国与全球化——华盛顿共识还是北京共识》，社会科学文献出版社2005年版。俞可平主编：《中国模式与'北京共识'》，社会科学文献出版社2006年版]

5 See Pan Wei, editor-in-chief, 2009, *The Chinese Model: Interpreting 60 Years of the People's Republic*, Central Compilation Press. Zhang Weiwei, 2011, *China Shaking: The Rise of a 'Civilized State'*, Shanghai People's Publishing House.[潘维主编：《中国模式：解读人民共和国的60年》，中央编译出版社2009年版。张维为：《中国震撼：一个'文明型国家'的崛起》，上海人民出版社2011年版]

6 Yan Yilong, 2017, *Building a Chinese School Based on Revival Practice* (People's Watch), *People's Daily*, 24 Sept, p.5. [鄢一龙：《基于复兴实践构建中国学派》（人民观察），《人民日报》2017年9月24日，第5版]

7 Yan Xuetong, 2018, 'Re-discussion on why there is no 'Chinese school', *International Political Science*, No. 9. 阎学通：《再论为何没有'中国学派'》，《国际政治科学》2018年总第9期。

8 For example, Kong Yingda believes that, 'Shuogua' says: 'Qian means strong and healthy'. speaks of the essence of sky, with health as its use. Wang Bi and Han Kangbo's commentary and Kong Yingda's commentary, 2009, *Zhou Yi Zheng Yi – The First Volume of the Zhou Yi Commentary*, China Zhigong Publishing House, p. 9. [例如，孔颖达就认为：《说卦》云：'乾，健也'，言天之体，以健为用。王弼、韩康伯注，孔颖达正义：《周易正义·周易注疏卷第一》，中国致公出版社2009年版，第9页]

9 For example, Cui Jing: 'The body is the form and quality, and the use is the subtle use of the form and quality.' Huineng: 'Determination is the body of wisdom, and wisdom is the use of determination.' 例如，崔璟：'体者即形质也，用者即形质之妙用也。'惠能：'定是慧体，慧是定用。'

10 For example, Zhu Xi: 'The essence has no place to be found, so it can only be seen in use.' 例如，朱熹：'本体无著莫处，故只可于用处看。'

11 For example, Hu Yuan: 'The ruler, the minister, the father and the son, the benevolence, righteousness, propriety and music, which cannot be changed through the ages, is the body; the actions and measures in the world can be used to govern the world, to make the people live in peace and obey the emperor's leadership, is the use.' [例如，胡瑗："君臣父子，仁义礼乐，历世不可变者，其体也；举而措之天下，能润泽斯民，归于皇极者，其用也。"]

12 Quoted in Fang Keli, 1984, 'On the Scope of Body and Use in Chinese Philosophy', *Chinese Social Sciences*, No. 5. [转引自方克立：《论中国哲学中的体用范畴》，《中国社会科学》1984年第5期]

13 Karl Marx, 2012, 'Theses on Feuerbach', *Selected Works of Marx and Engels, Vol. 1*, People's Publishing House, 2012, pp. 133-136. Originally in German: *Die Philosophen haben die Welt nur verschieden interpretiert; es kommt darauf an, sie zu verändern*, 1845, published in 1888, Stuttgart Verlag von J.H.W. Dietz. [马克思：《关于费尔巴哈的提纲》，《马克思恩格斯选集》（第1卷），人民出版社2012年版，第133—136页]

14 *Selected Writings of Lukács*, 2008, People's Publishing House, p. 115.[《卢卡奇文选》，人民出版社2008年版，第115页]

15 'Introduction to the Critique of Hegel's Philosophy of Right', 2012, *Selected Works of Marx and Engels*. Vol. 1, People's Publishing House, p. 11. [《黑格尔法哲学批判导言》，《马克思恩格斯选集》（第1卷），人民出版社2012年版，第11页]

16 Mao Zedong, 1999, 'Where Do People's Correct Thoughts Come From?', *Works of Mao Zedong*, Vol. 8, People's Publishing House, pp. 320–321. [毛泽东：《人的正确思想是从哪里来的》，《毛泽东文集》（第8卷），人民出版社1999年版，第320-321页]

17 Wang Shaoguang and Yan Yilong, 2015, *Big Wisdom and Prosperity: How China Makes a Five-Year Plan*, Renmin University of China Press. [王绍光、鄢一龙：《大智兴邦：中国如何制定五年规划》，中国人民大学出版社2015年版]

18 Cheng Yi, *Learning is to make people seek from the inside*. 'Seeking from the outside instead of inside is not the learning of a sage'. (The Suicide Note of Er Cheng, Vol. 25) [程颐："学也者，使人求于内也，不求于内而求于外，非圣人之学也。"(《二程遗书》卷25)]

19 See *President Xi Jinping's Series of Important Speech Readers*, 2014, Learning Publishing House, People's Publishing House, p. 101. [参见《习近平总书记系列重要讲话读本》，学习出版社、人民出版社2014年版，第101页]

20 *Song Dynasty* – Lu Jiuyuan, 'The Book of Discourses': 'Some people ask: Why don't you write a book?' He said: 'Six classics note me! I note six classics!' [宋·陆九渊《语录》："或问先生：何不著书？对曰：六经注我！我注六经！]

21 American scholar Womack put forward the concept of 'second-order continuity' in the process of researching Mao Zedong's political ideological changes around 1957. He believed that although Mao Zedong's behavior changed around 1957, his values and thinking methods still maintained continuity. See Brantly Womack, 2006, *The Foundations of Mao Zedong's Political Thought (1917–1935)*, Renmin University of China Press, p. 270. Originally published in 1982, University of Hawai'i Press. [美国学者沃马克在研究毛泽东1957年前后政治思想转变的过程中提出了"二阶连续性"的概念，认为1957年前后虽然毛泽东的行动方式发生转变，但是价值和思想方法仍然保持连续性。参见沃马克：《毛泽东政治思想的基础（1917—1935）》，中国人民大学出版社 2006 年版，第 270 页]

22 Karl Popper, 2008, *The Logic of Scientific Discovery*, translated by Zha Ruqiang et al., China Academy of Art Press, pp. 3-6, Originally *Logik der Forschung: Zur Erkenntnistheorie der modernen Naturwissenschaft*, 1934 [波普尔：《科学发现的逻辑》，查汝强等译，中国美术学院出版社2008年版，第3-6页]

23 Francis Bacon, 2010, *Novum Organum*, The Commercial Press, p. 106. Originally in Latin, 1620 [培根：《新工具》，商务印书馆2010年版，第106页]

24 He Xuefeng, 2014, 'Saturated Empirical Method: Understanding of Empirical Research Methods in Central China', *Sociological Review*, No. 1. [贺雪峰：《饱和经验法：华中乡土派对经验研究方法的认识》，《社会学评论》2014年第1期]

25 *The Chronology of Mao Zedong (1949-1976)*, 2013, Volume VI, Central Party Literature Publishing House, p. 488. [《毛泽东年谱（1949—1976）》第六卷，中央文献出版社2013年版，第488页]

PART 2
CHINA'S ECONOMIC MODEL

Developing a market economy under conditions of socialism represents a great pioneering effort undertaken by our Party. One of the key factors behind China's tremendous success in economic development is that we have simultaneously leveraged the strengths of both the market economy and the socialist system. Our market economy has developed under the essential conditions of socialist system and the leadership of the CPC. The term 'socialist' is the key descriptor, and this is something that we must never lose sight of.

– Speech by Xi Jinping at the 28th group study session of the Political Bureau of the 18th CPC Central Committee (23 Nov, 2015)

CHAPTER 3

Overall Knowledge Application Mechanisms: Understand the Five-Year Plan Under the Market Economy

[*The first draft of this article is the 16th lecture of the 'National Conditions Forum' of National Research Institute of Tsinghua University on 27 Nov, 2018. Published in the Summer 2019 issue of the Journal of Oriental Studies. Slightly revised for inclusion in this book本文初稿系2018年11月27日清华大学国情研究院《国情讲坛》第16讲演讲稿。刊发于《东方学刊》2019年夏季刊。收入本书时，略有修订。]

1. Has the national planning system failed?

A. *Failure theory of national planning: testing and rethinking*

As China entered its 14th Five-Year Plan period in 2021, the Five-Year Plan is now so well recognised that few would deny or even advocate its abolition; This was not the case in the 1990s when the prevailing view and theory was the 'national planning failure theory'.

The 1996 World Bank report 'From Plan to Market' gave a historic 'sentence' to the national planning system, arguing that national planning is inherently unfeasible because of its deep inefficiency. The report also analyses several aspects of the planning system, including: planners do not have access to sufficient information to substitute for the information conveyed by prices in a market economy; With relationships becoming an important factor, planning essentially becomes an individualised bargaining process; the planning system has proven to be unfavourable for industry, and even more so for agriculture; the suppression of individual motivation requires a tight set of controls.[1]

Fukuyama, an American political scientist, rashly threw out the 'end of history' conclusion, arguing that the socialist system that adopted the planning mechanism has failed, that history has come to an end, and that there is no alternative to capitalism for human society.[2] Even 'left-wing scholars' like Joseph Stiglitz also believe that planning is feasible only when it is concentrated at a very 'partial' level (e.g. urban planning, business planning), and that a national planning framework is not feasible.[3]

As the 1996 World Bank report title clearly stated, 'From Plan to Market', the only way out for socialist countries is to integrate with the Western capitalist system.

We can divide the socialist countries at that time into two categories: those in transition those that converged with the capitalist system, and those in transformation, that while borrowing from the Western system, persisted in the socialist path and promoted reforms on their own. After 30 years of practical tests, different results have emerged. In terms of the Human Development Index, the countries in transition have either stagnated and then grown slowly, or declined and then recovered. In contrast, countries in transformation have continued to rise, and China has continued to rise rapidly.

At the time, there was a perception among Western scholars that the transition process would involve a painful valley of tears,[4] also known as 'shock therapy', where a short period of shock was required to restore health. In hindsight, we find that this 'valley of tears' was so long that many of the countries in the transition had not recovered to their initial per capita GNP levels after 20 years, and countries such as Russia took more than a decade to recover (see Figure 1). 30 years on, China has changed dramatically in comparison to Russia and other Eastern European countries. In many respects, China has come from behind. This is profound proof that 'the path determines the destiny' and that the path chosen can affect the destiny of a country for a generation or even for several generations.

Some scholars have begun to reflect on the so-called 'National planning failure theory'. According to Professor Peter Nolan of the University of Cambridge, one of the lessons of the Soviet transition was the confusion between command economy with state planning. When the command economy was abolished, so was the planning. Whereas China succeeded in separating the two. It transitioned from a planned economy to a market economy, while retaining the planning system itself. Nolan believes that good planning should be able to identify the unique market failures that occur in a given country and provide flexible and practical solutions.[5]

János Kornai, regarded as an important critic of the planned economy, also began to reflect in his 2006 autobiography:

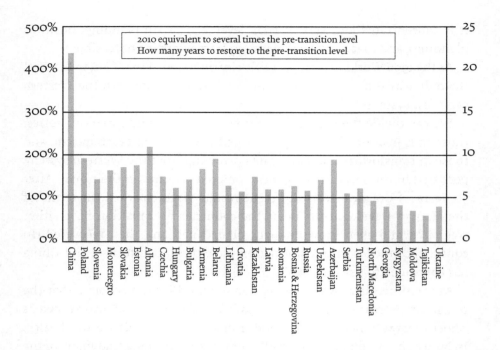

Figure 1 Changes in GDP per capita in transition (type) countries (1989-2010, calculated in 1990 international dollars)

Source of Data: J.Bolt and J.L.van Zanden, The First Update of the Maddison Project: Re-Estimating Growth Before 1820, Maddison Project Working Paper 4, 2013. <http://www.ggdc.net/maddison/maddison-project/home.htm> [4 May 2021].

Source of Data: Wang Shaoguang and Yan Yilong, 2015, 'Great Wisdom for a Prosperous Nation: How China Makes Five-Year Plans', Renmin University of China Press, p. 22.

'I think it is regrettable that the failure of the communist system should have discredited with the idea of planning...Perhaps one day, when the dire memories of old-style planning under a communist system have vanished, the idea of planning may enjoy a renaissance... Let me make a seemingly anachronistic suggestion: the introduction of medium and long-term planning. Not the kind of directive planning that has proved to be a failure in the socialist system, but an improved version of the kind of guided planning that was once used in France.'[6]

B. *The performance of China's planning system*

China began its first five-year plan in 1953 and is now in its 14th five-year planning period. Rather than disappearing with the reform of the market economy, China's five-year plans have shown increasing dynamism and have become China's super public policy second only to the reports of the Party Congress. China has demonstrated a strong ability to achieve its objectives, moving the country forward step by step through the implementation of five-year plans (planning) that determine the basic direction of China's development for the next five years. The Five-Year Plan (planning) has not only been a great success domestically but has also attracted worldwide attention, with many countries beginning to learn from China's five-year experience.

Robert F. Engle III, winner of the 2003 Nobel Prize in Economics, commented that while China is making five-year plans for the next generation, Americans are only making plans for the next election. This speaks of an important advantage of the planning system: because of planning, we can stand high and see far, and we can do things for a long time.

For example, the report of the 19th Party Congress (19th National Congress of the Communist Party of China) sets out the goal of building a powerful modern socialist country in an all-around way by 2050. This goal was not proposed today, but has been consistent since 1964, when we proposed the 'Four Modernisations', that is, to build a powerful modern socialist country with modern agriculture, industry, defence, and science and technology. After the reform and opening up, Comrade Deng Xiaoping proposed to achieve modernisation by the middle of the 21st century. Now we have advanced this goal by 15 years and aim to achieve this goal in 2035. At the same time, China also proposed to build a powerful modern socialist country in an all-around way by 2050. China has been able to continue to pursue the goal of modernisation for generations, with each five-year plan (planning) taking a step forward to gradually achieve the modernisation goal.

At the same time, there are many things we can do that we may not see obvious benefits from in the immediate future, but the next generation or the generations that follow will be able to enjoy the dividends. Comrade Mao Zedong and his generation scrimped and scraped to build a strong national defence system, an independent and complete industrial system and a national economic system.

Calculated at constant prices, the national consumption level in 1978 was equivalent to 1.8 times that of 1952, while the GDP was 4.71 times and the gross industrial output value was 16.6 times.[7] To this day, we are still enjoying this bonus. In the environment of fierce global competition, due to its strong national defence strength and complete industrial system, China can maintain a high degree of autonomy while promoting opening up without having to look up to others. It has the conditions to consolidate and upgrade its position as a global manufacturing centre, the status of the supply chain centre, and ultimately a global innovation and creation centre.

2. A new type of national planning: a five-year plan using holistic knowledge

Let's try to answer the question: why is there a need for national planning in market economy conditions?

A. Scattered knowledge versus holistic knowledge

To answer this question, we must first understand why the planned economy failed? There are various criticisms of the planned economy, including: incompatible incentives, insufficient autonomy, bureaucracy, and information asymmetry. One of the key criticisms was made by Friedrich Hayek.

Hayek believes that the fundamental reason for the infeasibility of centralised national planning is that the key information of economic activities is dispersed. 'The various 'local knowledge' and the knowledge of the circumstance, on which the economic system depends for its effective functioning, such as preferences, price measurement, technology, resource availability, etc., exist in a dispersed manner in various economic institutions. This knowledge never exists in a centralised or complete form, but only in incomplete and often contradictory forms mastered by separate individuals'.[8]

He argues that the problem with the planned economy system is not just that the central planners do not have enough computing capability; If it is just a lack of computing capability, it can be solved by using computers and supercomputers. The root of the problem is that the underlying data exists scattered and cannot be mastered centrally. This might sound a little abstract, but let's take an example. In a bakery at the east gate of Tsinghua University, how much bread should be produced every day can only be decided by the bakery owner. The reason is that some key information related to decision-making, including customer preferences, changes in passenger flow, material costs, price trends, etc., is only available to the owner.

What would happen if the quantity of production were specified by a national directive? Either too little bread is produced and some customers cannot purchase it, or too much bread is produced, with the excess being wasted as it eventually goes stale. So what is the tactic that is often adopted when the country specifies quantities? It is to keep production as low as possible to avoid a surplus. The shortage economy of the planned economy period is closely related to this.

One prominent feature of planned economy is that the planned economy at the early stage of socialist countries was very successful. The Soviet Union's 'First Five-Year Plan' and 'Second Five-Year Plan' achieved brilliant achievements, propelling the Soviet Union from a backward agricultural country to an emerging industrial one, while the European and American economies were in the Great Depression. China's 'First Five-Year Plan' has also made great achievements, with a completion rate of the planned targets at 84.4%, most of them are over-fulfilled, which has established the initial foundation for socialist industrialisation. However, as the economy's scale grew, the problem of information asymmetry became severe, and the planned economies of various countries experienced a decline in efficiency.

The problem with Hayek's criticism is that he overlooks another type of knowledge. In addition to what he calls scattered knowledge, holistic knowledge is highly important to economic and social activity. Holistic knowledge reflects the overall and long-term conditions of the economy and society, it exists in a centralised and systematic way and can be used by central planners (see Table 1). We also use the bakery example, where public information such as weather may also be important, in addition to the scattered information mentioned above. For example, when the weather changes, the store owner can also use this public information to judge whether the number of his customers would increase or decrease. This is at the micro-level, but more importantly, in the operation of the country at the macro level, this holistic knowledge is very important. For example, why should we fully liberalize the two-children policy? May we further encourage childbirth in the future? A very important indicator is the rapid decline in the total fertility rate, which is far below the level of generational replacement.

This means that China will sooner or later enter a stage of negative population growth. Why put forward the goal of poverty reduction and energy saving? In addition to the pursuit of expected objectives, it is also based on the overall knowledge of the country's long-term overall development.

Table 1 Comparison of scattered knowledge and holistic knowledge

	Scattered Knowledge	*Holistic Knowledge*
Scope of Application	Private Products	Public Affairs Governance
Source of Knowledge	Private, short-term scenarios	Holistic, long-term contexts
Knowledge attributes	Partly invisible knowledge	Visible knowledge
Variability	Constantly changing	Relatively stable
Decision-makers	Enterprise	Central Planners
Decision-making approach	Scattered	Centralised
Coordination mechanisms	Price system	Planning system

Businesses also need to have a plan. Why? As we often say, 'When a family has a thousand things to do, start with the toughest', the objectives pursued by enterprises are diverse, but the resources are limited, hence requiring a good plan to achieve optimal allocation of resources. The same applies to the governance of a country. There are many problems facing the country. Which one to solve first? How to solve it? National public governance affairs are complicated. Which one should we advance first? How do we move forward? All of them need to be coordinated by good national planning. The country needs to plan like an enterprise, and like an enterprise formulate the quantity and target of public goods in a certain period of time, to achieve the target. In other words, it is to use the planning to apply holistic knowledge to advance public affairs governance effectively.

Hayek's theory intentionally or unintentionally ignores the application of holistic knowledge. National planning is needed in a market economy because if we consider the market system as a system that applies scattered knowledge, then national planning is a system that uses holistic knowledge. These two types of knowledge application systems can complement each other and make economic and social operations more efficient.

B. *From economic planning to public affairs governance planning*

If you compare China's five-year plan today with the five-year plan of the planned economy period, you will find a big difference:

First, state planning no longer intervenes in microeconomic activities, but provides the overall framework for economic and social development. During the planned economy period, the vast majority of plans were physical quantity indicators, including the production of steel, coal, crude oil, grain, cotton and other physical products. Since the reform and opening up of the country, physical quantity indicators have been gradually eliminated, and since the 10th Five-Year Plan, physical quantity indicators have been completely eliminated. Today, the indicators of the five-year plan are macro indicators.

Second, the content of the plan ranges from economic construction to covering all aspects of national development. During the planned economy period, the plans mainly focused on economic planning; although there were also some social construction aspects, they were not the main ones. Since the reform and opening up, the coverage of the plan has been continuously expanded. The 6th Five-Year Plan changed the name of the five-year plan from the National Economic Development Plan to the National Economic and Social Development Plan, and after the 11th Five-Year Plan, it was changed to National Economic and Social Development Planning. However, it still does not cover its actual content. Today's five-year plan includes economic, cultural, technological, social, ecological, and other aspects, and it is already a complete national development plan.

Third, there was a shift in planning targets from economic to non-economic oriented. The 'Sixth Five-Year Plan' was the first five-year plan after the reform and opening up. The economic and non-economic indicators were split 60-40, with economic indicators accounting for 60.7% and non-economic indicators 39.3%. By the 12th Five-Year Plan, economic indicators accounted for only 12.5%, and by the 13th Five-Year Plan, only 16%, with the vast majority of indicators being non-economic indicators such as education, science and technology, resources and environment, and people's livelihood. Even if they are economic indicators, they are macro indicators related to economic growth rather than the physical indicators of the planned economy, including economic growth, employment, economic structure, etc. (see Table 2).

Table 2 Proportion of different types of quantitative indicators for each five-year plan (planning)

	'6th Five-year'	'7th Five-year'	'8th Five-year'	'9th Five-year'	'10th Five-year'	'11th Five-year'	'12th Five-year'	'13th Five-year'
Economic growth	15.2	21.4	26.9	23.5	10	9.1	4.2	4
Economic structure	45.5	35.7	30.8	23.5	23.3	13.6	8.3	12
Total of Economic indicators	60.7	57.1	57.7	47	33.3	22.7	12.5	16
Education and science	15.2	7.1	3.8	11.8	23.3	9.1	16.7	20
Resources and environment	3	3.6	7.7	11.8	20	27.2	33.3 (42.9)	40
People's livelihood	21.2	32.1	30.8	29.4	23.3	41	37.5	24
Total of non-economic indicators	39.3	42.9	42.3	53	67.7	77.3	87.5	84

Source: Yan Yilong: Governance by Objectives: The Visible Hand of Five-Year Planning, Renmin University of China Press, 2013, p. 160. The authors have made changes based on the latest data.

In short, China's five-year plan has been transformed from an economic plan to a public affairs governance plan. Of course, this does not mean that there is no economic content. Maintaining moderate economic growth, macro stability, and optimizing economic structure are also important components of public affairs governance.

C. Planning and the market: from substitution to complementary

A related question is, will the implementation of state planning in the market economy affect the free choice of enterprises? Future experts John Naisbitt and Doris Naisbitt have a very good evaluation of China's planning: plan forests to allow trees to grow freely.[9] The commonly used metaphor 'paramagnetism' is a concept in physics, which means that there are countless small magnetic needles in the magnet, pointing in different directions, and that when a magnetic field is given outside, not all of these small pins will point in the direction of the field, but still in all directions, but there will be more small magnetic needles pointing in the direction of the external magnetic field in probability. The larger the external magnetic field, the greater the probability that more small magnetic needles will point in the direction of the magnetic field. We can compare a small magnetic needle to a business and the external magnetic field to a plan. Planning does not interfere with the free choice of the firm, but rather enables the firm to form a joint force while it is free to choose, and the stronger the power of planning, the stronger the joint force will be (see Figure 2).

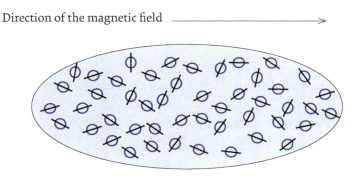

Figure 2 The relationship between planning and enterprise is similar to the relationship between magnetic field and small magnetic needle

The picture comes from: *Schrödinger: What is Life*, retranslated by Luo Laiou and Luo Liao, Hunan Science and Technology Press, 2015 edition, p.10.

In addition, when considering the relationship between planning and markets, it is not enough to observe only from the perspective of the state on the market empowerment relationship (赋权). A more important perspective is to endow the subject with certain abilities and energies (赋能). Empowerment is a positive-sum perspective, not a zero-sum perspective. Empowerment allows individuals to pursue their dreams, while to endow a subject with certain abilities and energies is to help individuals achieve their dreams. To a certain extent, planning also endows market entities' and individuals' abilities and energies. From the perspective of endowing the enterprises with certain abilities and energies, planning does not limit the freedom of the enterprise, but rather expands its substantive freedom. Because of planning, the enterprise can participate in it, which helps the enterprise to achieve its own objectives. Ann Lee, a professor at New York University in the United States, believes that the United States should learn from China to formulate plans and let business executives participate in medium and long-term planning, instead of suffering from chaotic policy signals.[10]

China's public affairs governance planning can be organically combined with the market mechanism. Like the market mechanism, it is not only an information utilisation mechanism, but also a resource allocation method. Under market economy conditions, it mainly plays three functions (see Table 3):

Table 3 The three functions of planning under market economy conditions

	Constrained planning	*Oriented planning*	*Predictive planning*
Type of resource	Public	Mixed	Mixed
Planning function	Ensures that public goods are supplied to meet objectives	Play a guiding role in industrial development	Provides expected macro signals

First, planning has a constraining function on the allocation of public-type resources.

The binding targets of national planning are the basis for the government to perform its duties. The objectives, tasks and projects formulated in the planning require the state to use public resources to promote the completion. Constrained planning enables the government to optimise the allocation of public resources.

Second, planning has a guiding function for the allocation of mixed resources that are of public interest.

Although enterprises and individuals are the main producers of mixed products, they have national strategic significance and require national strategic guidance. For example, planning can guide infrastructure investment, human capital development and industrial restructuring.

The most typical example is 'Made in China 2025' issued by the State Council in 2015, which is the first ten-year action plan of the Chinese government to implement a strong national strategy. The main body of manufacturing development is, of course, the enterprises, but the plan has formulated the roadmap for a strong manufacturing nation, and allocated relevant resources, which will effectively guide the behaviour of enterprises, scientific research institutions and individuals to form a strategic synergy.

Third, planning has a signalling function for allocating private social resources.

The signalling function of the five-year plan (planning) has stabilized society's expectations. For example, before the '13th Five-Year Plan' was released, society was uncertain about China's economic growth prospects in the medium to long term. The annual economic growth rate of no less than 6.5% stabilised market confidence to a large extent.

The positioning of the five-year plan (planning) in the market economic system has also undergone continuous changes. Among them, the most significant change occurred in the 'Ninth Five-Year Plan' after the establishment of the socialist market economic system reform goal. The 'Ninth Five-Year Plan' proposes that the overall plan should be of a macro, strategic and policy nature, and the indicators should be instructive and predictive in general. There is a view that the reason why the five-year plan was changed to five-year planning in the 11th Five-Year Plan is to better suit the market economy. In fact, this is not the case. The original intention of the drafters is that 'the word 'planning' originates from the 'gauge'

(规), which means drawing or correcting circles, having a more spatial and graphic overtone in its meaning' to highlight the spatial layout function of the five-year plan. The strongest market orientation should be the 'Ninth Five-Year Plan' and 'Tenth Five-Year Plan'. The reform orientation is to weaken the intervention of the plan on market entities, and use it only as a guiding tool at the macro level. However, in the process of market-oriented reform, there is also a problem that the plan is out of control. We evaluated the 'Tenth Five-Year' plan and found that there were four deviations in the implementation of the 'Tenth Five-Year' plan: First, the adjustment of the industrial structure deviates from the plan; Second, the adjustment of the employment structure failed to meet expectations; Third, energy demand and energy structure targets were not achieved; Fourth, the targets for reducing emissions of major pollutants were not achieved. The '11th Five-Year Plan' is instead an adjustment to radical market-oriented reforms. It re-emphasises the state's role, more appropriately handles the relationship between the government and the market, divides the types of indicators into anticipatory and binding, and defined the public service field for the first time. The 11th Five-Year Plan clearly states that, in addition to guiding market players, the plan is also the basis for the government to perform its public service responsibilities. The 12th Five-Year Plan continues this two-pronged approach. The 13th Five-Year Plan has been adjusted to a three-dimensional approach: First, it is the behavioural orientation of market players; Second, it is an important basis for the government to perform its duties; Third, it is a shared vision of the people of all ethnic groups in the country. This is similar to the three planning functions in a market economy that we mentioned earlier.

We then turn to another view, similar to that of Kornai mentioned earlier, which suggests that the new type of planning in China since the reform and opening-up is nothing more than a guiding economic plan similar to, or a modified version of, the guiding economic plan once practised in France, for example: When comparing the two dimensions of categorisation – the knowledge utilisation dimension and the product provision dimension – Soviet-style planning may have placed more emphasis on the directive aspect. At the same time, it also had a prescriptive and guiding function. Guiding economic planning emphasises steering the development of the economy in a market economy. However, both plans focused on economic or private product activities. China's five-year plans since the reform and opening-up have focused on the use of holistic knowledge and the governance of public affairs. This type of planning goes beyond the Soviet and the French models and is a new type of national planning. It is important not only for China's development, but also for the world's exploration of planning in the 21st century (see Table 4).

Table 4 Different types of national plans (planning)

	Scattered Knowledge	*Holistic Knowledge*
Private Goods	Directive economic planning (former socialist countries such as the USSR)	Guiding economic planning (post-WWII, France, etc.)
Public Affairs Governance	Daily Public Policy	Public Affairs Governance Planning (China since the 1990s)

3. Challenges facing national planning

There are, of course, some problems in our new type of national planning, which need to be constantly adjusted.

First, how to further rationalise the planning system? At present, it is a hierarchical and classified planning system. The central government, provinces, cities and counties have five-year plans, including national economic planning, special planning, professional planning, regional planning, and spatial planning. There is the problem of too much planning and the problem of the relationship between different types of planning. For this, the newly promulgated 'Opinions of the Central Committee of the Communist Party of China and the State Council on Unifying the Planning System to Better Play the Role of Strategic Orientation of National Development Planning' clarifies the basic principles, namely: national development planning plays a leading role, spatial planning plays a basic role, and special and regional planning plays a supporting role. The lower-level planning is subordinate to the upper-level planning, and the lower-level planning serves the upper-level planning.

Second is the status of planning in the macro-management system. Our macro-control system includes planning, land, financial, industrial, fiscal, and monetary policies. The report of the 19th National Congress of the Communist Party of China clearly put forward the need to strengthen the strategic guidance function of development planning. The 'Opinions of the Central Committee of the Communist Party of China and the State Council on Unifying the Planning System to Better Play the Role of Strategic Guidance of National Development Planning' clearly requires planning to set the direction, finance to guarantee and support, and other policies to coordinate and build a synergistic and working mechanism for development planning, finance, and other policies.

Third is the dynamic boundary between planning and the market. Theoretically, it can be said that planning must not overstep its bounds, but there is no clear, fixed boundary between planning and the market, and it needs to be constantly and dynamically adjusted according to practice. The general adjustment principle is that market planning has its own division of labour, with the market playing a role mainly in the field of scattered knowledge and the provision of private goods. In contrast, national planning plays a role mainly in the field of holistic knowledge and the governance of public affairs. At the same time, planning needs to compensate for market failures and empower market players.

Fourth is the relationship between individual planning and national planning. There is a common problem nowadays that people think planning is very lofty, and it is very far away from us. In the future, it is necessary to explore the use of information technology to further strengthen the connection among national planning, individual planning and enterprise planning, to explore a mechanism for the preparation of integrated planning from micro to macro, as well as a mechanism for the implementation of planning empowered from macro to micro.

Fifth, how should planning be transformed under the new information technology conditions? Some entrepreneurs proposed that a 'new planned economy' could be implemented. The so-called 'new planned economy' is a new platform economy, because the data required by the plan is concentrated in the platform enterprises, which is different from the national plan we are discussing.

At the same time, new information technologies have changed how knowledge is used. Let's also take the example of bakeries, where the use of scattered knowledge, as Hayek said, was still more based on individual experience. But with the advent of mobile payments, information on customer preferences can be accurately collected, stored and mined, not only enhancing the ability to anticipate production, but even customer flow information can provide the shop's credit base. In other words, implicit information has become visible, and the invisible hand has been made visible in the age of data.

At the same time, the emergence of these information technologies provides the conditions for what we said before was not computable, and the problems of information asymmetry and lack of computing capability faced by central planners have been largely resolved. In such an era of 'decentralisation' and 'strong centralisation', how to promote new plans will be a huge opportunity and challenge.

In short, since the reform and opening-up, China's five-year plans have achieved transformation and great success. The reasons for this are:

China has innovated a new type of national plan, which we call public affairs governance planning. Going beyond the Soviet-style planned economic system as well as the free-market economic system, China's public affairs governance planning is a system that uses holistic knowledge, which can be organically combined with the market economy and form compound advantages alongside it.

The transformation of China's five-year plan also has implications for understanding China's path since reform and opening-up:

First, when you pour out the bath water, keep the baby. Both an open and innovative spirit and a pragmatic insistence on following one's own path are needed. The successful experience of reform lies in this, and reform in the new era requires even more adherence.

Second, the Chinese Path of reform and opening-up has surpassed the Soviet and Western models. Instead, it has taken a middle path and formed a combined advantage.

Third, China's practice has created a successful example of national development planning in the 21st century, which is rooted in the Chinese system and has global significance.

---

1 *World Bank, 1996, World Development Report 1996: From Planning to Markets,* China Financial and Economic Press, pp. 1-2. [世界银行：《1996年世界发展报告：从计划到市场》，中国财政经济出版社1996年版，第1-2页]

2 Francis Fukuyama, 1989, 'The End of History?', *The National Interest*, No. 16, pp. 3–18. 又见Francis Fukuyama, 1992, The End of History and the Last Man, New York: Free Press

3 Joseph Stiglitz, 2011, *Where is Socialism Going: Theory and Evidence of Economic System Transformation*, translated by Zhou Liqun, Han Liang and Yu Wenbo, Jilin People's Publishing House. Originally *Whither Socialism*, 1994, MIT Press [约瑟夫·斯蒂格利茨：《社会主义向何处去——经济体制转型的理论与证据》，周立群、韩亮、余文波译，吉林人民出版社2011年版]

4 Ralt Dahremdorf, 1990, 'Europe's Vale of Tears', *Marxism Today*, May, pp.18–23

5 Peter Nolan, 2012, *The Rise of China and the Decline of Russia: Politics, Economy and Planning in the Transformation of Marketization*, translated by Sui Fumin, Zhejiang University Press, p. 331. Originally published in 1995, Macmillan [彼得·罗澜：《中国的崛起与俄罗斯的衰落——市场化转型中的政治、经济与计划》，隋福民译，浙江大学出版社2012年版，第331页]

6 János Kornai, 2006, *By Force of Thought: Irregular Memoirs of an Intellectual Journey*, Cambridge, MA: The MIT Press, p. 157.

7 Department of National Economic Comprehensive Statistics, National Bureau of Statistics: 'Compilation of Statistical Data for the Fifty-Five Years of New China', China Statistics Press, 2005 edition. [国家统计局国民经济综合统计司：《新中国五十五年统计资料汇编》，中国统计出版社2005年版]

8 F.A. von Hayek, 2003, Individualism and Economic Order, translated by Deng Zhenglai, Life, Reading and New Knowledge, p. 117, Originally published in 1948, Routledge Press. [F.A. 冯·哈耶克：《个人主义与经济秩序》，邓正来译，生活·读书·新知三联书店2003年版，第117页]

9 John Naisbitt and Doris Naisbitt, 2009, *China's Megatrends*, China Industrial and Commercial Union Press Ltd., p. 61. [约翰·奈斯比特、多丽丝·奈斯比特：《中国大趋势》，中国工商联合出版社有限公司2009年版，第61页]

10 Ann Lee, 2012, *What can the US learn from China?*, translated by Zhang Xiaoying, Red Flag Press, p. 85. [李淯：《美国能向中国学什么？》，章晓英译，红旗出版社2012年版，第85页]

CHAPTER 4

Five-Year Plan: A National-Target Governance System

[*The first draft of this article is the speech of the 16th lecture of 'National Conditions Forum' of the National Research Institute of Tsinghua University on 27 Nov, 2018, published in 'Five-year planning: a system of Governance-by-Objectives for national objectives', 2019, Culture Vertical, No. 3. Further revisions were made by the author for inclusion in this book. 本文初稿为2018年11月27日清华大学国情研究院《国情讲坛》第16讲演讲稿，刊发于《五年规划：一种国家目标治理体制》，《文化纵横》2019年第3期。收入本书时，作者作了进一步修订。]

1. Promise must be kept and action must be fruitful

A strong ability to achieve national objectives is an important feature of the Chinese system. As Mao Zedong proclaimed in the early days of the founding of New China, 'Our objectives must be achieved. Our objectives will certainly be achieved.'[1]

The five-year plan (planning) is a good object for assessing the achievement of China's national objectives. It reflects the country's quantitative objectives, and at the same time has continuity that covers almost the entire history of New China. China implemented the first five-year plan in 1953, and 2020 is the final year of the 13th five-year plan. We have evaluated the achievement of the objectives of the previous five-year plans. Two outstanding features can be identified: First, on the whole, China has a strong ability to achieve national objectives. Although there are some good and bad ones, the objectives are generally achieved. Second, in general, the post-reform and opening-up period has been better than the pre-reform and opening-up period, and the completion rate tends to increase, with 20 of the 22 indicators in the 11th Five-Year Plan completed and 23 of the 24 indicators in the 12th Five-Year Plan completed. 'The first four years of the 13th Five-Year Plan were very good, but in the last year, due to the impact of the Covid-19 pandemic, 5 of the 25 indicators may be difficult to complete, with an estimated completion rate of 80%.[2]

Table 1 Evaluation of completion of objectives of the previous five-year plans (planning)

Period	Number of indicators	Percentage of completed indicators (%)	The average percentage of completion (%)
1st Five-Year	32	84.4	136
2nd Five-Year	21	0.0	21
3rd Five-Year	51	46.9	101.3
4th Five-year	52	34.6	88
5th Five-Year	16	31.3	90
6th Five-Year	33	84.8	178
7th Five-Year	28	71.4	119
8th Five-Year	27	92.6	267
9th Five-Year	16	75.0	144
10th Five-Year	45	64.3	104
11th Five-Year	22	90.9	132
12th Five-Year	24	95.8	
13th Five-Year	25	80.0	

Note: The 'Second Five-Year Plan' is calculated based on the index values stipulated in the first plan in the 'Central Committee's Opinions on Approving the Second Five-Year Plan' revised at the Beidaihe Conference of the CPC Central Committee on 28 August 1958.

Source: Yan Yilong, 2013, *Governance-by-Objective: The Visible Hand of Five-Year Planning*, Renmin University of China Press, pp. 293–295, pp. 326–340. Modified based on the latest data.

It seems perfectly normal to have objectives and then have to achieve them, but it is not true. As former British Prime Minister Tony Blair said, in Western political culture, setting objectives merely conveys a general desire; China is a country that practices what it preaches, and once it sets a goal, it keeps its word until it is finally accomplished.[3] The Obama administration set out many objectives in his State of the Union address that year, including building high-speed rail, reducing the fiscal deficit and increasing the proportion of clean energy, but they had failed to achieve them. In his State of the Union address, he lamented that the whole of Washington was in a predicament of being torn apart and nothing was being accomplished.[4] Not only that, the series of measures taken by the Trump administration after taking office have almost emptied the few policy legacies of the Obama administration. In 2000, the European Union formulated the Lisbon Strategy for the new century's first decade. According to the post-assessment, the three main objectives proposed in the strategy had not been achieved: the target of 3% average annual economic growth was only reached by 1.42%; the target of a 3% increase in R&D investment funds as a proportion of GDP was actually only about 2%; and the target of a 70% increase in average employment was actually only reached by 63.7%.[5]

Why does China have a strong capacity to achieve national objectives? Why are some countries able to achieve national objectives while others are not?

The most straightforward explanation for this problem is state capacity. In the 1990s, Wang Shaoguang, Hu Angang and others began to emphasise the state's capacity, believing that without a strong state capacity, neither marketisation nor democratisation could achieve the transformation of a modern state.[6]

Since the beginning of the 21st century, Fukuyama, an American scholar who once advocated the 'end of history', has also begun to discuss nation-building, taking a strong nation as one of the three elements of modern politics.[7] National capacity is a powerful explanation for the achievement of national objectives, but national capacity is not the same as the ability to achieve national objectives. National capacity is only a necessary, but not a sufficient, condition for the achievement of national objectives.[8]

The realisation of national objectives depends not only on the strength of the state's ability, but also on the effectiveness of the market and society. The explanation for the competing state capacity is the 'spontaneous order theory', which holds that state objectives are the result of the autonomous efforts of decentralised subjects, rather than the result of state initiatives. The 'spontaneous order theory' rarely directly answers the question of national objectives – this explanation presupposes only individual objectives and organisational objectives, and it is inappropriate to propose national objectives. Hayek, for example, explicitly defines a free man as one who is not bound by the specific common objectives of the community in times of peace.[9]

Different from the above two theoretical explanations, this chapter argues that it is not enough to rely only on strong state capacity or on free markets and civil society to achieve national objectives; it also requires the formation of effective mechanisms of interaction among different agents of the state (central and local), society and the market. An attempt is made here to present a theory of goal-based governance to describe the mechanism that drives the achievement of China's national objectives. It is a combination of top-down and bottom-up governance mechanisms through which China has driven the achievement of national objectives. This type of governance is widespread across all branches of government, but is most evident in the five-year plans.

While the goal responsibility system was first applied to corporate management, the discussion on the government goal responsibility system began in the 1980s. The author proposed a conceptual framework of goal governance based on China's five-year planning system in 2013, and scholars have subsequently conducted related research. An attempt at a theoretical summary of the target governance system based on the established research will now be presented.

2. Institutional safeguard for management by objectives

Peter Drucker, a management scientist, put forward the theory of 'Management by Objective' in his book *The Practice of Management* in 1954. He believed that 'managing a business means managing it according to objectives'. He divided the management of the enterprise into three areas: management of the enterprise, management of managers, and management of workers and work, while management by objectives links the objectives of different management units and individual objectives to collectively point to the performance objectives of the enterprise. Management by objectives is not top-down control, but 'management by self-control instead of management by domination'. It achieves the matching between individual objectives and organisational objectives through participatory goal setting and self-control.[10]

While Drucker talks about management by objectives at the corporate level, China's strong ability to achieve national objectives is mainly due to the formation of a Governance by Objective system at the national level.

We define a Governance by Objective system as a way of national governance that uses holistic knowledge to develop national plans, mobilise all parties, and guide the allocation of resources to jointly promote the realisation of objectives through a combination of bottom-up and top-down approaches. This definition includes the following connotations.

Firstly, it is a way of governance of the state. It is different from the administrative directives of a planned economy. It is not simply top-down administration, but the governance of public affairs in which multiple subjects, including the central government, localities, enterprises, and the people, participate and work together through administrative methods, social networks, and market mechanisms.

Secondly, it is a model of governance that uses holistic knowledge to deliver public goods. Governance by objectives operates on the basis of holistic knowledge. Not only is the holistic knowledge the basic data of decision-making, but the coordination between different subjects is also done through holistic knowledge. Through the top-down transfer of holistic knowledge, the roles and functions of dispersed subjects in the overall picture are thus defined.

Thirdly, it is a governance model guided by centralised planning. Holistic knowledge dictates that decision-making should be carried out in a centralised manner, which of course does not mean that other subjects cannot participate in decision-making, but rather that there is a need for centralised arrangements and plans for public affairs and the setting of corresponding objectives.

Governance by objectives is essentially a goal-driven power transmission mechanism formed through the interaction between different subjects, and this mechanism can be broken down into three aspects as follows.

The first is the goal matching mechanism. Similar to enterprises achieving goal management through self-control, goal governance in the state is first and foremost through goal matching. It refers to the matching of objectives of different subjects through interaction, thus making the conscious implementation of secondary decision-making subjects an important way to achieve objectives. Goal matching is mainly achieved through participatory decision-making processes, political guidance and goal convergence. The national objectives themselves incorporate the demands of dispersed subjects, while the formulation and promotion of national objectives become a process of political consensus building and the release of national political signals, thus leading dispersed subjects to adjust their objectives and seek to match them with the national objectives.

The second is the goal implementation mechanism. It refers to promoting the realisation of the goal by providing incentives to influence the behaviour of the target executive body. In the goal implementation process, the target decision-making subject and the implementation subject are principal-agent relationships, and the secondary subject realises the goal of the superior subject rather than its own. The goal implementation mechanism is mainly through the goal responsibility system, comprehensive-incentive, project system and other ways to solve the incentive incompatibility and information asymmetry problems in the principal-agent relationship.

The third is the goal adjustment mechanism. It refers to a mechanism for adjusting objectives and institutional frameworks based on implementation. The assessment of objectives identifies problems, creates a feedback mechanism and makes adjustments to the objectives and the institutional framework on which they are based (see Figure 1).

Figure 1 China's Governance-by-Objectives System

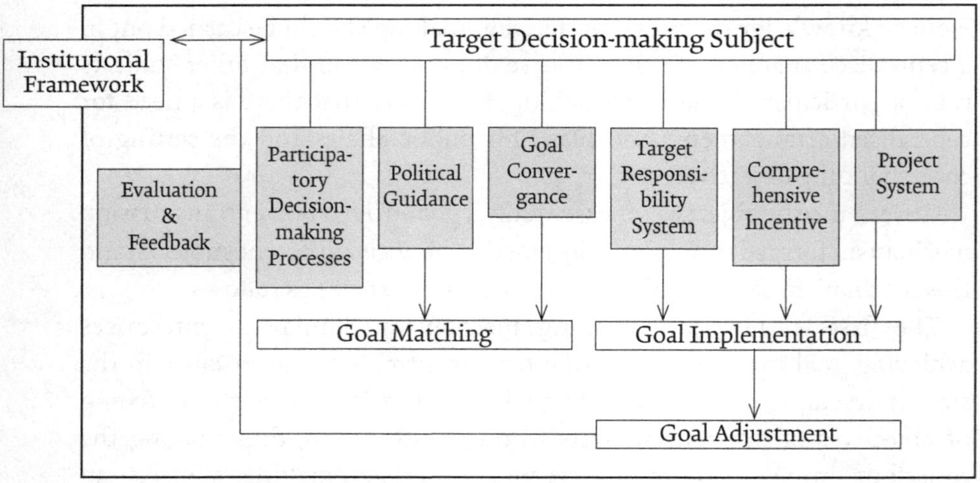

China's Governance-by-Objectives system has its roots in the planning and management system, which was developed during the planned economy to allow the state, departments, regions and enterprises to carry out planning and management according to their different competencies and responsibilities. In planning, the method of 'two down and one up' is generally adopted: Firstly, only the control figures (one down) including the outline of the plan are issued step by step; Secondly, based on the control figures issued, the lower levels prepared draft plans, taking into account their own situation, and submitting them step by step (one up); Thirdly, based on the submitted draft plans, the state will carry out a comprehensive balance, coordinate arrangements to prepare a formal plan, and issue it at each level for implementation (another one down). Once the plan has been issued, regular supervision and inspection are carried out, the completion of the plan is assessed, and the plan is revised in accordance with certain procedures.[11]

The planning system, even in the planned economy, could hardly be summed up in terms of a monocentric system of so-called 'command and order'; the planning and management system was generally a hierarchical system under the premise of a unified national plan. The planning management centres have never been monolithic and a large number of economic activities are not included in directive plans, but are planned or independently arranged.

Following the reform and opening-up, with the reform of China's economic system, the planned management system was gradually transformed into a governance by objective system, which is certainly not monocentric, nor is it polycentric. Polycentric governance assumes that multiple autonomous centres can coordinate with each other based on a system of rules (legal and macro-institutional frameworks) without relying on a central authority. However, such spontaneous coordination mechanisms are costly and inefficient to operate. For a rapidly developing and transforming country like China, relying only on polycentric governance is not sufficient to meet the complex challenges of national governance.

Governance by objectives is a combination of polycentric and monocentric governance mechanisms, which we call the '1+N' central governance model. It combines top-down and bottom-up governance with the participation of multiple actors, including the central government, local governments, enterprises, and the people. Governance by objectives is widespread in China's national governance, and this chapter uses the five-year plan as an example.

3. Three mechanisms of governance-by-objectives system

A. *Goal matching mechanism*

The most important mechanism of governance by goal is the goal matching mechanism. This is similar to the management-by-objective theory of enterprises, not through the directive domination of superiors over subordinates, but through 'self-control' to match individual objectives with organisational objectives.

While the objectives of decision-makers depend on their interests, they are also subject to their perceptions, and goal matching is achieved primarily by influencing participants' perceptions through information exchange.

The first is participatory goal-setting. China has developed a 'Collective wisdom' type of decision-making in preparing its five-year plans, in which numerous staff from different systems and levels have been involved in the nearly two-year-long process of preparing the plans. Through jointly thinking about the development path for the next five years, sharing information, and consulting with each other, they reach a consensus on the future direction of development.[12]

Participatory goal-setting is a two-way process of information transfer and cognitive influence. While higher-level decision-makers need to incorporate the opinions of subordinate decision-makers, the subordinate decision-makers also seek to position themselves according to the guidance of higher-level decision-makers. For example, the most characteristic feature of China's policy-making process is the large number of research activities carried out. Such research is, on the one hand, to understand the situation on the ground and listen to the views of the grassroots. While on the other hand, it conveys the central government's intentions and propositions and guides the local community's next direction. The consensus reached in the process of national planning formulation constitutes a conscious implementation mechanism, which can promote the achievement of the planning objectives through daily policy formulation and daily work promotion.

The second is political guidance. The central government effectively guides local initiatives to the central policy objectives through political guidance.

During the preparation of the five-year plan, the local five-year plan shall be reviewed and approved by the local people's congress. The approval of local five-year plans precedes that of the central government to ensure that the local five-year plans are consistent with the spirit of the central government—mainly through political guidance. After the Central 'Recommendation' was passed, the local party committee held a meeting to study the spirit of the Central Committee to guide the preparation of the local 'Recommendation' and 'Outline'. The Recommendations of each local party committee began with a preamble, stating that the basis for formulating this document was to implement the spirit of the Central Government's Plenary Session. A provincial five-year plan drafter told us, 'When the standing committee of the provincial party committee considered the report we drafted for review, it was most concerned about whether the spirit of the central government is well-reflected.' In addition, the Five-Year Plan will be widely publicised and mobilised for organisational study throughout society after it has been drawn up, which is a kind of information transmission mechanism.

The third is the planning interface mechanism. Local five-year plans need to be aligned with national five-year plans. For example, during the '12th Five-Year Plan' period, China took the initiative to promote the transition from rapid development to scientific development, and the central government took the initiative to lower the economic growth target. However, many local governments still pursued high growth. At the end of 2010, the '12th Five-Year Plan' and 'Recommendations' of the local party committees were successively issued, with ten provinces, autonomous regions, and municipalities still setting high growth targets of more than 10%, of which seven provinces, autonomous regions, and municipalities proposed a goal of doubling the number in five years. (such as a growth rate of 14%). In January 2011, the National Development and Reform Commission (NDRC) specifically requested local governments to lower their regional GDP targets. Since then, most of the provinces that had previously proposed excessively high regional GDP growth targets lowered their targets, especially those that had proposed doubling their targets. Finally, the average economic growth rate for the provinces in the 12th Five-Year Plan was 10.6%, still well above the 7% that the central government had proposed, but considerably lower than the requirements of the Recommendations of the provinces (see Table 2).

Table 2 Some provinces, autonomous regions and municipalities have lowered their targets for regional GDP in the 12th Five-Year Plan

Region	Target in Recommendations (10%)	Targets of Outline (10%)
Hubei	Above 10	7
Guangxi	Regional GDP double	10
Fujian	Regional GDP double	Above 10
Shanxi	Key economic indicators double	13
Chongqing	Regional GDP double	14
Heilongjiang	Regional GDP double	Above 12
Anhui	Strive to double GDP	Above 10
Guizhou	Province aims to double its gross domestic product	Above 12
Yunnan	Above 10, strive to double	Above 10

Source: The author compiled according to the 'Recommendations' of the provincial party committees on the '12th Five-Year Plan' and the 'Outline' of the '12th Five-Year Plan' of each province.

Table 3 Proportion of consistency index between local and national five-year plans (planning)

	'6th Five-year'	'7th Five-year'	'8th Five-year'	'9th Five-year'	'10th Five-year'	'11th Five-year'	'12th Five-year'
All indicators	64.7	77.5	77.9	43.2 (42.1)	53.2 (46.6)	83.2 (89.3)	74.9 (76.9)
Economic indicators	56.4	81.0	79.2	27.1	25.3	59.9	34
Non-economic indicators	89.3	70.7	76.0	62.8	66.4	95.5	86.7

Source: Yan Yilong: Governance by Objectives: The Visible Hand of Five-Year Planning, Renmin University of China Press, 2013, p. 176.

The proportion of the consistency index between the provincial five-year plan (planning) and the national five-year plan (planning) accounted for 64.7%, and then continued to rise. The 'Ninth Five-Year Plan' saw a relatively significant decline, then rose again. In the 12th Five-Year Plan, it fell a little further. Overall, 70% to 80% of the indicators in the 11th and 12th Five-Year Plans are consistent with the central government (see Table 3).

As can be seen, the goal matching mechanism ensures that national objectives are achieved through the local implementation of their own objectives.

Goal matching mechanisms can also influence the choice of a company's own objectives. Many enterprises formulate five-year plans or medium and long-term plans for enterprise development that are synchronised with the national five-year plan, or take the initiative to set up public policy departments to study the direction of national strategies. National objectives and national strategies constitute the external potential for business development. Planning conveys the signal of the macro trend of national development and provides a platform for enterprises to participate in national planning to achieve their own development.

B. *Goal implementation mechanisms*

If goal matching primarily drives goal attainment through influencing perceptions, goal implementation relies heavily on driving goal attainment through aligning interests. Specifically, there are the following mechanisms.

First is the goal responsibility system. The implementation of the five-year plan is a typical example of the operation of the goal responsibility system. In the 11th Five-Year Plan, China introduced a division between binding and expected targets. Binding targets are the work requirements set by the central government for local governments and relevant central government departments in the areas of public services and public interest. Their implementation is based on the goal responsibility system. The goal responsibility system consists of four main components: goal decomposition, goal evaluation, goal supervision, and goal assessment. Goal decomposition is mainly to decompose the ambitious objectives and clarify the work arrangements and responsible subjects. After the five-year plan is drawn up, the arrangement of the division of work should also be clarified, and the departments should carry out the decomposition. The decomposition should be carried out at different levels, and on a yearly basis. After the planning objectives are decomposed, it is necessary to follow up and supervise them, establish an assessment system for binding indicators, incorporate binding indicators into the comprehensive evaluation and performance assessment of economic and social development of various regions and departments, and incorporate certain key indicators into the performance assessment of leading cadres in various regions. The '13th Five-Year Plan' specifically issued a document, which clearly requires that 'local governments at all levels should incorporate the indicators of the 'Outline' into the scope of work division, monitoring and evaluation, supervision and evaluation.'[13]

The goal responsibility system can even extend to enterprises. For example, the energy-saving targets in the 11th Five-Year Plan have been broken down into enterprises, and the 'Thousand Enterprises Energy Saving Initiative' has been launched. The selected thousand enterprises account for 33% of the total energy consumption in the country. This initiative alone is expected to achieve energy savings of around 100 million tonnes of standard coal. The main body of the Thousand Enterprises Energy Saving Initiative is state-owned enterprises. In addition, local governments have also identified key energy-consuming enterprises in their regions and issued energy-saving assessment indicators to the relevant enterprises.

The second is a comprehensive incentive mechanism. The incentive mechanism of the planning is the result of the comprehensive use of political, legal, administrative, and economic means. For enterprises, it is mainly economic incentives. The economic incentive mechanism affects the business activities of the enterprise itself. In terms of input elements, if it does not comply with the national goal orientation, it will not be able to obtain land approval from the state. It will also be difficult to obtain bank loans, or other forms of financing. At the same time, compliance with national objectives also affects the enterprise's balance sheet, including tax incentives, financial subsidies, pricing policies, etc.

The third is the project-based system. Projects and programs are not only the specific starting point for the 'implementation' of national planning objectives, but also the most important 'planning plate' for local governments to compete for national resources. An important manifestation of socialism's concentrated efforts to accomplish major events is that resources such as human, financial and material resources are concentrated to the key projects and works identified in the plan. Every year, a large amount of special funds from the central government are allocated to local governments through the 'project-based' approach. In addition to the 'special transfer payments' from the government, there are also funds transferred to local governments through central ministries and commissions, and local governments also adopt the 'project-based' approach to allocate funds at each level. In addition to financial funds, elements such as land are also linked to the project. The project is also a platform for integrating social resources. The market and social subjects, as the ultimate undertaker of the project, need to invest in the corresponding resources in addition to obtaining the project through competition on the basis of merit.[14]

For example, the 13th Five-Year Plan has identified 165 major engineering projects, including both hard projects in the area of engineering construction and soft projects in the area of environment. Once these projects are determined, they become platforms for integrating multiple resources from the government, enterprises and society, in addition to determining the division of responsibilities, establishing task lists, setting up and implementing ledgers, and conducting online monitoring in accordance with the management by objectives. In addition to financial investment and land use security, the government also guides the participation of social capital and social forces through innovative investment and financing mechanisms.[15]

C. Goal adjustment mechanism

The goal adjustment mechanism enables the national objectives to be adjusted according to the actual situation. Douglas North has pointed out that the key to long-term growth is adaptive rather than allocative efficiency.[16] Not only economic growth, but the key to the long-term sustainability of institutions is adaptive efficiency.

China's governance by goal system leaves ample room for spontaneous adaptation. Different from the plans in the planned economy period, the Five-Year Plan does not intervene in microeconomic activities and does not interfere with the free choice of market entities.

In addition, there is conscious adaptability, that is, the proactive adaptation and adjustment of human beings to the environment. Governance by objectives in China provides a source of conscious adaptability and a mechanism to bridge the gap between perception and reality. The goal implementation process is a test of the gap between belief systems and objective reality, where the achievement of a goal validates the correctness of the belief system, and where failure indicates that the belief system may be wrong.

The strong implementation capacity itself constitutes a key aspect of institutional adaptability. Many studies put the focus of adaptability on the free expression of opinion. The problem is that if there is a lack of executive power, no matter how many opinions are expressed, it will only be reduced to empty talk, and will not bring about substantial institutional adjustment. For example, every once in a while in the United States, there will be shootings in public places such as campuses, which will also cause widespread and free discussion throughout society, but once the hot spot passes, everything will be the same as before, and nothing will change.

The deeper logic of goal adaptation lies in the understanding that humans change mechanisms through cognition. The practice is a two-way transformation process between the objective and subjective worlds. Only by trying to change the world can we better understand the world. Learning by doing exists not only at the organisational level, but also at the national level, and learning by doing is precisely the key to understanding the Chinese model. Just as some people understand the market system as a micro-level learning mechanism through trial and error, planning is also a macro-level learning mechanism through practice.

Thus, Governance-by-Objectives in China is a two-way adjustment mechanism, whereby cognition is adjusted to reality through planning and implementation, and reality is adjusted to cognition by revising cognition and objectives based on feedback from implementation results. The gap between cognition and reality is narrowed through an ongoing policy cycle of 'goal-implementation, new-goal-implementation'.

The system's adaptability mainly comes from the feedback mechanism, and the main mechanism of planning adjustment is realised through a five-year planning cycle, mid-term evaluation, and annual monitoring. This one-year, two-and-a-half-year, and five-year cycle of planning policies constitutes the iterative innovation mechanism of the planning system, which enables the continuous transformation and innovation of planning.

The cycle of planning formulation and implementation in the five-year cycle is also a cycle of policy learning. When formulating the five-year plan, we will review the implementation of the previous five-year plan, sum up experience and lessons, analyse changes in domestic and foreign situations, rethink the development direction for the next five years, and carry out the strategic design.

Mid-term evaluations were first introduced in China in the 10th Five-Year Plan. Planning evaluation is precisely the connection between cognition and reality. On the one hand, it allows for the adjustment of deviations in the implementation of objectives and promotes the realisation of objectives; On the other hand, if there are significant deviations from the plan, the plan can be adjusted according to the planning assessment. 'The 13th Five-Year Plan' has introduced annual monitoring to keep track of the plan's implementation and make dynamic adjustments to the plan as needed.

The adaptability of the five-year plans is also reflected in the combination of continuity and innovation of the objectives. As can be seen from the evolution of the indicators in the five-year plans since the Sixth Five-Year Plan, there is a clear continuity in the development objectives of the five-year plans. On average, 43% of the indicators are derived from the previous five-year plan (planning), of which the 'Seventh Five-Year Plan' is the highest, reaching 65%. At the same time, an average of 62% of the five-year plan (planning) indicators are updated index, of which 52% are newly added indicators, which shows the innovation of the five-year plan (planning). This is particularly the case when there are major changes in development strategies. The updating of indicators is more evident; for example, 78% of the indicators in the Sixth Five-Year Plan were new (see Table 4) on page 90.

4. Challenges of the governance-by-objectives system

The Governance-by-Objectives System is an important institutional advantage of China, but it also faces major challenges.

The first challenge is the ability of the government to integrate its objectives. The objectives of the central government and local governments are not completely consistent. For example, the national five-year plan (planning) abolished the financial and investment targets very early, from the 'Ninth Five-Year Plan'. However, two-thirds of the provinces still had fiscal targets, and half had set investment targets until the 12th Five-Year Plan. China's five-level government system tends to magnify this inconsistency, with a cascading effect. For example, in the 11th Five-Year Plan, the national target for GDP growth was 7.5%, but at the provincial

Table 4 Proportion of retention and updated indicators relative to the previous five-year plan (planning)
('6th Five-Year' – '11th Five-Year')

Plan (Planning)	Retention indicators	Updated Indicators		
		Adjusted Indicators	New Indicators	Total
6th Five-Year	17	4	78	82
7th Five-Year	65	12	23	35
8th Five-Year	30	7	63	70
9th Five-year	50	19	31	50
10th Five-Year	20	5	75	80
11th Five-Year	50	10	40	50
12th Five-Year	61	11	38	49
13th Five-Year	52	13	35	48
On average	43	10	48	58

level, it reached 10.1%, at the prefectural level, it reached 13.1% on average, and at the county level, it reached 14.2%, almost double the national target.

This corresponds to a cascading attenuation effect. The lack of local motivation makes things 'hot on the top, warm in the middle and cool under the bottom'. Some well-intentioned public policies fail in the implementation process and fail to achieve the purpose set by the original policy. Authorities at all levels are acting as middlemen only to pass the documents, the meetings, and the plans.

This is not only true for vertical levels, but the horizontal levels also have a problem of goal fragmentation. Departmental planning will undoubtedly reflect the interests of the department. But as the objectives of different departments may cancel each other out, national objectives will likely fall short. The reform of the ministerial system since the 18th National Congress of the Communist Party of China has not only strengthened the integration of different departments, but also emphasised a high degree of political centralisation and unity, which is conducive to solving the problem of goal fragmentation.

The second challenge is the problem of excessive quantitative assessment.

Governance by objectives largely relies on quantitative indicators, which can only be measured, compared, and evaluated when quantified. But imposing the quantitative assessment and evaluation on unquantifiable things can cause many adverse problems. Using the same yardstick to measure a thousand different things stifles creativity, initiative, and motivation while erasing differences. Many things that cannot be quantified and assessed require the government to actively rely on dispersed subjects to exert their autonomy and creativity to achieve.

The third challenge is the problem of 'irregularisation'. Governance-by-Objectives is a goal-oriented governance approach, rather than a rule-oriented one. The Governance-by-Objectives system needs to mobilise resources from all parties to promote the realisation of objectives. As objectives change, the direction of resource allocation will also change, often in the form of 'policy swings.' In order to achieve new objectives, other aspects are ignored. For example, in the past few years, in the process of promoting environmental protection measures and combating haze, we ignored the problems of the economy and people's livelihood. Some enterprises were 'one-size-fits-all' shut down, and local heating could not keep up. Now we are going back to adjust.

A related problem is a mismatch between the planning period and the change of government. The five-year planning cycle does not match the change of local government cycle, which causes many places to change their practices after a change of leadership, and the plans made by their predecessors become 'planning hanging on the wall'.

China's strong ability to achieve national objectives lies in the Governance-by-Objectives system, which consists of three main mechanisms: goal matching, goal implementation, and goal adaptation. Governance by objectives is neither monocentric nor polycentric, but a combination of both.

Governance by objectives is a concentrated expression of China's institutional advantages, which include both formal system arrangements and effective system arrangements formed through long-term exploration. The institutional premise for the effective operation of the Governance-by-Objectives system is, firstly, the long-term governance of the Communist Party of China and the work tradition of seeking truth from facts, which enable the planning of long-term objectives and the conscious adjustment of the objectives according to the implementation situation, and avoid the 'short-term tyranny' of competitive electoral systems.[17] The second is

China's tradition of democratic centralism and the mass line, which requires a dialectical interaction between decision-makers and implementers (sub-decision-makers) as a teacher-student relationship.[18] The third is the 'ubiquitous political nature' of the Chinese system. The logic of China's political system is not one of political-administrative dichotomy, but rather one of political-administrative indistinguishability. The local government's response to the central government's objectives is mainly political response, followed by administrative compliance. This 'ubiquitous political nature' also guides the whole society to form a consensus on objectives and strategies. It gives full play to the enthusiasm and creativity of all parties under the common national strategic framework. Fourth, the Chinese government has a large amount of public resources and a wider range of powerful policy tools at its disposal, which enable it to use a combination of economic, political, legal and planning instruments to provide incentives for market players to comply with national objectives.

Of course, the Governance-by-Objectives system has its drawbacks and limitations. Not all areas are suitable for the Governance-by-Objectives system, so it needs to be combined with other forms of governance to maximise strengths and avoid weaknesses wherever possible.

---

1 Mao Zedong, 1999, 'Striving to Build a Great Socialist Country', *The Collected Works of Mao Zedong*, Vol. 6, People's Publishing House, p. 350. [毛泽东：《为建设一个伟大的社会主义国家而奋斗》，《毛泽东文集》第6卷，人民出版社1999年版，第350页]
2 Hu Angang and Yan Yilong, 2020, 'Economic and Social Evaluation during the "Thirteenth Five-Year Plan" Period', *China Study*, 2020 Special Issue, No. 4. (see Table 1). [胡鞍钢、鄢一龙：《"十三五"时期经济社会评价》，《国情报告》2020年专刊第4期 (见表1)]
3 'China's "bottom-up" drive for low-carbon growth', VOA Chinese, 29 Mar, 2011, Beijing. [《中国"自下而上"推动低碳增长》，美国之音中文网，2011年3月29日，北京]
4 U.S. President Barack Obama delivers his State of the Union address on 24 Jan, 2012, Transcript, the Office of the White House Press Secretary. *References*, No. 16, 2012. [美国总统奥巴马2012年1月24日发表国情咨文，白宫新闻秘书办公室文稿。《参考资料》2012年第16期]
5 Hu Angang and Huang Yu, 2013, 'Catching up comprehensively, surpassing partially – China's prospects from a comparison of long-term development performance between China and Europe', *People's Forum – Academic Frontiers*, No. 21.[胡鞍钢、黄瑜：《全面追赶，局部超越——从中欧长期发展绩效比较看中国前景》，《人民论坛·学术前沿》2013年第21期]
6 See Wang Shaoguang, 1991, 'Building a Strong Democratic State', *Papers of the Centre for Contemporary China Studies*, No. 4; Wang Shaoguang and Hu Angang, 1993, *Report on China's State Capability*, Liaoning People's Publishing House. [参见王绍光：《建立一个强有力的民主国家》，《当代中国研究中心论文》1991年第4期; 王绍光、胡鞍钢：《中国国家能力报告》，辽宁人民出版社1993年版]
7 See Fukuyama, 2007, *State-Building: Governance and World Order in the 21st Century*, China Social Sciences Press, Originally published in 2004, Cornell University Press; Fukuyama, 2012, *The Origins of Political Order: From Prehuman Times to the French Revolution*, Guangxi Normal University

Press, Originally published in 2011, Profile Books. 参见福山：《国家构建:21世纪的国家治理与世界秩序》，中国社会科学出版社2007年版。福山：《政治秩序的起源——从前人类时代到法国大革命》，广西师范大学出版社2012年版]

8 See Wang Shaoguang, 2014, 'State governance and state capacity – China's philosophy of governance and institutional choice', *Economic Journal*, No. 6; Wang Shaoguang, 2018, 'Reform and opening-up, state capacity and economic development', 25 September, National Research Institute, Tsinghua University, State of the Nation Forum, Lecture 7. Ou Shujun, 2013, *The Foundations of National Basic Capabilities*, China Social Science Press; Fan Peng, 2017, Social Transformation and State Coercion, China Social Science Press. [参见王绍光：《国家治理与国家能力——中国的治理理念与制度选择》，《经济导刊》2014年第6期。王绍光：《改革开放、国家能力与经济发展》，2018年9月25日，清华大学国情研究院《国情讲坛》第七讲。欧树军：《国家基础能力的基础》，中国社会科学出版社2013年版。樊鹏：《社会转型与国家强制》，中国社会科学出版社2017年版]

9 F. A. Hayek, 2000, *The Fatal Conceit*, Chinese Social Science Press, p. 69, Originally published in 1988, University of Chicago Press. [哈耶克：《致命的自负》，中国社会科学出版社2000年版，第69页]

10 Peter F. Drucker, 1989, *The Practice of Management*, Workers' Publishing House, pp. 14, 19, 157, Originally published in 1954, Harper & Row; Drucker, 2013, *Task, Responsibility and Practices*, Machine Industry Press, pp. 56-68, Originally published in 1973, Harper & Row. [德鲁克：《管理的实践》，工人出版社1989年版，第14页、第19页、第157页；德鲁克：《使命、责任与实务》，机械工业出版社2013年版，第56—68页]

11 See Chen Xian, 1984, *Planning Workbook*, China Financial and Economic Press, pp. 423-450. [参见陈先：《计划工作手册》，中国财政经济出版社1984年版，第423—450页]

12 For details on the decision-making process of the five-year plan, please refer to Wang Shaoguang and Yan Yilong, 2015, *Big Wisdom and Prosperity: How China Makes a Five-Year Plan*, Renmin University of China Press. [五年规划决策过程具体参见王绍光、鄢一龙：《大智兴邦：中国如何制定五年规划》，中国人民大学出版社2015年版]

13 The General Office of the Central Committee of the Communist Party of China and the General Office of the State Council issued the 'Opinions on Establishing and Improving the Implementation Mechanism of the National "13th Five-Year Plan" Outline'. [中共中央办公厅、国务院办公厅印发《关于建立健全国家"十三五"规划纲要实施机制的意见》]

14 See Qu Jingdong, 2012, *Project-based System and Grassroots Government Mobilization*, China Social Sciences Press; Zhou Feizhou, 2012, 'Specialization of Financial Funds and Its Problems: A Concurrent Discussion on Project Governance', Society, No. 1; Zheng Shilin, 2016, 'Research on the Project System of Chinese Government's Economic Governance', *China Soft Science*, No. 2. [参见渠敬东：《项目制与基层政府动员》，中国社会科学出版社2012年版；周飞舟：《财政资金的专项化及其问题：兼论项目治国》，《社会》2012年第1期；郑世林：《中国政府经济治理的项目体制研究》，《中国软科学》2016年第2期]

15 The National Development and Reform Commission issued the 'Opinions on Coordinating and Promoting the Implementation of 165 Major Engineering Projects in the 13th Five-Year Plan' (Development and Reform Planning [2017] No. 730).《国家发展改革委印发〈关于统筹推进"十三五"165项重大工程项目实施工作的意见〉的通知》（发改规划〔2017〕730号）。

16 Douglass C. North, 1994, 'Economic Performance Through Time', *The American Economic Review*, Vol. 84, No. 3, Jun, pp.359-368.

17 Zhang Yongle, 2015, 'Institutional Confidence and the Reform of China's Political System', in Yan Yilong, Bai Gang, Zhang Yongle, Ou Shujun, He Jianyu, *A Journey to the Great Road: The Communist Party of China and Chinese Socialism*, Renmin University of China Press, pp. 54-64. [章永乐：《制度自信与中国政治体制改革》，载鄢一龙、白钢、章永乐、欧树军、何建宇：《大道之行：中国共产党与中国社会主义》，中国人民大学出版社2015年版，第54—64页]

18 Bai Gang, 2018, 'Dialectics of Teacher and Student: Chinese Socialism's Inheritance and Transcendence of Leninism', in Yan Yilong, Bai Gang, Lu Dewen, Liu Chenguang, Jiang Yu and Yin Yiwen, *The World is Public: Chinese Socialism and the Long 21st Century*, Renmin University of China Press, pp. 34-39. [白钢：《师生辩证法：中国社会主义对列宁主义的继承与超越》，载鄢一龙、白钢、吕德文、刘晨光、江宇、尹伊文：《天下为公：中国社会主义与漫长的21世纪》，中国人民大学出版社2018年版，第34—39页]

CHAPTER 5

Construction of a Minsheng State in the New Era

[*Yan Yilong: 'Construction of Minsheng State in the New Era', Journal of the Central Institute of Socialism, No. 1, 2018. The author made substantial revisions for inclusion in this book.鄢一龙：《新时代民生国家建设》，《中央社会主义学院学报》2018年第1期。收入本书时，作者作了大幅修订。]

The issue of people's livelihood is the issue of people's survival in the world and the issue that is closely related to their own life interests. Ensuring and improving people's livelihood is an important aspect of building socialism with Chinese characteristics in the new era. The report of the 19th National Congress of the Communist Party of China pointed out that one of the basic strategies of socialism with Chinese characteristics in the new era is to insist on ensuring and improving people's livelihood in the development process. It puts forward seven 'insurances' in the field of people's livelihood – insuring access to childcare, education, employment, medical services, elderly care, housing, and social assistance.

China is neither a free market economy nor a welfare state, but a Minsheng state. Entering the new era, the main contradiction in our society has transformed into the contradiction between the people's ever-growing needs for a better life and unbalanced and inadequate development. An important aspect of unbalanced development is the unbalance between people's well-being and economic development. To deal with this unbalance, we need to further safeguard and improve people's livelihood during development.

1. Building a Minsheng state

The free market assumes that people's livelihoods depend entirely on the degree of an individual's success in the market mechanism, and that individuals are solely responsible for their own well-being. For working people, who make up the vast majority of the population, the way to participate in the market relies primarily on selling their labour and, as

Polanyi argues, separating labour from the other activities of life and making it subject to the laws of the market is, in effect, the atomism of survival.[1] Modern society is a society with high survival costs. Under the condition of individual atomisation, not only the disadvantaged groups, but also the vast majority of workers in society cannot solve livelihood problems such as housing, medical care, and education only through individual strength.

The emergence of the welfare state is actually to provide individuals with a state protection system outside the market. This kind of protection is only a low-level assistance with strict qualifications for the free welfare system. Even if a universal welfare system is implemented, the level of welfare that can be provided is extremely low, subject to its contribution level and financial strength. And the relatively wealthy groups in society still purchase higher levels of welfare through the market. Without unique natural resource conditions, small population sizes, and high levels of development, it is impossible to provide the relatively high levels of universal access to benefits that the Nordic countries have. Many countries have fallen into the 'welfare trap' of overstretching their finances.

China is not a welfare state in any sense. All welfare states are embedded in the capitalist system, and the decommodification of the welfare state is merely a remedial and reverse movement to the capital-dominated and market-driven system. China is a socialist country, and during the classical socialist system, it relied on the state and the collective community to solve the people's livelihood problems. After the reform and opening-up, China introduced a market economy, but China's market economy is embedded in the socialist system, not the other way around.

China has embarked on a path of a Minsheng state, surpassing both the free market and the welfare state. It is based on China's socialist system and relies on a new type of socialist community to solve the people's livelihood issues. The Minsheng state is the middle way between efficiency and fairness, and it pursues 'efficient fairness', rather than merely prioritising fairness or efficiency. The Minsheng state has a dual function: one is the function of social protection, which guarantees the basic living needs of the disadvantaged in a market economy; the other is the function of promoting economic efficiency, that is, through the universal development of human resources, it can generally improve the ability of the people to compete in the market, thereby promoting economic development and social equity. In people's lives, the state plays different roles. The liberal state is like a public service store, the classic socialist state is like a father, the welfare state is like a nanny, and the Minsheng state is like a counsellor who will focus on helping the students who are lagging behind, but that is mainly to bring them up to the same level as everyone else.

The path of the Minsheng state has its roots in China's pursuit of a commonwealth society, which has been pursued since ancient times. The traditional Chinese pursuit of a commonwealth society means that all people can enjoy their lives, that everyone is close to each other and that everyone is happy. Therefore, people not only support their parents, not only raise their children, but also enable the elderly to live their lives, the middle-aged to serve society, and the young children to have a place where they can grow up healthily. 'And the old without wives, the old without husbands, the young without fathers, the old without sons, and the disabled can all be supported by society. Men have jobs and women have a home. People hate the act of throwing their possessions on the ground, but they do not necessarily want to keep them for themselves; they are willing to do their best for the common good, but not necessarily for their own personal gain'.[2] According to Confucius, the three steps of governing a country are to increase the population, enrich them, and educate them.[3] It is also necessary to take good care of people's livelihood issues as the key to governing the country.

Mencius also paints a picture of people living and working in peace and contentment, 'Five acres of residential land, planted with mulberry trees, and men in their fifties will be able to wear silk fabrics. When raising chickens, pigs, and dogs, don't delay their breeding opportunities, and men in their seventies will be able to eat meat. Don't delay the farming season for a field as large as one hundred mu, and a family of several people can be free from starvation. Education should be set up seriously, and the principle of respecting parents and elder brothers should be repeatedly taught to the people, so that elderly people with grey beards will not be walking on the road with heavy objects on their backs or their heads. A man of seventy can wear silk fabrics and eat meat, and the common people are not starving and freezing. There has never been anyone who has achieved this but cannot unify the world and become king.'[4]

Sun Yat-sen inherited the 'ideology of great harmony in the world that Confucius hoped for' and advocated livelihoodism, making the solution of the livelihood of the people, such as food, clothing, housing, and transport, the primary concern of those who governed, and the 'driving force of all social activities'. Sun Yat-sen repeatedly declared: 'My humble aim is to promote industry and to implement livelihoodism, with socialism as the final destination, so that all the people of the country, without a single poor person, can enjoy the happiness together'. 'The livelihoodism is socialism, also known as communitism, which is the cosmopolitanism.'[5]

At the early stage of socialist construction, when China's economic development was still at a very low level, people were provided with basic livelihood protection through the unitary system in the cities and the collective economic system in the countryside. At the same time, according to the principle of 'Take part from the surplus to make up for the deficit,' extremely limited public resources were allocated more to the disadvantaged groups through the unified purchase and sale of grain, rural cooperative medical care, universal primary education, etc., the basic livelihood of hundreds of millions of people has been solved to a large extent despite the low level of income.

Since the reform and opening-up of China, in the process of promoting market-oriented reforms, with the disintegration of the urban corporate system and the rural collective economic system, atomised individuals were thrown into the tide of the market economy. For a period of time, the problem of 'one leg being long and the other being short' in terms of economic development and people's livelihood emerged. Since the beginning of the 21st century, China has strengthened the state's function of protecting and supporting the people's livelihood. The report of the 17th Party Congress put forward the 'five insurance' of building people's livelihood, namely 'Let people have better access to education, employment, medical services, elderly care, and housing.' This is a response to the traditional ideal of a commonwealth society and a strengthening of socialist features in the construction of socialism with Chinese characteristics. The report of the 18th Party Congress requires continuous achievement in the 'five insurance'. The 19th Party Congress report further upgraded the goal of building people's livelihoods to 'seven insurance', that is, 'insuring access to childcare, education, employment, housing, medical services, elderly care, and social assistance'. Since the 21st century, China has made a new leap forward in building people's livelihoods. It established a medical and pension insurance system covering both urban and rural residents. It built a safety net for basic social security, significantly reducing the number of people living in poverty, and rapidly improved people's education and health standards.

China has made great achievements in improving people's livelihood. In 1949, 80% of China's population was illiterate, the life expectancy of the population was only 35 years, and the vast majority of people lived below the poverty line. By 2020, China has built a moderately prosperous society, with a basic medical insurance coverage rate of over 95%, and an average life expectancy of 77.3 years, 4.7 years higher than the world average of 72.6 years. The expected number of years of education for the population is 13.9 years in 2018, already higher than the world average of 12.7 years.[6] Absolute poverty has now been completely eradicated.

2. Minsheng state versus welfare state

Costa Espin-Anderson divides the Western welfare state into three clusters of institutional types, namely the 'liberal welfare state' of the Anglo-Saxon countries, including the United States, Canada, Australia, etc.; the 'conservative welfare state' of continental Europe, including Austria, France, Germany, Italy, etc.; and the Nordic 'social-democratic welfare states', including Sweden, Norway, Denmark, etc.[7]

The Minsheng State is a unique path that China has explored that is different from both the liberal state and the welfare state. The Minsheng State is different from any type of welfare state in the following ways.

First, the underlying philosophy is fundamentally different. A basic idea of the welfare state is 'corporate statism', and the 'conservative welfare state' is mainly derived from this idea. The welfare system is to maintain class and status differences, promote class cooperation and national unity. Social rights are attached to the class status of the individual in society.[8]

Another fundamental concept of the welfare state is the need to provide social security against the risks faced by individuals living in a market economy. The Beveridge Report proposed the need for the state to provide living security for those whose income is interrupted or who have lost their earning capacity, or whose families have special needs (e.g. families with many children), and proposed the creation of a unified social security system.[9]

Another basic idea of the welfare state is social rights of citizens, which is to regard the need for the state to provide welfare to citizens as an integral part of civil rights. T.H. Marshall regarded social rights as the development of citizenship in the 20th century, and constituted one of the three dimensions of citizenship, namely, civil, political, and social.[10]

The closest thing to a socialist philosophy in the welfare state is the idea that the state should correct inequalities in market distribution through secondary distribution, and that the goal of the welfare state is to promote greater social equality. This is a more broadly Keynesian concept of the welfare state, a concept that has been widely adopted by socialist democratic welfare states.

Different from the concept of the welfare state, the core concept of Minsheng state is the concept of the socialist community. The socialist community itself is an inseparable community of interests, responsibility, and destiny which needs to be built and shared by the members of the community. Safeguarding and improving people's livelihood is an important connotation of socialism. The various ideas of the welfare state are incorporated in the construction of the Minsheng state in China, but they do not constitute the theory of the Minsheng state, but only the method of the Minsheng state. The members of the community are not just individual citizens, but are also people in the sense of the whole, with not only individual rights but also common rights. The members of the community do not have a rigid social claim to the community, but have a common responsibility for the development of the community and a common right to share the fruits of development. The Minsheng state is a system for improving people's well-being centred on promoting people's ability to develop and is shared by individuals, communities and the state. People's livelihood problems need to be solved jointly through individual, collective and national forces. Unlike the welfare state, which emphasises individual rights and state responsibilities, the Minsheng state is about shared rights and shared responsibilities. The goal of the development of the socialist community is to promote the all-round development of human beings. The Minsheng state has also established a social security system. After achieving the basic security of people's livelihood issues, people can be liberated from lifelong struggle to solve the problems of survival, and pursue more meaningful life, to truly realize the all-round development of human beings.

Second, the relationship with development is different. The welfare state also has system arrangements linked to development, but in general, it is designed to solve the problems brought about by development based on market mechanisms, without considering it as a means to promote development. Whereas the main function of the social-democratic welfare state is redistribution, the function of the Minsheng state is that production, primary distribution and redistribution all play a role.

The Minsheng State is a system arrangement centred on improving people's ability to develop. It focuses on developing human resources for the people through investment in health and education to improve people's ability to compete in the market. The original meaning of 'people's livelihood' comes from 'Zuo Zhuan: The Twelfth Year of Xuangong', 'The livelihood of the people lies in hard work, and if you work hard, you will not lack food and clothing', which well reflects that the Minsheng state is a system arrangement that encourages diligence and does not support laziness. In terms of employment policy, the emphasis is not on unemployment benefits, but on the policy of creating jobs and promoting reemployment. Every five-year plan (planning) since the '6th Five-Year Plan' has set the goal of creating new jobs. During the '12th Five-Year Plan' period, China has created 64.31 million new urban jobs. While the 13th Five-Year Plan calls for the creation of more than 50 million new jobs in urban areas in five years, but the actual figure is 65.67 million, exceeding the planned target. In terms of poverty alleviation policies, emphasis is also placed on strengthening the 'hematopoietic' function (Stimulating the endogenous motivation of the poor to get out of poverty) of poverty-stricken areas and poor populations, improving the self-development ability of poor populations through education, employment, and industrial poverty alleviation.

For example, from the perspective of welfare policy in the United States, helping low-income families is generally a kind of assistance policy, including the provision of subsidies, income support, cash benefits, medical assistance, and temporary assistance.[11] In contrast, China's poverty alleviation policy is primarily a development support policy. For a long time, China's poverty alleviation has emphasized not only providing a 'blood transfusion' mechanism, but also improving the poor people's own 'hematopoietic' ability. Sustainable and endogenous poverty alleviation is achieved by improving the development capacity of poor areas and poor people. Although the models of rural poverty alleviation are very diverse, they are all fundamentally about improving the development capacity of farmers and villages themselves, and China's poverty alleviation policy is essentially a development-supported, development-linked poverty alleviation policy.

In June 2017, the author investigated the poverty alleviation project of China Resources Hope Town in Jinggangshan, a model of poverty alleviation by state-owned enterprises (SOEs), which promotes poverty alleviation by introducing state-owned enterprises in the countryside. State-owned enterprises have strong market operation capabilities, and at the same time, a strong sense of social responsibility. Based on the 'one town, one product' industry, China Resources (华润) drives local development. For example, the China Resources Hope Town in Baise develops sheltered grapes, cherry tomatoes, chickens raised in forests, high-quality laying hens in Xibaipo, and ecological kiwi fruit in Jinzhai. etc.; in Jinggangshan, it develops the rural tourism industry. According to the characteristics of Jinggangshan as a red education base and rich tourism resources, rural tourism development is driven by the hotel + homestay model. China Resources has invested heavily in the local area to improve the rural environment, including the hardening of roads and the reconstruction of rural infrastructure. At the same time, China Resources has used its extensive experience in hotel operations to not only build a branded hotel chain under the Jinggangshan, but also drive extensive participation of local residents through the development of B&Bs, helping farmers to operate them more professionally. In addition to driving farmers to wealth，the proceeds from the rural tourism industry, can also be invested in the construction of rural communities by building nursing homes and kindergartens in cooperation with professional institutions, rebuilding rural culture, and solving the problem of rural public services. China Resources Hope Town is a typical example of sustainable poverty alleviation through state-owned enterprises leading the development of rural industries and rebuilding rural communities.

In September 2016, the author investigated targeted poverty alleviation in Zhonghe West Town, Dalat Banner, Ordos, and Inner Mongolia. The town adopted a poverty alleviation model of improving development capacity plus full coverage of public services. For poor households, it mainly helps them develop planting industries, including new economic crops such as wolfberry and oil peony; develop breeding industry, provide them with piglets, lambs, etc., and provide production materials such as three-wheeled agricultural vehicles. It also introduces poor households to work in some local communities and helps solve their children's education problems.

At the same time, Inner Mongolia implements 'ten full coverage' to achieve full coverage of public services in rural areas through government subsidies, including: the renovation of dangerous houses, safe drinking water, hardening of streets and alleys, village electricity and power grid upgrades, radio and television access to every village, construction and safety improvement of school buildings, standardised clinics, cultural activity rooms, convenience stores, and pension and medical insurance for the permanent resident population. The town's rural roads and other infrastructure have been repaired, and many people live in new houses through self-financing and government subsidies. More than 60% of the poor households have been lifted out of poverty through migration and relocation.

In September 2019, the author conducted research on a self-media short video platform. In the era of attention, short video social software has created a new model of poverty alleviation through information flow empowerment, which solved the problem of attention poverty among the poor. By helping farmers master the new skills of the information age, such as short video filming and live video broadcasts on mobile phones, empowered farmers with information flow, some villages have been lifted out of poverty.

For example, in some remote Miao cottages, mobile internet has successfully created the persona, scenery, and objects of the internet celebrity villages through unique scenic spots, ethnic songs, and dances, and ethnic costumes, which has attracted massive attention, thus driving the development of the countryside and achieving poverty alleviation. The village of Yugouliang in Zhangjiakou, Hebei province, is remote and lacks resources, with villagers living in poverty and young adults mostly working outside the village. Lu Wenzhen, the secretary of the village party branch, led the elderly in the village to practice yoga, creating a unique yoga exercise for farmers. While exercising, he uploaded short videos to platforms such as Kuaishou. Because the villagers' collective practice of yoga has attracted a lot of attention, Yugouliang Village has become a yoga net-celebrity village, which has driven rural tourism and the sale of quinoa, potatoes and other special agricultural products, achieving poverty alleviation.

Third, the sources of funding are different. Socialist public assets allow the Minsheng state to have more ways to raise funds than the welfare state. Unlike the welfare state, which can only rely on taxation and social financing channels to finance people's livelihood and welfare, China has a large number of public assets, which can provide new sources of investment in the field of people's livelihood. The Third Plenary Session of the 18th

Central Committee of the Communist Party of China proposed to increase the proportion of state-owned capital gains to be turned over to 30% by 2020, with more being used to protect and improve people's livelihood. In November 2017, the State Council issued the 'Implementation Plan for Transferring Part of State-owned Capital to Enrich the Social Security Fund', which clearly required that some central enterprises and provinces would be selected for pilot projects from 2017, and 10% of the state-owned equity of enterprises would be uniformly transferred to enrich the social security fund.

Fourth, the subjects of responsibility are different. The welfare state believes that under the market system, individuals cannot be fully responsible for their livelihoods due to income disparity and social risks. The state is needed to regulate and guarantee them. The main subjects of responsibility are the individual and the state. The construction of a Minsheng state is based on the construction of a socialist community, where individuals, families, collectives (employment units, residential space) and the state all have different degrees of responsibility for people's livelihood, with different actors participating and providing together.

The 'social-democratic welfare state' system is de-familial and considers the individual the basic unit. China has had a tradition of attaching importance to the family since ancient times, and to this day, the family is still the basic unit for solving livelihood problems. In solving problems such as education and pension, the role of family members must be fully utilised, and cannot be replaced by any other mechanism. China's livelihood policy is strongly family-oriented and aims to enhance the function of the family in people's livelihood. For example, in the targeted poverty alleviation programme, low-income households are identified and assisted on a household basis, and so is the re-employment policy, which proposes the need to avoid 'zero-employment families' at the stage of lay-offs and re-employment.

The 'welfare state trap' is largely due to the fact that the state has taken on too much responsibility for its citizens and is therefore overburdened. In the early years of socialist construction, there was an important community between the state and the individual – the collective, which referred to the commune and the production team in the countryside and the enterprise units in the cities. With the disintegration of the collective economy and the unit system, atomised individuals are thrown into the torrent of the market. In a market-oriented environment, with the rising prices of necessities for people's livelihood, such as housing, education, and medical care, the individual as a worker can no longer solve these problems on their own, no matter how hard they try. A new type of organised community solution mechanism should be actively explored to encourage employment units, communities and social organisations to undertake the supply of livelihood goods actively.

Under market economy conditions, employers also need to assume important responsibilities for people's livelihood. On the one hand, employers are important subjects of social security contributions. On the other hand, qualified employers are encouraged to become important providers of employee benefits, such as providing employees with canteens, setting up kindergartens and schools, raising funds to build houses, etc.

The 'enterprises run society' and 'employment units run society' cannot be considered inefficient. Compared to the market mechanism, the community has the advantage of providing livelihood products with fewer intermediate links and, more importantly, the capital of trust accumulated through long-term contracts, which enables it to provide higher quality livelihood products at a lower cost.

Some internet companies are reviving the 'employment units run society' system that was once considered backwards. But of course, this is not a traditional enterprise-take-all system, but rather a system that provides good benefits and builds more interest and emotional ties with employees. For example, some private enterprises have established kindergartens within their headquarters. In August 2019, the author investigated an internet company in Beijing. This is an online game development company with mainly young employees and good benefits. It is similar to a 'new employment unit system', with a canteen providing three meals a day, a gym with a full-time trainer and a special children's activity room, where employees' children are transported to after classes. The staff are comfortable in this kind of working environment and are more engaged in their work as they have no worries.

Fifth, the degree of decommodification varies. As Costa Espin-Anderson has pointed out, the degree of decommodification of social benefits dominated by social assistance in the 'liberal welfare state' is low, because the eligibility for assistance is very strict, and only 'market losers' are able to access the meagre relief. 'This, in fact, reinforces the degree of commoditisation, where the vast majority of people get their benefits through the purchase of private sector services'.

Compulsory social insurance in the 'conservative welfare state' is also less de-commoditised as the number of contributions is highly dependent on employment. Even the 'social-democratic welfare state', which has the highest degree of decommodification, mainly refers to a high degree of decommodification in terms of eligibility for benefits.[12]

The de-commodification attribute of the Minsheng State is embedded in its socialist system itself, mainly referring to the de-commodification of the supply mechanism. People's livelihood products are necessities with extremely low price elasticity. Hence, the livelihood sector cannot be done as an industry, but it must adhere to the public welfare direction of the reform of the people's livelihood field. In fact, the reforms that need to be promoted in these areas are to de-market and return to public welfare reforms.

For example, medical reform is a problem in the world. China is also faced with the high cost of getting medical services, difficult access to health care, and constant conflicts between doctors and patients. What is the cause? Due to information asymmetry, patients have no choice but to trust doctors' professional competence and professional ethics. However, in a system where 'medicine feeds doctors', individual doctors see their patients as a tool to make money and differentiate between productive and unproductive clients. Therefore, the medical reform model in Sanming City, Fujian province, has a significance of weathervane. According to CCTV reports, just one month after the introduction of the medical reform programme in Sanming, the commonly used hospital drug omeprazole sodium has dropped from 256 yuan a box sold before the reform to 6.9 yuan, a 37-fold drop. What a shocking profiteering in the industrial chain of medicine. In the three years since the medical reform, Sanming City has saved a total of 1.795 billion yuan in drug costs, equivalent to an average saving of nearly 700 yuan in drug costs per person. Not only is it cheaper for the common people to see a doctor, but the income of medical staff has risen significantly, and the medical insurance fund has turned from a deficit to a surplus.[13] How did Sanming do it? Fundamentally, it adheres to the public welfare and socialist direction of medical reform. Sanming City broke the profit-seeking mechanism of hospitals at its source and did not allow doctors to see patients as tools to earn money but as objects of service. The annual salary of doctors in public hospitals is linked to the workload of the post, medical ethics and social evaluation, rather than the income from drugs, tests and consumables, which fundamentally removes the incentive for doctors to prescribe large prescriptions, and restores the professional dignity of doctors to save lives and help the injured. At the same time, the comprehensive reform of the medical and health care system, which links medical care, medicine and health insurance, has allowed only two VAT payments for drugs from the factory to the warehouse, thus controlling the problem of inflated drug prices in the distribution of drugs.

The central government has proposed that 'houses are for living and not for speculation', the core of which is to return housing to its use-value. At present, many places have introduced a policy of shared ownership housing, which has achieved a certain degree of decommodification and changed the financial attribute of housing. The price of shared ownership housing is lower than the market price, and the house can be used for living or inherited. It can also be traded after meeting certain conditions, but it does not have the financial attributes of value preservation and appreciation. However, as eligibility conditions strictly limit such a system, the scale of supply is small, and the proportion of non-commercialised preferential treatment is very low, which in practice does not have a significant effect on solving the housing problems of residents. Fundamentally, it is still necessary to return to the essential features of socialism, as some scholars have proposed, to explore ways of rationing livelihood products based on the use value and shared by the community, and to implement a rent-to-buy system of inclusive shared ownership.

3. Imbalance between people's well-being and economic development

As the level of development increases, the demand for people's livelihood in China is increasingly shifting towards high-quality demand, while the unbalanced and inadequate supply of people's livelihood has become a prominent contradiction. An important aspect of unbalanced development is the imbalance between the well-being of people's livelihood and economic development.

A paradox has emerged in our development. Economic development is increasing, but the pressure on people's livelihoods has increased instead of being reduced in many ways. Different livelihood issues arise at different

Table 1 Comparison of Minsheng state with different types of welfare states

	Minsheng State	Liberal Welfare State	Social Democratic Welfare State	Conservative Welfare State
Representative countries	China	United States, Canada, Australia, etc.	Sweden, Norway, Denmark, etc.	Austria, France, Germany, Italy, etc.
Basic philosophy	Socialist community	Social assistance and social security	Universal social rights, secondary distribution to promote equality	Stability and unity of different classes
Relationship with Development	Focus on Social Protection & Economic Efficiency Promotion	Focus on the redistribution based on civil society rights, with no emphasis on the relationship between production and development		
Source of funds	Public asset dividends, taxation, socially raised funds	Taxation, socially raised funds		
Subjects of responsibility	Individual family, collective, country	Individual, country		
Degree of Decommodification	Highest	Low	High	Moderate

stages of development. Currently, China's subsistence-oriented livelihood issues have not been completely eliminated, development-oriented livelihood issues are prominent, while developed livelihood issues are beginning to come to the fore, and it is at a stage where the three types of livelihood issues are superimposed.

Subsistence-oriented livelihood problems refer to the issues in which people's basic livelihood is difficult due to the low level of development. After more than 70 years of development, livelihood issues related to people's basic livelihoods have generally been resolved. However, this problem still persists in the long term due to uneven development. After all the poor people have been withdrawn by the end of 2020, there will still be a large number of underprivileged people and low-income groups in China, and the problem of relative poverty in urban and rural areas will remain prominent.

Development-oriented livelihood issues refer to the people's livelihood issues arising in the course of development, and have become the main contradiction in the livelihood sector. On the one hand, livelihood issues emerge along with development. Currently, the most prominent ones are environmental protection, health and safety, and other livelihood issues. On the other hand, as the level of development increases, the demand for a higher-quality supply of livelihood products is not met, which is mainly reflected in the people's desire for better education, medical care and elderly care services, which are not effectively met.

Developed livelihood problems are those that arise after development, which has become prominent in China today. Developed livelihood problems are a common problem in developed countries around the world. Even the United States, with a GDP per capita of over $60,000, has not been able to solve this problem. Nearly half of American households still face difficulties with basic expenses, with 23.1% unable to meet food expenses and 9.3% struggling to afford housing-related costs.[14] 40% of Americans are unable to pay an extra $400. The middle class, the backbone of society, has been reduced to the so-called 'Miserable class'. The failure to address livelihood issues has become a major cause of social unrest in the US.

Development cannot cure all diseases. Comrade Deng Xiaoping said in those days that 'now we can see that the problems after development are no less than when development did not take place'.[15] As we enter the high-income stage, the pressure on people's livelihoods remains enormous. According to the World Bank's definition of a high-income economy, Beijing, Tianjin, Shanghai, Jiangsu and Zhejiang are already high-income economies, and the problems of developed livelihood issues become prominent.

Firstly, the cost of livelihood expenditure has risen, and income has increased, but people do not feel that the actual standard of living has improved much. A large number of the so-called social elite and gold-collar class also feel the huge pressure of survival. Most of their income is spent on basic living needs such as a house, children's education, business insurance, and pension savings. Secondly, the gap between the rich and the poor has widened, and the problem of relative poverty has become prominent. Finally, the livelihood problems brought about by the ageing population, and low birth-rate stage began to become prominent. Developed livelihood problems are not solved by marketisation; on the contrary, they are precisely the result of excessive marketisation to a large extent. The skyrocketing housing prices in fully commoditised and financialised first-tier cities, which far exceed the purchasing power of workers, is a striking example.

4. Promoting the construction of an all-round and all-cycle Minsheng state

After building a moderately prosperous society in all respects in 2020, China has entered the stage of the 14th Five-Year Plan, which is also the beginning stage of the second 100-year goal. During this period, China's economic development generally enters the track of high-quality development, and promoting the national construction of a full-cycle and all-round Minsheng state will become one of the key tasks of the 14th Five-Year Plan.

What we are building is not a cradle-to-grave welfare system, but a system that can be relied upon throughout the entire life cycle, from birth to death, in different life situations such as clothing, food, housing, transport, education, health care and retirement, in order to solve the livelihood problems faced by individuals in different life situations, with a particular focus on the disadvantaged.

The overall layout of socialist construction with Chinese characteristics in the new era is the 'five-in-one' approach to economic, political, social, cultural and ecological civilisation construction. The construction of a comprehensive Minsheng state means not only ensuring and improving people's livelihood in social construction, but also integrating the connotations of a Minsheng state into the overall layout of the 'five-in-one', thus forming an all-round and full-life-cycle state system that offers people good livelihood.

From the perspective of economic construction, a mechanism for linking economic development with the construction of the Minsheng state should be established. While constantly improving people's livelihoods during economic development, we should also avoid whetting our appetite for high growth and instead set the bottom line for economic growth by meeting the needs for employment, improvement of people's livelihoods and financial resources for social security. It is necessary to ensure that the growth rate of the disposable income of urban residents, the net income of rural residents, and investment in the field of people's livelihood are not lower than the growth rate of GDP.

Increase the supply of public goods for people's livelihood and expand the total social demand. In the new era, China has generally bid farewell to the era of shortage economy and entered the era of relative surplus. By increasing the supply of public goods for people's livelihood, we can, to a certain extent, boost social demand and promote economic development.

From the perspective of political construction, livelihood issues are not only economic and social issues, but also major political issues. It is necessary to promote democracy with people's livelihood and to drive people's livelihood with democracy. A Minsheng state is also an important way to realise people's democracy. The survey shows that the most important thing Asian peoples understand about government democracy is to solve people's livelihood issues, with the proportion of Asian people holding this view reaching 54.7%, and the proportion of Chinese people reaching 67.1%,[16] much higher than those who see freedom of election, criticism, etc. as attributes of democracy.

In terms of social construction, it is necessary to promote social construction in a comprehensive and balanced manner with the focus on ensuring and improving people's livelihood, and continue to improve people's livelihood issues such as employment, medical care, housing, health, and education, narrow the income gap and the gap between the rich and the poor, innovate social governance methods and ensure people's livelihoods through more flexible and diversified mechanisms.

From the perspective of cultural construction, the focus should be on promoting the construction of people's culture. People are not only the subjects of cultural consumption, but also the subjects of cultural creation and cultural participation. Various mass cultural activities are carried out to educate, entertain, and build a core socialist value system.

From the perspective of ecological civilisation, a beautiful ecological environment is a demand for people's livelihood. Focusing on the environment, we should vigorously address environmental pollution issues, such as water, gas, sound and soil that people are concerned about, and focus on environmental issues closely related to people's interests, such as rural source pollution, drinking water safety and ecological poverty.

The path of the Minsheng state is a new path based on the system of Chinese characteristics, which differs from the welfare state. It better manages the relationship between development and the improvement of people's well-being, thus ensuring the continuous improvement of people's welfare while avoiding falling into the 'welfare state trap'.

There are several reasons why the Minsheng state does not fall into the welfare state trap: firstly, the Minsheng state and economic development promote each other. The level of livelihood protection is linked to development and can be adjusted to the level of development, while at the same time, development is promoted by improving the people's ability to develop. Secondly, the Minsheng state relies not only on the state but, more importantly, on mutual assistance between different community levels. Thirdly, the public resources shared by the members of the society provide access to finance beyond taxation and, at the same time, make it possible for the society to supply public goods for people's livelihoods in a non-market-based rationing system.

The institutional advantage of socialism with Chinese characteristics lies in the organic combination of the socialist system and the market economy. Compared with the capitalist system, socialism clearly has institutional advantages in solving livelihood issues. As we enter a new era and face new contradictions, we need to promote de-marketing reforms in the field of people's livelihoods, give full play to the advantages of the socialist system and advance the construction of a Minsheng state, thereby creating a higher and more sustainable level of livelihood achievements than those of developed capitalist countries.

The Minsheng state is fundamentally designed to change the situation of ordinary people who have to work all their lives to meet their basic needs, to liberate workers from the 'slavery of things', and to promote the 'comprehensive development of the human being' that belongs to all people.

---

1 See Karl Polanyi, 2007, *The Great Transformation: The Political and Economic Origins of Our Time*, Zhejiang People's Publishing House, Originally published in 1944, Farrar & Rinehart. [参见波兰尼：《大转型：我们时代的政治与经济起源》，浙江人民出版社2007年版]
2 *Book of Rites: The Conveyance of Rites* [《礼记·礼运》]
3 *The Analects of Confucius – Zi Lu* [《论语·子路》]

4 *Mencius – On King Hui Liang* [《孟子·梁惠王上》]

5 Sun Yat-sen, 1981, 'Livelihoodism', *Selected Works of Sun Yat-sen*, People's Publishing House, p. 802. [孙中山：《民生主义》，《孙中山选集》，人民出版社1981年版，第802页]

6 Source of data: UNDP: <http://hdr.undp.org/en/data>, [4 May 2021]

7 Cøsta Esping-Andersen, 2010, *The Three Worlds of Welfare Capitalism*, translated by Miao Zhengmin and Teng Yuying, Commercial Press, Originally published in 1990, Princeton University Press. [哥斯塔·埃斯平-安德森：《福利资本主义的三个世界》，苗正民、滕玉英译，商务印书馆2010年]

8 Cøsta Esping-Andersen, 2010, *The Three Worlds of Welfare Capitalism*, translated by Miao Zhengmin and Teng Yuying, Commercial Press, p. 62. [哥斯塔·埃斯平-安德森：《福利资本主义的三个世界》，苗正民、滕玉英译，商务印书馆2010年版，第62页]

9 William Beveridge, 2004, *The Beveridge Report*, China Labour and Social Security Press, Originally published in 1942, His Majesty's Stationery Office. [贝弗里奇：《贝弗里奇报告》，中国劳动社会保障出版社2004年版]

10 T.H. Marshall, 1950, *Citizenship and Social Class and Other Essays*, Cambridge: Cambridge University Press.

11 Diana DiNitto, 2016, *Social Welfare: Politics and Public Policy*, Renmin University of China Press, pp. 274–316, Originally published in 1983, Prentice Hall PTR. [迪尼托：《社会福利政治与公共政策》，中国人民大学出版社2016年版，第274—316页]

12 Cøsta Esping-Andersen, 2010, *The Three Worlds of Welfare Capitalism*, translated by Miao Zhengmin and Teng Yuying, The Commercial Press, pp. 50-52. [哥斯塔·埃斯平-安德森：《福利资本主义的三个世界》，苗正民、滕玉英译，商务印书馆2010年版，第50—52页]

13 'The "Sanming Path" of Medical Reform in Deep Water Zone, CCTV, 12 Dec, 2015. [《医改深水区的"三明路径"》，央视网2015年12月12日]

14 Quoted from Wei Nanzhi and Wang Congyue: 'Division and Consensus: Prospects for the 2020 U.S. Election', ' Blue Book of the United States: Annual Research on Report of USA (2020)' [转引自魏南枝、王聪悦：《分裂与共识：2020美国大选展望》，《美国蓝皮书：美国研究报告(2020)》]

15 *The Chronology of Deng Xiaoping (1975–1997)*, 2004, Vol. 2, Central Literature Publishing House, p. 1364. [《邓小平年谱(1975–1997)》下卷，中央文献出版社2004年版，第1364页]

16 <http://www.eastasiabarometer.org chinese/news.html>, [4 May 2021]

CHAPTER 6

Dealing with Insufficient Effective Demand with New Demand Management

[*The first draft of this article was a presentation made by the author at the Forty People Forum on China Finance biweekly roundtable seminar on 1 Sept, 2017. Officially published in World Socialist Studies, No. 10, 2018. It was not revised for inclusion in this book. 本文初稿是作者2017年9月1日参加中国金融四十人论坛双周圆桌研讨会的发言。正式刊发于《世界社会主义研究》2018年第10期。收入本书时未作修订。]

1. The fundamental challenge to China's economic development lies in the lack of effective demand

China's economic development has entered a phase of relative abundance from a phase of scarcity, and the main contradiction in economic growth has been transformed, mainly in the form of three contradictions in supply and demand associated with economic growth: The first is low supply efficiency, the second is insufficient effective supply, and the third is insufficient effective demand. As President Xi Jinping pointed out: the supply side and the demand side are the two basic means of managing and regulating the macro economy. Demand-side management focuses on solving total quantity issues. Supply-side management focuses on solving structural problems.[1] Among these three contradictions, insufficient effective demand is the contradiction in terms of total quantity, and insufficient effective supply and supply efficiency are the contradictions in terms of structure.

In response to the problem of low supply efficiency, some advocate measures such as tax and fee reductions to reduce business costs and deregulation to motivate businesses. These policies have some effect in the short term, but their effect diminishes in the long term.

As price increases in broad factors of production are a natural process of economic development and do not expand market space, the effect of such policy adjustments is actually quite limited. According to a survey conducted by the China Academy of Fiscal Sciences on cost reduction from 2014 to 2016, the rigid costs of raw materials, energy and land use, labour and logistics are mainly rising faster, and the room for institutional adjustment is quite limited. For example, the average value of 'total taxes as a proportion of the overall cost burden of the enterprise' was 5.42%.[2] At the same time, the process of cost reduction is a redistribution of benefits across different sectors, with upstream companies providing resources and funding benefits, including government tax revenues and basic benefits for employees, all being affected.

The problem of insufficient effective supply is due to the fact that the potential demand in the market is not effectively supplied. The main solution to this problem is to achieve transformation and upgrading of economic development through innovation drive and structural adjustment. From the practice of recent years, structural reforms have been very effective, with significant changes in the industrial structure, factor input structure and division of labour in the value chain, and the flourishing of new industries and new kinetic energy as new hotspots for economic growth. More effective supply reform has appeared precisely because it stimulates potential demand and expands effective demand. However, innovation drive and structural adjustment will also encounter the bottleneck of insufficient effective demand. The cycle of innovation is getting shorter and shorter, new products are released one by one, and the market space is immediately filled again. At the same time, the change of supply form promotes the improvement of supply efficiency, and will cause further overcapacity.

A more fundamental challenge to China's economic development lies in the lack of effective demand. Insufficient effective demand refers to the fact that the total demand of society with purchasing willingness and purchasing power is lower than the total social supply. The concept of insufficient effective demand emerged in the 1920s and was systematically discussed by Keynes in 1936 in his General Theory of Employment, Interest and Money.

The concept of insufficient effective demand is at the heart of the Keynesian economic revolution. In the view of the supply school, there is no problem of insufficient effective demand, because supply automatically creates demand (a simple expression of Say's Law), and saving is considered to be saving for future consumption. Keynes pointed out that there is no such a 'parallel line axiom' that demand always equals supply. Total social demand can be divided into investment and consumption (here refers to an economy under closed conditions). Due to the marginal propensity to consume, the marginal efficiency of capital and liquidity preference, there is no spontaneous coordination between investment and consumption, that is, savings cannot be spontaneously converted into investment. As a result, capitalist economies have a problem of insufficient effective demand (or the equivalent concept of 'underemployment'), which needs to be driven by government investment to fill the gap and avoid the economy falling into a depression.

The so-called 'Keynesian revolution', although much attacked by the defenders of Western classical economics, was in fact quite moderate. Keynes is careful not to let his analysis touch the capitalist economic system. As he has repeatedly stated, he was conservative in most areas, except for minor differences from classical economics.

His analysis of insufficient effective demand does not touch on more fundamental factors such as production mode and distribution mode, but takes social structure and technical level as given factors. To truly understand the reasons for the lack of effective demand, it is necessary to penetrate the scalpel of ideas into the field of circulation, production, and distribution, as Marx said in his book 'Das Kapital'.

Fundamentally, the lack of effective demand is determined by the production mode of capital that chases profit maximisation and the corresponding unbalanced distribution mode under the condition of a market economy. As productivity gets higher and higher, the speed of demand cannot keep up, so there will be insufficient effective demand, or overproduction. We can analyse this in terms of the three components of total social demand: consumption, investment and exports.

First, capital income far exceeds labour income, resulting in insufficient consumer demand. Under conditions of wage labour, wealth is concentrated in favour of the owners of capital because of imbalances in the distribution mechanism, where capital income far exceeds labour income. Piketty and his fellow researchers found that the global net rate of return on capital (typically 4-5%) was significantly higher than the global economic growth rate over the course of history, with the gap between the two narrowing in the 20th century and widening again in the 21st century.[4] The phenomenon of 'poverty in abundance' occurs in societies where, on the one hand, there is a surplus of production and, on the other, the poor are in a stage of scarcity.

The country is also experiencing a steady decline in the share of labour remuneration in gross national income and an excessive Gini coefficient in the distribution of wealth and income.

Even economists like Keynes said that 'considerable inequality of wealth and income is justified, but the degree of inequality should be smaller than the gap that currently exists'.[5] When the main contradiction of economic growth lies in the supply side, a certain degree of inequality may help to promote economic growth, but when the main contradiction of economic growth is insufficient effective demand, the wealth gap reduces the marginal propensity to consume for society as a whole because the rich have a lower marginal propensity to consume than the poor, leaving society as a whole with insufficient effective consumption demand.

Secondly, a decline in the return on capital leads to a lack of effective investment demand. The infinite accumulation characteristics of capital can lead to a decline in the rate of return to capital. Adam Smith had been aware of this, he said that If a country's capital increases, profitable investment opportunities decrease, and competition for capital intensifies, the profits generated by capital must decrease.[6] Marx identified the declining average rate of profit as a fundamental law of capitalism.[7]

It is difficult for scholars to agree empirically on this because of the different methods of measurement and data used, but there does appear to be a large body of empirical research supporting the idea that capital margins have fallen. According to Brenner's calculations, the G7's net profit margin fell from 26.2% in 1950-1970 to 15.7% in 1970-1993.[8] In 2001, US nonfinancial corporate profit margins were at their lowest levels since the war.[9]

In recent years, China's economy has also experienced a decline in the return on capital in the real economy. An article by Liu Renhe and others published in Economic Research points out that China's return on capital has declined year on year from 9.82% in 2008 to 3.02% in 2014.[10] Research by relevant institutions has found that the return on investment in China's real economy has continued to decline since 2008. By 2014, it was lower than the financing cost ratio, and only slightly recovered after 2016. At the end of 2016, the return on investment in China's real economy was 4.2%, still lower than the risk-free rate of return in the financial market.[11] The decline in the return on investment in the real economy, to a certain extent, shows that China's investment growth has been slow in recent years, and economic development is facing huge pressure from the real to the virtual economy.

Third, unbalanced globalisation has suppressed global trade growth, resulting in insufficient export demand. Developed capitalist countries integrate developing countries into the capitalist system through globalisation to open up the global market, to solve the problem of inadequate domestic effective demand, and find a way out of the crisis of excessive capital accumulation. The developed countries promote the transformation of their industries to higher value-added, extracting high profits and transferring middle and low-end industries overseas, transforming the employment relationship between domestic capital and labour into a value chain deprivation relationship between different nation-states, which constitutes an uneven development relationship in the global capital system.[12] If developing countries fail to achieve sustainable and endogenous development, the huge potential demand of these countries will not be converted into actual purchasing power.

Of course, the lack of effective demand and the relative overcapacity are corresponding concepts, which are said in terms of both supply and demand, respectively. How to restore the state of supply greater than demand to the equilibrium state of supply and demand depends on different understandings of the equilibrium state. One way is to achieve a negative balance by cutting supply, a path that can easily lead to economic growth entering a recessionary cycle. The contraction of production leads to the reduction of the total social income, and triggers the contraction of investment and consumption, thus allowing a surplus to be cleared at the contraction level. The other way is to focus on boosting effective demand and achieving a positive balance, which in turn helps drive growth into a boom cycle. The expansion of demand allows supply to clear at a higher level, leads to higher total social income, and drives economic growth through higher demand. These two different equilibria will lead to different economic competition scenarios. Just as Keynes said, in the former competition, only companies with excellent performance can survive, while in the latter competition, ordinary companies can develop well.

2. The 'six carriages' on the demand side and new demand management

Under the capitalist economic system, the total social demand is nothing more than the 'troika'- investment, consumption, and export. In the socialist market economy system, an additional dimension of private and public can be added. Thus, the 'troika' becomes the 'six carriages': public investment, public consumption, global potential demand, business investment, private consumption, and exports (see Table 1). The classification dimension of public and private here is not classified from the sector of demand, but from the realisation mechanism of potential demand. Public investment and public consumption are not equivalent to but include government purchases, which refer to investment and consumption that are led through public mechanisms.

Table 1 The 'six carriages' on the demand side

	Production	Consumption	Foreign Countries
Public Mechanism	Public Investment	Public Consumption	Global Potential Demand
Private Mechanism	Business Investment	Private Consumption	Export

Under the new classification framework, we can see that there is a large amount of potential demand that has not been effectively supplied, which can be tapped and transformed into actual effective demand, thereby supporting the medium-to-high-speed growth of the Chinese economy in the medium and long-term.

China still has plenty of room for public investment needs, including infrastructure upgrades, infrastructure development in less developed regions and investment in various areas such as public health, education, ecology and environment, national defence and water conservancy, etc. There are still many outstanding debts. At the same time, public investment will also stimulate the growth of investment demand by private enterprises. In the field of public consumption, in addition to further promoting the equalisation of public services, a large number of people's basic needs still have not yet been met. In the field of private consumption, due to the large gap between the rich and the poor, the consumption demand of a large number of people with middle and lower incomes has not been effectively released. Globally, the countries of the South, which account for the vast majority of the world's population, still have huge demand potential, and the problem of supply failure of global public goods is prominent.

This new classification is not about juggling or playing concept games, but about lifting the veil that covers the huge potential demand that already exists. The concept of effective demand implies that there is a huge amount of unrealised potential demand under the surface of the water, and that the lack of effective demand means that the potential demand is not fully realised. Under capitalism, potential demand can be transformed into effective demand only when market entities have the will and the purchasing power, which makes a large number of potential demands unable to be realised by relying on market mechanisms. Due to the mismatch between consumer demand and purchasing power, the mismatch between long-term demand and short-term benefits, and the mismatch between public demand and private revenue, it is difficult to convert it into real effective demand.

Under the conditions of socialist market economy, in addition to the market mechanism, there are also public mechanisms to realise the potential demand, so as to create a larger space for effective demand.

The demand management policy proposed by Keynes is based on the capitalist economic system. Since variables such as consumption tendency and marginal efficiency of capital cannot be intervened, the variables that demand management can intervene are mainly to make up for the investment gap through government investment. Therefore, demand-side management policies were often referred to as stimulus policies, and were treated as an exception in times of economic depression, with several negative consequences. In the 1970s, there was a problem of 'stagflation' in Western countries, and Keynesianism was widely criticised, which contributed to the subsequent neoliberal revival of classical economic ideas.

To distinguish it from Keynesian demand management under capitalist conditions, we call the policy of giving full play to the advantages of socialism and responding to the lack of effective demand, under the conditions of a socialist market economy, the New Demand Management. China implements a socialist market economy, which is different from the Western capitalist market economy. Demand management is not a stimulus policy in essence, but uses the institutional advantages of socialism to address the challenge of insufficient effective demand fundamentally. In other words, these policies are persistent in the socialist market economic system, rather than discretionary external stimulus policies. For example, Keynes once implicitly suggested that a fundamental solution to the problem of insufficient effective demand required addressing the gap between rich and poor, and put forward the proposition of socialisation of investment. This kind of proposal is too radical for a capitalist economic system, and Keynes is also known as 'Marx's Keynesianism', and these measures were merely the right thing to do for a socialist market economy.

3. Dealing with the lack of effective demand with new demand management

New demand management is mainly to give full play to the advantages of the socialist system, expand the space for effective demand, promote the sustainable and coordinated development of the economy by promoting public consumption, public investment and tap global potential demand. Specifically, the following measures can be taken:

First, actively regulate the distribution of wealth and income, and increase the marginal propensity to consume in the whole society.

The income gap and wealth gap in the country remain large. According to data from the National Bureau of Statistics, the Gini coefficient of China's resident income reached 0.4910 in 2008, then began to decline. After 2015, it rose again to 0.4670 in 2017, which is even higher than that of the United States. The Gini coefficient of the United States in 2016 was 0.415.[13] Of greater concern than the large income gap is the large wealth gap and the uneven distribution of assets across society. Survey data from the China Household Finance Survey and Research Centre of Southwest University of Finance and Economics shows that in 2013, the richest 10% of households in China owned 60.6% of social wealth, while the poorest 10% of households accounted for only 0.1% of social wealth.[14]

The large income and wealth gaps not only reflect the imbalance between regions and urban-rural areas, but also reflect the imbalance between capital and labour, and the imbalance between speculative capital and industrial capital in the distribution pattern.

The first step is to start with primary distribution to proactively regulate it. In recent years, while the rate of return on industrial capital has declined, speculative capital has harvested a large amount of social wealth through the rapid appreciation of real estate and other assets. At present, more than 60% of residents' wealth is the net value of the real estate. There is a need to increase the rate of return on industrial capital through policy regulation, regulate the scope for profiteering of virtual capital, strictly regulate the improper income from speculation, and crack down on grey industries.

At the same time, the proportion of labour remuneration in the primary distribution and the proportion of residents' income in the national income is relatively low, and the continuous downward trend has not been effectively curbed. It is necessary to explore the mechanism of universal sharing of public assets, form innovative common property rights, mixed property rights and other methods, and gradually form a new type of property rights jointly owned by labour and capital and shared between them, so that labourers can share the benefits of capital, thus curbing the polarisation between capital and labour, while also expanding the effective demand of the whole society.

Second, it needs to be regulated through strong state redistribution levers. High-net-worth groups are often groups with strong tax avoidance and tax evasion capabilities, so it is necessary to increase tax collection and supervision of property holdings and transfers. At the same time, there is a need to increase the fiscal expenditure to further utilise the leverage of fiscal expenditure, promote a high level of parity in public services, actively encourage and regulate the development of public welfare and charity, and increase its income regulation function.

Second, explore a non-monetised basic public consumption system.

Explore the gradual implementation of the basic public consumption system, and establish online and offline basic public consumption areas for clothing, food, and use. Basic public consumption also includes the free opening and provision of parks, fitness facilities, libraries, museums, and public social places.

Creatively restore the ticket system. The ticket system in the past was the 'second currency' for the shortage economy, and the new public consumption voucher system is the 'second currency' for the surplus economy.

According to their income and wealth status, each citizen receives public consumption vouchers according to a certain quota, which are not redeemable for cash and can only be used in the basic public consumption area. The commodities in the public consumption areas are subject to the planned price guide. There are two ways to use the vouchers: Free consumption with the voucher and using the voucher to offset a certain amount of cash. Suppliers' consumption voucher income can be used to deduct tax, obtain governmental subsidies and equivalent social donations.

At the same time, the resale of goods in the public consumption area is prohibited. This system arrangement can be combined with the sharing economy and social service points to avoid becoming a system for raising lazy people. The rich can donate or transfer public consumption vouchers (tax deduction or in exchange for exemption from social service obligations) to low-income people.

This system arrangement is essentially a kind of adjustment system between the rich and the poor that 'Takes part from the surplus to make up for the deficit'. Through the basic public consumption voucher system, the basic survival needs of all people can be gradually met, and at the same time, the consumption power of low-income groups can be improved, and potential social needs can be released.

Third, build a socialist financial community to stimulate potential public investment.

Stimulating potential public investment is not simply a matter of relying on investment to stimulate the economy, but of building a financial community between the state and the market to stimulate potential demand. As public investment is characterised by its large scale, long lead time and strong externalities, market capital is often reluctant to enter, resulting in the coexistence of relative excess of overall social capital and insufficient funds for national construction. It is necessary to guide market funds to serve the long-term development of the country through effective institutional design.

For example, Shi Zhengfu proposed that a quasi-market strategic investment umbrella fund system that shoulders the national strategic mission can be formed by setting up a national development strategy fund of one trillion yuan. The central bank and the national finance provide guidance funds to form a long-term investment fund led by national strategies, national capital, and mixed with multiple capitals. Funds can be invested in different strategic fields such as water conservancy, disaster mitigation, national defence, social security, science and technology, etc. Although it is difficult for such funds to generate returns in the medium and short term, they have sustained and stable investment returns in the long term.[15]

This institutional design, which combines the advantages of the market with those of socialism, also provides a long-term and stable channel for residents' investments, allowing people to share the dividends of the country's long-term development.

Fourth, make livelihoods a priority area for public investment and public consumption.

There is undoubtedly a huge potential consumer demand and investment demand in the areas of people's livelihood, such as housing, pension, education, health, etc. Products in the field of people's livelihood are necessities with extremely low price elasticity, and cannot be regarded as the so-called 'sunrise industry' and become a capital carnival feast.

The fundamental direction of China's reform is to promote the socialisation of investment and consumption in the livelihood sector. In addition to introducing the socialised investment mechanisms mentioned above into the livelihood sector, at the same time, we must adhere to the public welfare direction of the reform in the livelihood sector and insist that the way of supplying people's livelihood cannot be excessively commercialised and financialised, and that the consumption of people's livelihood products requires individuals, employers and the state to share responsibilities.

Explore the rationing system of people's livelihood products based on use-value. Taking housing as an example, if the first house of the residents, according to certain conditions, is provided in the form of a shared-ownership house, which is only allowed to be used and not traded, the Chinese dream of 'home ownership' can be realised at a very low cost.

Fifth, implement the 'domestic and international economic cycle strategy' to expand the market demand space.

At the beginning of the reform and opening-up, economist Wang Jian once proposed a strategy of international economic cycle, which is to communicate the cycle of China's agriculture and heavy industry through the international market conversion mechanism.[16] This strategy was proposed against the background of China's economic transition from closed to open at that time.

Today, more than 40 years after the reform and opening-up, China has become a highly open economy, and has shifted from a shortage economy to a surplus economy. China needs to stand in front of the world map and plan its domestic and international economic cycles strategy, promote internal and external development, provide greater space for demand for China's economic development and achieve a win-win situation for both China and the world.

Firstly, China needs to consolidate and enhance its position as a global manufacturing and supply chain centre, and gradually become a global innovation and creation centre. Due to its vast territory, China has huge room for economic development. Also, it has comprehensive advantages in capital, technology, labour and management, a complete industrial and supply chain, and vast domestic market space, so it does not need to make the same mistakes as the hollowing out of industries in Japan and the US.

Secondly, China needs to form a complete strategic layout for common development and prosperity, mainly for the countries of the South. Through the implementation of the 'One Belt, One Road' and 'Two Continents' (Africa and South America) strategy, we are accelerating the outward expansion of enterprises, increasing investment and technical assistance to countries in the South, and helping them to build infrastructure, develop their own manufacturing industries and create local jobs.

By laying out the domestic and international production and markets, we promote a global economic cycle in the following areas: a major cycle of resource products – manufacturing, a major cycle of manufacturing – construction projects, a major cycle of agricultural and light industrial products – consumer markets, and a major cycle of productive services – investment and trade.

While promoting overseas investment, we will expand the sources of imports of resource goods and form a big cycle of resource goods manufacturing. By helping local development, the purchasing power of developing countries will be boosted, and a great cycle of agricultural products, light industrial products and consumer markets will be formed. Through the construction of international engineering projects, the output of supporting manufacturing products will be stimulated, and the great cycle of manufacturing-construction projects will be realised. By promoting Chinese investment, China will go global and drive Chinese standards, improving the global service capacity and global service radius of China's production service industry, realising the great cycle of producer services industry-investment and trade.

The global economic cycle strategy will not only provide huge space for China's industrial development, but also provide huge opportunities for the world to achieve mutual benefit for both China and the world.

In short, 'New Demand Management' looks like an anti-market radical 'utopian' policy, but it is not. It is proposed to address the shortcomings of the fundamentalist market economy, overcome the crisis of insufficient effective demand for economic growth, give full play to the advantages of socialism, to better reflect the essential characteristics of China's socialist market economy, to create more space for China's economic development, and to promote a more coordinated and healthy economic development.

---

1 Xi Jinping, 2016, *Speech at the Symposium on Studying and Implementing the Spirit of the Fifth Plenary Session of the 18th Party Central Committee for Major Leading Cadres at the Provincial and Ministerial Levels*, People's Publishing House, p. 30. [习近平：《在省部级主要领导干部学习贯彻党的十八届五中全会精神专题研讨班上的讲话》，人民出版社2016年版，第30页]

2 The Cost Reduction Group of the China Academy of Fiscal Sciences, 2017, 'Cost Reduction: Survey and Analysis in 2017', Public Finance Research, No. 10. [中国财政科学研究院"降成本"课题组：《降成本：2017年的调查与分析》，《财政研究》2017年第10期]

3 John Maynard Keynes, 1999, *General Theory of Employment, Interest and Money*, retranslated edition, translated by Gao Hongye, Commercial Press, chapters 8-18, Originally published in 1936, Palgrave Macmillan. [参见凯恩斯：《就业、利息和货币通论》（重译本），高鸿业译，商务印书馆1999年版，第8-18章]

4 Thomas Piketty, 2014, *Capital in the Twenty-First Century*, translated by Basu Song et al, CITIC Press, p. 364, Originally Le Capital au XXIe siècle, 2013, Éditions du Seuil. [皮凯蒂：《21世纪资本论》，巴曙松等译，中信出版社2014年版，第364页]

5 John Maynard Keynes, 1999, *General Theory of Employment, Interest and Money*, retranslated edition, translated by Gao Hongye, Commercial Press, p. 387. [凯恩斯：《就业、利息和货币通论》（重译本），高鸿业译，商务印书馆1999年版，第387页]

6 Adam Smith, 2005, *The Wealth of Nations*, translated by Tang Risong et al, The Commercial Press, pp. 47-53, Originally published in 1776, London. [亚当·斯密：《国富论》，唐日松等译，商务印书馆2005年版，第47—53页]

7 *Das Kapital*, 2004, Vol. 3, People's Publishing House, pp. 235-257. [《资本论》第3卷，人民出版社2004年版，第235-257页]

8 Robert Brenner, 2016, *The Economics of Global Turbulence*, translated by Zheng Jiwei, Renmin University of China Press, p. 5, Originally published in 1998, New left Review. [罗伯特·布伦纳著：《全球动荡的经济学》，郑吉伟译，中国人民大学出版社2016年版，第5页]

9 'Interviewed by Quan Zhen', 2009, translated by Jiang Hongda and Zhang Ludan, 'Brenner believes that overcapacity is the root cause of the world financial crisis', *Foreign Theoretical Trends*, No. 5. [荃镇采访，蒋宏达、张露丹译：《布伦纳认为生产能力过剩才是世界金融危机的根本原因》，《国外理论动态》2009年第5期]

10 Liu Renhe, Chen Yingnan, Ji Xiaomeng, Su Xuejin, 2018, 'China's Return on Capital: Estimation Based on Q Theory', *Economic Research*, No. 6. [刘仁和、陈英楠、吉晓萌、苏雪锦：《中国的资本回报率：基于q理论的估算》，《经济研究》2018年第6期]

11 Liu, Chen J., 2018, 'Economic Pattern and Family Wealth Management in the New Era', Financial View, No. 3. [刘陈杰：《新时期经济格局与家庭财富管理》，《金融博览》2018年第3期]

12 Robert Brenner, 2016, *The Economics of Global Turbulence*, translated by Zheng Jiwei, Renmin University of China Press, p. 3. [罗伯特·布伦纳：《全球动荡的经济学》，郑吉伟译，中国人民大学出版社2016年版，第3页]

13 World Bank: World Development Indicators Database, https://data.worldbank.org.cn, [4 May 2021].

14 China Household Finance Survey and Research Centre, Southwest University of Finance and Economics, 'Report on the Distribution of Chinese Household Wealth and High Net Worth Household Wealth', January 2014, <https://wenku.baidu.com/view/a19bbd21f7ec4afe04a1dfc9.html>, [4 May 2021]. [西南财经大学中国家庭金融调查研究中心：《中国家庭财富的分布及高净值家庭财富报告》，2014年1月]

15 Shi Zhengfu, 2016, 'Solving Structural Overcapacity with Structural Investment', *Economic Herald*, No. 2; Shi Zhengfu, 2013, *Extraordinary Growth: China's Economy from 1979 to 2049*, Shanghai People's Publishing House, pp. 127–131. [史正富：《用结构性投资化解结构性产能过剩》，《经济导刊》2016年第2期。史正富：《超常增长——1979—2049年的中国经济》，上海人民出版社2013年版，第127–131页]

16 Wang Jian, 1988, 'What is the international economic cycle', *Journal of the Sichuan Institute of Building Materials*, No. 3. [王建：《什么是国际经济大循环》，《四川建材学院学报》1988年第3期]

PART 3
CHINESE POLITICAL SYSTEM

The best way to evaluate whether a country's political system is democratic and effective is to observe whether the succession of its leaders is orderly and law-based, whether the people can manage state and social affairs and economic and cultural undertakings in accordance with the law, whether the public can express their needs through open channels, whether all sectors of society can effectively participate in the country's political affairs, whether the country's decision making can be conducted in a rational and democratic manner, whether people of all fields can join the state leadership and administrative systems by way of fair competition, whether the governing party can lead state affairs in accordance with the Constitution and the law, and whether the exercise of power is subject to effective checks and oversight.

– Xi Jinping's speech at the celebration of the 60th anniversary of the founding of the National People's Congress (5 Sept, 2014)

CHAPTER 7

Comparison of Chinese and American Political Systems: 'Seven divisions of power' versus 'Separation of three powers'

[*The first draft of this article was delivered on 24 June 2019 at the National Research Institute of Tsinghua University's State of the Nation Forum, published in the 'Dongfang Journal' on 1 Sept, 2020. Details were revised when it was included in the book. 本文初稿系2019年6月24日清华大学国情研究院 '国情讲坛' 讲稿刊发于 '东方学刊' 2020年9月1日收入本书时有细节修订]

Aristotle once said that when people are troubled by problems, they are like being bound by ropes.[1] When people are misled by wrong concepts, they cannot move, as if hypnotised by a 'spell'.

Western mainstream theories often attach two 'spells' to the Chinese political system:

One is 'totalitarianism'. 'Totalitarianism' is used to describe a political system that has absolute authority over society and seeks to do everything possible to control public and private life. The monopoly of political power is summarised in six characteristics: a single official ideology; a single political party, whose typical characteristic is that the leader acts arbitrarily; the control of the media; the central control and guidance of the national economy through the bureaucracy; secret police system; monopoly of armed forces.[2]

Due to the study and introduction of the Soviet political model at the beginning of the founding of the People's Republic of China, the Chinese political system was once regarded as 'totalitarian'. The highly centralised power takes total control over the country through ideological construction and the organisation of the party, government and military.[3] The omnipotent state power control permeates all aspects of society. Due to its strong ideological constructs, the concept of 'totalitarianism' is losing its own meaning and explanatory power, it is even less convincing to be used as the label of China's political system. In the era of planned economy, the influence of state power on society was more based on mobilisation and persuasion, rather than the one-way central totalitarian control described by totalitarian theory. After the 1970s, Western scholars had the opportunity to observe China's political system in person. Especially since the reform and opening-up, the adjustment of China's political system has made most Western scholars realise that the Chinese political system cannot be classified as 'totalitarian'.

The second is 'authoritarianism'. After the 'totalitarian' interpretation became invalid, 'authoritarian' analysis became the mainstream concept in Western political science to analyse China's political system.[4] This theory holds that China, as a country in transition to a modern era, has gradually begun to grow its social power, but in the process of the decline of traditional authority, state authority is required to keep its transition process stable, resulting in the emergence of a transitional 'authoritarian' regime.

This is the most popular term, and is still the most common label used to describe China's political system. This can't even be regarded as the tinted glasses they must wear when looking at China. The scholar Wang Shaoguang calls it stickers that are stuck everywhere.[5] As long as we do a simple search, we can find that the label of 'authoritarianism' is affixed everywhere in Chinese studies, and social movements, media commercialisation, and the policy processes of decentralisation reform have been labelled with various 'authoritarian' labels.[6] This kind of label is not only affixed to China's political system, but as long as it is a political system that is not recognised by the West, it may be labelled as 'authoritarian'. For example, Singapore has been called 'authoritarian' under the rule of law, and Turkey, post-Soviet Russia, and post-Cold War hybrid regimes have all been placed under the umbrella of 'authoritarianism'.[7]

'Authoritarianism' is a theory of very low resolution. The vitality of theory lies in explaining reality, but in explaining the Chinese political system, 'authoritarianism' has appeared in an embarrassing dilemma. Scholars have found that the term 'authoritarianism' no longer properly explains the Chinese political system, so they resorted to qualifiers, which led to the emergence of various descriptions of 'authoritarianism' in China's political system. We have counted more than 30 'authoritarianisms'.[8]

It is interesting that the qualifier and subject are often contradictory. 'Authoritarian' is a derogatory term, while the qualifier 'legitimate, responsible, participatory, responsive, resilient, adaptive, elastic etc.,' are mostly praise words in an attempt to correct the 'authoritarianism' that cannot explain the achievements and vitality of China's political system, and describe China as a 'bad system' that is not so bad. In fact, it is not a problem of qualifiers at all, but the word 'authoritarianism' itself is wrong. Just as the scholar Wang Shaoguang called for, it is time to abandon the use of this outdated concept to describe the Chinese system.

Here, on the basis of previous research, the author makes a new generalisation of China's political system, namely the 'seven divisions of power' system, and compares China's 'Seven divisions of power'[9] system with the US 'Separation of three powers' system in terms of the principles of political operation, the way government officials are elected and policy changes, in order to provide a background for the analysis of the political system in the US-China strategic game. Under the conditions of Sino-US strategic competition, China's political system has its unique advantages, which can effectively support the long-term Sino-US strategic competition.

1. China's 'Seven divisions of power' political system

Based on China's practice, this book summarises China's political system as the 'seven divisions of power'. The system of 'seven divisions of power' is different from the 'separation of three powers', and it is also different from the system of the integration of deliberation and action. The state power is constituted not by a separation but by a division of labour. It includes three types of division of labour: the first is the division of functions; the second is the vertical division of labour between 'big power' and 'small power'; the third is the division of labour in the power operation chain.

In terms of the division of functions, seven systems exercise powers of a different nature. The first is the leadership of the Party Central Committee, the second is the legislative power of the National People's Congress, the third is the executive power of the State Council, the fourth is the military power of the Central Military Commission, the fifth is the supervisory power of the State Supervisory Commission, the sixth is the judicial power of the Supreme People's Court and the Supreme People's Procuratorate, and the seventh is the consultative power of the consultation of the National Committee of the Chinese People's Political Consultative Conference (CPPCC). Of course, this division is not absolute, and the powers of different branches are intersected, coordinated and restricted.

In terms of the vertical division of labour, there is an overall three-tier structure. The leadership of the Party Central Committee is at the top of the vertical division of power, a unifying force that plays a leading role in the overall direction of national development and has a dominating and unifying function over the other six state powers. The legislative power of the National People's Congress (NPC) and the consultative power of the National Committee of the Chinese People's Political Consultative Conference (CPPCC) are at the second level of the vertical division of power. The legislative power of the NPC is also a unifying power, the President and Vice-President of the State are appointed and removed by the NPC, and 'the State administrative organs, supervisory organs, judicial organs and procuratorial organs are all elected by the People's Congress, responsible to it and under its supervision'.[10] The CPPCC also performs its consultative powers under the leadership of the Party Central Committee. The executive, supervisory, judicial and military powers are at the third level of the vertical division of powers, operating under the unified leadership of the Party Central Committee and accountable to the legislative power and subject to its supervision.

In terms of the division of labour in the chain of power operation, it includes the division of labour between decision-making, implementation and supervision. The leadership of the Party Central Committee, the legislative power of the National People's Congress and the consultative power of the National Committee of the Chinese People's Political Consultative Conference are, on the whole, powers in the decision-making chain and jointly ensure scientific decision-making; the administrative power of the State Council and the military power of the Central Military Commission are, on the whole, powers in the execution of state and military affairs, safeguarding the effective implementation of decisions; the judicial power of the Supreme People's Court and the Supreme People's Procuratorate and the supervisory power of the State Supervision Commission are, on the whole, powers in the supervision chain, ensuring the effective implementation of national laws and party regulations and to avoid abuse of power.

The author believes that the 'seven divisions of power' is China's actual political power structure. The seven-state powers are clearly reflected in the 'Constitution of the People's Republic of China'. The leadership of the Party Central Committee is fundamentally established in the general outline of the Constitution. The legislative power of the National People's Congress, the administrative power of the State Council, the military power of the Central Military Commission, the supervisory power of the State Supervisory Commission, the judicial power of the Supreme People's Court and the Supreme People's Procuratorate is clearly stipulated in Chapter III of the Constitution on State Institutions. And the consultation power of the CPPCC is clearly reflected in the preamble of the Constitution.

The 19th Party Central Committee is generally based on a division of labour based on seven systems of power. The Standing Committee of the Politburo, the Politburo members working in the Central Committee and the Secretary of the Central Secretariat are all located in these seven systems of power. At the same time, the central-level state institutions are also distributed among these seven systems of power.

The Party Central Committee is the pivot of the highest political leadership in China and exercises leadership in state affairs. The leadership of the Party Central Committee lies at the heart of the seven power systems, and the leadership of the Party Central Committee over the State is manifested through the following four levels:

The first is the highest decision-making core. The Party's Central Committee, the Central Political Bureau and the Standing Committee of the Central Political Bureau are the core of decision-making for the leadership of the Party and the State. The Politburo Standing Committee and Politburo members are responsible for the work of various central parties and state institutions. The Politburo Standing Committee and Politburo meetings convened by the General Secretary of the Central Committee are themselves the highest state affairs conference in the country.

After a long period of exploration, China has developed the system arrangement of uniting the General Secretary, the State President and the Chairman of the Military Commission, which in itself is a confirmation of the leadership of the State by the Party Central Committee.

The third is the Party's leadership over other branches of state power. Through the committee system, the leading group system, the party group system, and system arrangements such as the Party Central Committee's working meetings in various fields, the Party Central Committee is able to achieve overall leadership over all branches of power. For the legislative power, it is guided to participate in decision-making consultations, form consensus on decision-making, and deliberate on and adopt proposals and ideas put forward by the Party. For the executive power, the Party Central Committee's guidelines and policies are effectively implemented through the division of labour between the party and the government. For the supervisory power, the Party's disciplinary power and state supervisory power are organically integrated through the integrated operation of discipline inspection and supervision. For military power, direct and absolute leadership is achieved through the 'Party commands the gun' system. For the judicial power, the main purpose is to lead the judiciary in the correct implementation of the Party's line and policy, without specifically interfering with the independent exercise of the judiciary's powers. With regard to consultative power, it is guided to carry out its political participation and deliberations around the centre and general situation determined by the Party Central Committee.

The fourth is the leadership function of the Party's central leadership system itself. That is, the party manages the line, the party manages the cadres and the party manages the ideology.

The National People's Congress is the highest organ of state power. The National People's Congress exercises legislative power. The narrow legislative power includes the creation of powers with legal functions and norms, and the broad legislative power includes all the powers centred on the narrow legislative power, mainly including the legislative power, the right to vote, the right to make decisions and the right to supervise.

The Chinese People's Political Consultative Conference (CPPCC) is an organisation of the patriotic united front of the Chinese people and an important institution for multi-party cooperation and political consultation under the leadership of the Communist Party of China.[11] The CPPCC's right to consultation is a right to speak, which refers to providing opinions and suggestions, participating in decision-making, and discussing national issues in the political process. In addition to political consultation, the CPPCC also has the functions of democratic supervision and participation in political affairs.

The State Council is the highest state administrative organ. Executive power is a kind of implementation right. The State Council is not only the executive organ of the highest authority of the state, but also the main supporting organ for implementing the decisions of the Party Central Committee. Executive power is undoubtedly the most extensive power, covering all domestic and foreign affairs of the country.

The supervisory power of the State Supervisory Commission is the power to conduct specialised supervision. The Central Commission for Discipline Inspection (CCDI) is a specialised agency for intra-Party supervision. It supervises Party organisations at all levels and all Party members, with the duty to supervise, enforce discipline and hold accountable.[12] The National Supervisory Commission is the country's highest supervisory organ, supervising all public officials exercising public power. Its main functions include supervision, investigation and disposal.[13]

The Supreme People's Court and the Supreme People's Procuratorate exercise judicial power. Judicial power is the specialised activity of applying the law to a specific case. Judicial power in a narrow sense only includes the right to trail, while a slightly broader definition includes procuratorial power. The people's courts are the judicial organs of China. China has established special people's courts such as the Supreme People's Court, local people's courts at all levels and military courts, with the Supreme People's Court being the highest judicial organ of the country. The people's procuratorates are the legal supervisory organs of the state, and China has established specialised people's procuratorates such as the Supreme People's Procuratorate, local people's procuratorates at all levels and military procuratorates, with the Supreme People's Procuratorate being the highest procuratorial organ.[14] The party's leadership of judicial power is mainly macro-level leadership, and does not intervene in specific cases. The courts and procuratorates exercise judicial and procuratorial powers independently in accordance with the law.

The Central Military Commission exercises military power, which includes military leadership, command, construction and execution, decision and declaration of war.[15]

The General Secretary of the Central Committee of the Communist Party of China is also the Chairman of the Central Military Commission. The National People's Congress has the power to decide on issues of war and peace; the President declares the state of war and issues mobilisation orders; the State Council leads and manages the national defence construction industry; the Central Military Commission leads the armed forces of the country and implements the chairman responsibility system. The Chairman of the Central Military Commission is responsible to the National People's Congress and the Standing Committee of the National People's Congress. The General Secretary of the CPC Central Committee concurrently serves as the chairman of the Central Military Commission.

2. Division of labour and coordination versus division of power and checks and balances

Generalising the principles of how a country's highly complex political system works is risky.[16] The purpose of this chapter is not to conduct a systematic study of the American political system, but to extract the most critical elements to provide a strategic perspective for the comparison of the Chinese and American political systems.

The core operating principle of the American political system is the separation of powers and checks and balances, which includes two aspects:

One is the separation of powers. Madison said: 'There is no political insight that has more intrinsic value than power, and can better embody the authority of a liberty defender with an Enlightenment thinker.'[17] The first is segregation of functions: a function is performed by a branch of government. Each branch can only perform its own functions, and cannot violate other branch functions beyond its authority. The United States divides state power into three branches: the first branch is the branch that makes laws, that is, the legislative power exercised by Congress; the second branch is the branch that implements the law, that is, the executive power exercised by the president; the third is the branch of interpreting laws, the judicial power of the Supreme Court. Secondly, to realise the separation of personnel, if a person serves in one branch of the government, he cannot serve in any of the other two branches at the same time.

The second is the checks and balances of power. Montesquieu said, 'In order to prevent the abuse of power, power must be controlled by power through the coordination of things'.[18] Madison said: 'But the great security against a gradual concentration of the several powers in the same department, consists in giving to those who administer each department the necessary constitutional means and personal motives to resist encroachments of the others... Ambition must be made to counteract ambition.[19] The United States not only decomposes state power into three branches, but also sets up three branches of power in its constitution: legislative, executive, and judicial, but also designs a political power structure that checks and balances each other. Legislative power can check and balance executive power, and Congress can impeach the president and other federal officials, approve federal appointments, and override presidential vetoes with a two-thirds majority. The checks and balances of the legislative power on the judicial power are reflected in the approval of the appointment of federal judges, the establishment of courts lower than the Supreme Court, etc.

Executive power can check and balance legislative power, including proposing legislative bills, vetoing Congressional legislation, and convening special sessions of Congress. Judicial power can check and balance legislative and executive powers by declaring laws unconstitutional and administrative actions unconstitutional. This kind of design idea similar to mechanical balance is difficult to operate in reality. In practice, the operation of American political power relies heavily on the coordination of different branches of power, and power is increasingly concentrated on the president. Nonetheless, the United States can still be seen as a political system with a high degree of separation of powers and checks and balances.

The excessive separation of powers and checks and balances in the United States has made it difficult for the government to move forward, and it is difficult to form a consensus on policy decisions when there is 'discussion without decision', or to form collective action when there is 'decision without action'. Fukuyama said: 'It is easy for different departments within the government to interfere with each other. Coupled with the judicialisation of politics and the extensive penetration of interest groups, the government structure shaped by the American political system finally undermines the basis of collective action and forms the so-called 'veto politics'. The U.S. political system has more severe checks and balances than other countries, or, in other words, there are many so-called 'veto points' that make collective action more costly and even impossible to move forward'. [20] Thomas Friedman: America is no longer a democracy, America has become a vetocracy, a system designed to prevent anyone from doing anything.[21]

This is not only reflected in the mutual checks and balances of legislation, executive, and judiciary, but also in other aspects, such as the checks and balances between the federal and state, the checks and balances between the ruling party and the opposition parties, and the constraints of interest groups. To give an example of high-speed rail, the United States almost started to have a high-speed rail dream with China. President Obama talked about the high-speed rail dream of the United States many times in his State of the Union address. For example, in 2011, he said: 'In the next 25 years, our goal is to get 80% of Americans on the high-speed rail.' Ten years later, when the Chinese dream has become a reality, the American dream is still a distant dream. In 2020, the total mileage of high-speed rail in China has reached 37,900 kilometres, which is more than double the total mileage of high-speed rail in other countries in the world, while the high-speed rail in the United States is only 735 kilometres. It took only two years to complete the Beijing-Shanghai high-speed rail in China, and the California high-speed rail plan, which was once ambitious to become a model for high-speed rail in the United States, has become what Trump called 'the unfinished project of the century' more than ten years later. The outstanding problem of the American system is that it is difficult to integrate fragmented interests and viewpoints. 'Ten people have ten justices, a hundred people have a hundred justices'. Everyone and each group have their own interests and ideas, but there is no effective force to promote common interests, common ideas and common actions.

Different from the US principle of separation of powers and checks and balances, the operating principle of China's political system is the division of labour and coordination. This also includes two aspects:

One is the division of power. Different from the idea that the division of power system splits the state power into different branches of power, and each branch of power has different sources of legitimacy, the division of power system believes that the state power is integral, and the divided parts are the governance power under the authorisation of the overall power, or according to Sun Yat-sen's expression, 'the division of power',[22] where Political power and sovereignty are unified, and division of labour refers to the division of labour in governing power.

The integrity of state power is reflected in two aspects: First, the Communist Party of China is the highest political leadership force in China and the highest organisational form of the Chinese people, representing the fundamental and broadest interests of the Chinese people and the Chinese nation, and other branches of state power under its unified leadership. Second, the National People's Congress is the highest organ of state power, and the executive power, supervisory power, judicial power, and military power are derived from and accountable to it.

Unlike the separation of functions and personnel in a system of separation of powers, the division of powers does not separate powers completely but recognises the intersection and coordination between them. First of all, it is shown that power operates in the way of collective leadership and division of responsibilities. Although each has its own division of power, this division of labour is subject to collective leadership and collective decision-making, and the operation of each power system is supervised by the collective leadership mechanism. Secondly, power functions overlap with each other, it is difficult to separate the powers of the party and government, and other powers also overlap. Finally, personnel flow laterally in different systems, and public officials in different power systems belong to the cadre system and can be mobilised across departments.

The second is functional synergy. A system of separation of powers is a confrontation of ambition against ambition[23] by separating and checking powers against each other, with the basic objective of limiting state power in order to avoid its evil, but constituting a constraint on collective action. The system of division of power is to achieve a mutual division and coordination of powers through the unification and intersection of powers in order to achieve public functions more efficiently, with the basic objective of effectively matching state power to promote the goodness of the community.

The different branches of power work together, coordinate with each other and operate around a central task. The different branches of power work together around the central task in order to ensure that the division of labour system can operate efficiently and jointly promote the achievement of national objectives. The principle of the operation of power is democratic centralism, that is, a combination of centralisation on the basis of democracy and democracy under the direction of centralisation.

The advantage of China's 'seven division of powers' system is that it has higher efficiency, can effectively integrate resources, and jointly promote the realisation of national objectives. China has a strong ability to achieve national objectives. 20 of the 22 targets in the 11th Five-Year Plan have been completed, and 23 of the 24 targets in the 12th Five-Year Plan have been completed.[24]

Any political system needs to address the issue of how to avoid corruption of power. China has not followed the Western path of separation of powers and checks and balances because that will lead to a decline in the efficiency of the power operation. The separation of powers and checks and balances prevents bad people from doing bad things and restricts good people from doing good things. While ensuring the division of power and cooperation, China has established a strict power supervision system, 'let the people supervise power, let power operate under the sun, and lock power in the cage of the system.' The 19th Party Congress report has designed a system to build a unified Party command, comprehensive coverage, authoritative and efficient supervision system, with the Party's internal supervision as the main focus, and with the supervision of state organs, democratic supervision, judicial supervision, mass supervision, and public opinion supervision in a coherent manner. The Fourth Plenary Session of the Nineteenth Central Committee made further system and mechanism design, which not only allows good people to do good things, but also prevents bad people from doing bad things, thus creating a system that is both efficient and clean.

3. Competitive selection versus competitive election

The main way in which national leaders are selected in the United States is through competitive elections, while government officials are also selected through appointments and examinations. The main way of selecting national leaders in China is competitive selection, while government officials are also selected through elections and examinations.

Members of the U.S. legislative system and the president of the executive system are all elected through competitive elections. The 435 members of the House of Representatives serve two-year terms and are elected every two years. Seats are allocated according to the population of each state. The Senate consists of 100 members, serving a six-year term, one-third of which is re-elected every two years, and two senators are elected from each state. The President is elected every four years for a four-year term, and the winner is the person with the highest number of electoral college votes.

Apart from competitive elections, a large number of officials in the United States are appointed. To this day, a large number of senior positions remain appointed by the President, who can appoint around 7,000 government officials, including hundreds of federal judges and top leaders in the military and diplomatic field, of whom around 500 require

Senate approval.[25] In fact, the 'pork barrel' system in the United States was not completely abolished with the establishment of the civil service. The president's decision to appoint usually considers repaying his supporters and implementing his own policy intentions. Trump's use of his power to appoint and remove these officials is very personal, and many senior US officials are only aware of their removal through Trump's tweets. Although the United States has the 'Anti-Nepotism Act', this has not stopped Trump from appointing his son-in-law Kushner as a senior adviser to the White House and entering the centre of executive power. Under a system like China, where the appointment and removal of officials have strict qualifications and need to go through strict organisational procedures, it would be inconceivable to have similar conditions to appoint and remove officials in the way that Trump has done.

Chinese leaders are selected through a competitive selection system. The selection and appointment of party and government leaders and cadres has clear basic conditions and basic qualification requirements, and requires promotion at each level, with a few being able to break the rules, as well as going through analysis and research and motion, democratic recommendation, inspection, discussion and decision, and public announcement. At the same time, China also uses elections to select public officials, with direct elections for village and neighbourhood committees, direct elections for county and township people's congress deputies and indirect elections for people's congress deputies at or above the county level. Staff members of state organs at all levels are elected by the people's congresses and their standing committees at all levels, respectively, and delegates and committees of the Party congresses at all levels are also elected through elections. China's electoral system is often combined with selection. The 19th Central Committee of the Communist Party of China was born through the combination of selection and election.[26] At the same time, there are also examination methods, such as civil service examination, public institution examination, open selection, etc. Generally, there are qualification requirements, and admission is based on merit through public examinations.

Chinese leaders have grown up gradually through experience in multiple positions, especially through long-term practice at the local and grassroots levels. Many of China's provinces have a population of tens or hundreds of millions of people, equivalent to the population size of large countries in the world, and ruling a province is equivalent to ruling a country. After familiarising themselves with the local situation, they also have to familiarise themselves with the national situation through their experience as Politburo members before they can join the Politburo Standing Committee.

'The prime minister must come from the fundamental department, and the fierce general must be from the front line.' (宰相必起于州部，猛将必发于卒伍。) The competitive selection system ensures that government officials have rich practical experience and, more importantly, they are tested by practice rather than by votes. Only after going through experience, testing and selection at all levels, can they finally become leaders of the country. China's competitive selection system is a way of selecting a practical and professional governance team, and as Lee Kuan Yew said, it is the most distinguished people among the billions of Chinese people who are at the helm.

By contrast, Trump can become president without any political experience, which goes against common sense. We know that any position in society, whether it is a teacher, a doctor, a civil servant, or a business operator, most of them have to start from a low-level position step by step, but the position of the President of the United States does not seem to require any professional qualifications. One step up to the highest office can be achieved by passing an election. The competitive election system in the United States is an 'open audition' system. The qualifications for congressmen and presidential candidates are only a basic qualification. One is the age requirement, the second is the citizenship period requirement, and the third is the residence period requirement. The House of Representatives is the loosest, the Senators second, and the President is relatively strict.

Of course, the possible institutional logic assumes that through the electoral system the unqualified can be screened out and the strongest can be selected. However, as the American saying goes, 'Elections are poetry, governance is prose', a good poet is not necessarily a good prose writer, and being good at elections is not necessarily good at governance; being good at governance is not necessarily being good at elections. Trump is certainly very good at 'electioneering', good at manipulating issues, has strong influence, is good at using new media, and has his own traffic. All of these qualities are the reasons why he can stand out in a brutal election campaign, but this does not mean that he is good at governing the country. Elections were originally for governance, but today the concept has been distorted as governance is also about elections. It is necessary to constantly brag about political achievements and attack political opponents on Twitter in order to win the next round of elections. What happened recently in Ukraine's election sham is a good example of the alienation of the 'open audition' system. In 2019, Zelensky, the hero of the national TV series 'The People's Servant', turned his traffic into an election and was actually elected as the sixth president of Ukraine, and the TV series' studio 'Kvartal 95' formed the 'People's Servant Party', which became the ruling party.

Sun Yat-sen saw very early on that the serious flaw of this 'open audition 'system was that there were no restrictions on the qualifications of candidates. He said: 'There are also many disadvantages of popular elections ... to remedy them, it is not a good idea to restrict the electorate alone. The best way is to restrict the elected ... If there is no standard, a single universal election will have many problems ... A person who is a member of parliament or an official must have talent and virtue or have some kind of ability. It is not possible to have money alone'.[27] He suggested that the remedy was to use examinations, but of course, examinations alone would not do, if all exams are used, it will result in the promotion of those who do not do a good job, but those who do well in the examinations. More sensible is still what is currently practised in China, where examinations are only a solution to the entrance problem and promotion is still a matter of selection by grade through practical tests.

4. Cumulative adjustment versus swing adjustment

All political systems require some degree of balance between continuity and adjustment. China's system is a cumulative system of adjustment, where the Chinese Communist Party has been in power for a long time and is able to engage in long-term strategic planning and to pursue national objectives consistently for decades. For example, China's socialist modernisation is a century-long strategy, subdivided into three major strategic steps of 30, 40 and 30 years. The first strategic step is to build an independent and complete industrial system and national economic system in the first 30 years; the second strategic step is to spend 40 years building a moderately prosperous society by 2020; and the third strategic step is to achieve the goal of a strong socialist modernisation in the next 30 years, by 2050.

At the same time, the Chinese system has also shown a strong ability to adapt, and it can continuously push forward changes and adjustments with the times. Since the reform and opening-up, China has undergone radical changes, as if it had changed into a whole new country. Since the 18th National Congress of the Communist Party of China, China has entered a new era in which systematic and fundamental changes are taking place. At the same time, China's adjustment is not a push-back, but a succession. The two stages before and after the reform are not mutually negative relationships, but successive relationships. The same is true of the changes since the 18th National Congress. For example, since the 18th National Congress, a new development concept has been proposed, which itself is the continuation and development of the scientific concept of development; the proposal to alleviate poverty with precision and to eliminate absolute poverty by 2020 is itself a strategic continuation and development, basing on decades of achievements in poverty reduction. Our calculation of the indicators of the five-year plan (planning) shows that, on average, 43% of the indicators are derived from the previous five-year plan (planning), and 48% are new indicators.

The US elections, which take place once every few years, are a mechanism for adjusting the US political system, but this adjustment is often a swing adjustment. Before leaving office, President Obama once said that 'The U.S. presidency is a relay race, and each of us has a time limit for our responsibilities to the country and that I will pass the baton to the next one when the time comes. ' There is no significant problem about the system, the problem is that after Trump took over the baton, he did not run in the original direction of Obama, but in the opposite direction. Washington pointed out the problems caused by the rotation of the two parties in power. 'The rule of one party over the other will become harsh governance due to the revenge that naturally arises from the discord between the parties'.[28] This view still holds true to this day. When George W. Bush took office, he pursued the ABC (All but Clinton) policy of doing everything, just not what Clinton had done. The Trump policy is still the same, all the policies that Obama adopted on health care, regulation, arms control, climate change, foreign affairs, immigration, race, transgender, etc. have been reversed and started all over. This will cause a swing effect in US policy following the election, which will not only cause the policy to sway from left to right, but also cause many efforts to fail and continue to toss. TPP is a typical example. The United States began to dominate the TPP strategy several years before

China proposed the 'One Belt, One Road' initiative, which was considered a major geostrategic strategy to contain China. But Trump announced his withdrawal from the TPP on the first day he took office. It means that the efforts of the Obama administration for many years were in vain. Today, the 'One Belt, One Road' initiative proposed by China has become the most ambitious and influential geo-development initiative in the 21st century. The Biden administration came to power as a 'new broom sweeps clean', burned Trump's political legacy and the US is experiencing another round of policy changing.

The political system of any country is the product of its own historical practice, and there is no one-size-fits-all political model applicable everywhere. At the same time, different political systems need to face some common problems (such as the efficiency of political systems, prevention of abuse of power, etc.), and explore the corresponding solutions. Human beings need the least bad politics (limited government), also need to pursue better politics (effective government), not only to restrict bad people from doing bad things, but also to encourage good people to do good things.

The 'separation of seven powers' political system is an institutional model with Chinese characteristics. The basic operating principle is the division of labour and coordination, but there is also supervision and checks and balances, which is an effective governance structure. The basic operating principle of the 'separation of powers' in the United States is the separation of powers with checks and balances, and there is also coordination in between, which is the structure of a limited government.

China's leadership team is a professional governing team, which is mainly selected competitively at each level, and its tenure is mainly based on professional governing ability, and the selection mechanism is practically tested. The U.S. leadership collective is a group of politicians, selected primarily through competitive elections, with tenure-based primarily on electability and a selection mechanism of elections.

The long-term rule of the Chinese Communist Party allows for a long-term strategic perspective in Chinese decision-making, while self-adjustment through mechanisms such as party congresses is a cumulative adjustment; the two-party rotating rule in the US also constitutes an adjustment mechanism, but with a swing effect.

1 Aristotle, 2003, *Metaphysics*, Renmin University of China Press, p. 37. [亚里士多德：《形而上学》，中国人民大学出版社 2003 年版，第 37 页]
2 C. J. Friedrich and Z. Brzezinski, 1956, *Totalitarian Dictatorship and Autocracy*, Cambridge, Mass.: Harvard University Press
3 Richard L. Walker, 1995, *China under Communism: The First Five Years*, New Haven: Yale University Press; A. Doak Barnett, 1960, *Communist China and Asia: Challenge to American Policy*, New York: Harper & Brothers; John W. Lewis, 1963, *Leadership in Communist China*, Ithaca, N.Y: Cornell University Press; Franz Schurmann, 1966, *Ideology and Organization in Communist China*, Berkeley: University of California Press
4 Richard Curt Kraus, 2004, *The Party and the Arty in China: The New Politics of Culture (State and Society in East Asia)*, Oxford: Rowman & Littlefield Publishers
5 See Wang Shaoguang, 2014, *China·Politics*, Renmin University of China Press, p. 31. [王绍光：《中国·政道》，中国人民大学出版社 2014 年版，第 31 页]
6 Daniela Stockmann, 2008, *Media Commercialization and Authoritarian Rule in China*, Cambridge University Press; Pierre F. Landry, 2008, *Decentralized Authoritarianism in China*, Cambridge University Press; Christopher Heurlin, 2017, *Responsive Authoritarianism in China*, Cambridge University Press; Mary E. Gallagher, 2017, *Authoritarian Legality in China*, Cambridge University Press; Xi Chen, 2014, *Social Protest and Contentious Authoritarianism in China*, Cambridge University Press; Timothy Hildebrandt, 2013, *Social Organizations and the Authoritarian State in China*, Cambridge University Press
7 Jothie Rajah, 2012, *Authoritarian Rule of Law*, Cambridge University Press; Graeme Gill, 2016, *Building an Authoritarian Polity*, Cambridge University Press; Steven Levitsky & Lucan A. Way, 2010, *Competitive Authoritarianism*, Cambridge University Press; Arat, Yeşim, and Şevket Pamuk, 2019, *Turkey between democracy and authoritarianism*. Cambridge University Press
8 For example, 'adaptive authoritarianism', 'resilient authoritarianism' by David Shambaugh, 'soft authoritarianism' by Minxin Pei, 'revolutionary authoritarianism' by Liz Perry, 'flexible authoritarianism' by Jean-Pierre Cabestan, 'populist authoritarianism' by Edward Friedman, 'legitimate authoritarianism' by Gunter Schubert, 'responsible government under authoritarian condition' by Linda Li, 'authoritarian yet participatory' from a study commissioned by the German Government, 'contentious authoritarianism', 'bargained authoritarianism', 'responsive authoritarianism', 'plutocratic authoritarianism', 'elite authoritarianism', etc. See Wang Shaoguang, 2014, China·Politics, Renmin University of China Press, pp. 30-31; Yang Zhijun, 2013, 'Central and Local, State and Society: The Dual Dimensions of Promoting the Modernisation of State Governance', *Journal of Gansu University of Administration*, No. 6
9 See Yan Yilong, 2017, 'The Division of Six Powers: A New Exploration of the Overview of China's Political System', *Journal of Tsinghua University* (Philosophy and Social Sciences Edition), No. 1. [鄢一龙：《六权分工：中国政治体制概括新探》，《清华大学学报（哲学社会 科学版）》2017年第1期]
10 'Amendment to the Constitution of the People's Republic of China' (adopted at the first session of the 13th National People's Congress on 11 Mar, 2018)
11 The Constitution of the Chinese People's Political Consultative Conference (revised on 15 Mar, 2018)
12 The Constitution of the Communist Party of China (partially revised at the 19th National Congress of the Communist Party of China, adopted on 24 Oct, 2017)
13 'Supervision Law of the People's Republic of China' (adopted at the first session of the 13th National People's Congress on 20 Mar, 2018)
14 See 'Constitution of the People's Republic of China' (adopted at the Fifth Session of the Fifth National People's Congress on 4 Dec, 1982)

15 Ma Ling, 2011, 'Military Powers in the Constitution', the full text is divided into three parts: 'Politics and Law', No. 1; 'Learning and Exploration', No. 2; 'Law', No. 2. [马岭：《宪法中的军事权》，全文分三部分：《政法论丛》2011 年第 1 期，《学习与探索》2011 年第 2 期，《法治论丛》2011 年第 2 期]

16 Many scholars have conducted in-depth discussions on the American political system. For example, Ostrom once proposed 13 theorems for the design of the American political system based on the Federalist Papers. Vincent Ostrom, 1999, *The Political Theory of Compound Republics*, Shanghai Sanlian Publishing House, pp. 72–85, Originally published in 1971, Public Choice, VPI&SU

17 Hamilton et al, 2015, *Fifty-one articles of The Federalist Papers*, translated by Cheng Fengru, Zai Han and Shu Xun, Commercial Press. [汉密尔顿等：«联邦党人文集» 五十一篇，程逢如、 在汉、 舒逊译，商务印书馆 2015 年版]

18 Montesquieu, 2012, *The Spirit of Law*, Commercial Press, Originally published in 1748. [孟德斯鸠：«论法的精神»， 商务印书馆 2012 年版]

19 Hamilton et al, 2015, *Fifty-one articles of The Federalist Papers*, translated by Cheng Fengru, Zai Han and Shu Xun, Commercial Press

20 Francis Fukuyama, 2011, 'Oh for a democratic dictatorship and not a vetocracy', *Financial Times*, 22 Nov, <http://www.ft.com/intl/cms/s/0/d82776c6-14fd-11e1-a2a6-00144feabdco.html#axzz28PC8kNpJ>, [4 May 2021]

21 <http://www.nytimes.com/2012/04/22/opinion/sunday/friedman-down-with-everything.html?ref=opinion#>, [4 May 2021]

22 see Sun Yat-sen, 2011, 'Civil Rights: The Fifth Lecture', *The Complete Works of Sun Yat-sen* (Volume 9), Zhonghua Book Company 2011 Edition, pp. 314–355. [参见孙中山：《民权主义·第五讲》，《孙中山全集》（第 9 卷），中华书局 2011 年版，第 314–355 页]

23 Hamilton et al., 2015, *Fifty-one articles of The Federalist Papers*, translated by Cheng Fengru, Zai Han and Shu Xun, Commercial Press

24 See Chapter 4 of this book for details

25 James McGregor Burns et al., 2007, *Government by the People: American Government and Politics*, Renmin University of China Press, p. 359, Originally published in 1989, Prentice Hall

26 'Should the historical responsibility to create a great cause of rejuvenation – the birth of the new Central Committee of the Communist Party of China and the Central Commission for Discipline Inspection of the Communist Party of China', Xinhua News Agency, Beijing, 24 Oct, 2017

27 See Sun Yat-sen, 2011, 'Speech at the Guangdong Education Association', in *The Complete Works of Sun Yat-sen*, Vol. 5, China National Book Co., p. 488

28 George Washington, 2012, 'Farewell Address', *Washington Anthology*, Commercial Press, 2012, p. 303

CHAPTER 8
Collective Wisdom Decision-Making System

[*The content of this part is mainly based on Wang Shaoguang and Yan Yilong: 'Great Wisdom and Prosperity: How China Makes a Five-Year Plan', Renmin University of China Press, 2015 edition.]

1. Collective wisdom decision-making model

As mentioned earlier, Westerners have long used the label of 'authoritarianism' to observe China's political system. This label was used in the period of the Beiyang warlords, and it is still the case today. Fragmented 'authoritarianism' is an influential theory in the West to explain China's decision-making process. It believes that China's decision-making is firstly authoritarian because of the lack of participation of social forces; secondly, it is fragmented, because the central control is not so strong, forming a fragmented game of interests.

This is a kind of mechanical thinking mode. It is like a symbol of 'authoritarianism' engraved on the boat. Although the boat has travelled 108,000 miles away, this symbol is still used to salvage the sword under the boat (刻舟求剑). Dispelling Western theoretical myths requires the academic consciousness of Chinese scholars. Many scholars are exploring the localisation theory of China's policy process, including Xue Lan, Wang Shaoguang, and Chen Ling from Tsinghua University's School of Public Administration, Ning Sao from Peking University, and Peng Fan from the Academy of Social Sciences. Our efforts are also part of this academic self-awareness.

We refer to the decision-making process of the Chinese central government as a Collective wisdom-based decision-making model based on the five-year plan (planning) decision-making process. Why is it possible to make good decisions? The secret of China can be concluded as 'collective wisdom' (集思广益).

'Collective wisdom' is from Zhuge Liang: 'Those in charge of state power must gather the thoughts of all people and listen to good opinions.

If you alienate people who have a quarrel with you and have difficulty in discussing with them, the affairs of the state will suffer. Disregard previous grievances, communicate with them, and listen to their pertinent opinions, like throwing away ragged shoes to get pearls and jewels.'[1] It means that if we discuss matters together, there is no way to remove the falsehoods and preserve the truth if we cannot be open and honest and discuss them repeatedly. This passage can be said to have captured the essence of collective wisdom.

Collective wisdom type decision-making refers to the decision-making process of continuously optimising the policy text through the arrangement of certain procedures and mechanisms in which the views of different parties are pooled. For example, when a student writes a doctoral dissertation or a master's thesis, how can he write well? It is definitely not enough to write in a hurry. You need to constantly consult different teachers to give opinions, and constantly revise and improve according to the opinions of others. The same applies to the collective wisdom decision-making model.

A leader in charge of planning once said: 'We are not worried about the low quality of planning, as long as all the procedures are in place, just think about how many people will check for us?' This explains the high quality of the plan: the preparation of the plan is a long-term process that involves many steps and countless people, concentrating the wisdom of countless people and undergoing numerous polishings.

We consciously use traditional language to describe the five-stage model of 'Collective wisdom' decision-making. (1) Make everyone offer good ideas: Mobilise all parties to offer suggestions and recommendations in the early stage of compiling the policy text, which is the 'Collective wisdom' in the early stage of policy formulation. (2) Collecting ideas broadly: The drafting group implements the instructions of the state leaders, integrates the opinions of all parties, collects relevant information, and drafts phased policy texts. (3) Extensive consultation: After the phased policy text is formed, opinions are solicited from all parties and amendments are made to form a policy draft.[2] (4) Collegial decision: The decision is discussed collectively in a formal meeting at different decision-making levels to form a formal policy document. (5) Informing the public: The policy document is communicated to all parties and implemented.

Table 1 Five Stages

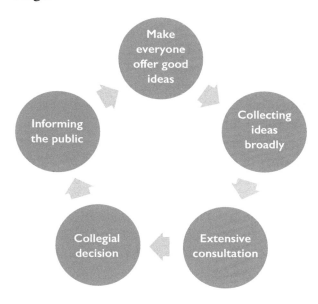

Source: Wang Shaoguang, Yan Yilong, 2015, 'Big Wisdom and Prosperity: How China Makes a Five-Year Plan', Renmin University of China Press, p. 51. The author has made revisions.

2. Historical evolution of decision-making

Through a systematic review of the preparation process of the Five-Year Plan (Planning), the evolution of the Five-Year Plan (Planning) can be divided into four types according to the characteristics of its decision-making, going through a total of five stages.

The five-year plan (planning) decision-making has gone through four generations of decision-making models. In the early period from the '1st Five-Year Plan' to the '2nd Five-Year Plan' period, a collective decision-making model within the government with extensive consultation and collective decision-making has been formed. Internal collective decision-making includes the following characteristics: (1) Although one agency of the bureaucracy is in charge of the compilation process, bureaucratic agencies at different levels and departments are involved in the compilation process. (2) Different organs of the state make joint decisions in accordance with legal procedures. (3) Decisions on important matters are made collectively by the leaders of the state. (4) The decision-making process is based on democratic centralism and is made realistically.

This model was then destroyed with the launch of the Great Leap Forward. From the latter stage of the Second Five-Year Plan until the Fourth Five-Year Plan, China's decision-making entered into a non-institutionalised decision-making period. This decision-making model was characterised by an emphasis on the absolute authority of the individual in the decision-making process, the absence of a fixed procedure for decision-making, and the arbitrary nature of the decision-making process. Although a certain range of decision-making subjects participated in the decision-making process, they did not actively express their opinions, and the decision-making process fell into a 'follow-the-leader effect'.

During the 'Fifth Five-Year Plan' and 'Sixth Five-Year Plan' periods, the internal collective decision-making model was rebuilt, and the decision-making process was restored.

From the Seventh Five-Year Plan onwards, experts, scholars and other social institutions began to participate extensively, and the five-year plan (planning) entered into a consultative decision-making mode. In addition to the internal collective decision-making character, the scope of decision-making consultation was extended to include elites outside the government, professional research institutions and personnel, people from outside the Party and business elites also participated in the decision-making process through different mechanisms

Marked by public participation, the five-year plan (planning) since the 'Tenth Five-Year Plan' has entered the mode of Collective wisdom decision-making. Despite the twists and turns, the democratic decision-making mode of the Five-Year Plan has been consistent and has been constantly improved, with procedural steps being developed and innovation and progress being made.

3. Decision-making process

Taking the '12th Five-Year Plan' as an example, we verified the five steps of decision-making proposed by this model. It takes more than two years to prepare the planning, which is divided into three stages and 11 steps. The first stage is to compile the 'Basic Ideas', which will take more than a year.

The second stage is to compile the 'Suggestions', which will take more than half a year. The third stage is the preparation stage for the official 'Outline', which will take nearly half a year. Each stage has gone through five steps: Make everyone offer good ideas, collect ideas, extensive consultation, collegial decision, and inform the public. The preparation of each stage lays the foundation for the preparation of the next stage.

The research stage of 'Basic Ideas', including mid-term evaluation, preliminary investigation, the drafting of opinions on basic ideas, etc., requires the collection of opinions from all parties by commissioned research on the subject, internal research on the subject, preliminary investigation, listening to suggestions from relevant parties and collecting opinions from all parties by asking for ideas from departments and localities. A draft of 'Basic Ideas' was formed based on this basic work. This will be followed by consultation with the relevant parties, such as holding meetings, that is, regional symposiums divided into eastern, western, north-eastern, and central regions, to seek local views; It also includes holding expert committee meetings to solicit opinions from development planning experts. After a consensus is formed, it will be notified to all parties to unify understanding, mobilise, and lay the foundation for the next step.

As we enter the preparation phase of the 'Suggestions', a new round of wisdom collection begins. It is necessary to carry out major topic's thematic studies. The NPC and CPPCC will start a long-term investigation and offer suggestions after the two sessions. The drafting team will also conduct research and issue a notice to solicit opinions from the whole party to collect opinions from all parties. The subsequent drafting process should focus on studying and compiling opinions from all aspects. The first draft is followed by extensive consultation within and outside the Party, mainly through two rounds of consultation. Four Politburo standing committees and two Politburo meetings are held to discuss it, and it is finally adopted at the Fifth Plenary Session of the 17th Party Central Committee before it begins to be officially announced, publicised and mobilised.

Formal 'Outline' preparation stage: The 'Outline' was compiled simultaneously with the 'Suggestions', but after the 'Suggestions' were passed, it will turn into a draft with the framework of the 'Outline'. The public proposal is specifically aimed at society as a whole, with research and proposals from the Chinese People's Political Consultative Conference (CPPCC) being carried out to make people offer good ideas. The State Council set up a '12th Five-Year' planning (compiling) group with the participation of 12 departments to promote the drafting of the 'Outline'. After the draft was formed, it entered the extensive consultation session, and the prime minister and vice-premier would listen to relevant opinions. The opinions of relevant scholars were solicited in writing, and three meetings of the '12th Five-Year Plan' Expert Committee were held to solicit opinions from all aspects. Subsequently, it was studied and discussed at the State Council executive meeting, the State Council plenary meeting, the Politburo Standing Committee meeting and the Politburo meeting, and finally considered and adopted by the Fourth Session of the Eleventh National People's Congress before a new round of publicity and mobilisation began.

Table 1 'Collective wisdom' decision-making mechanism in the three stages of the 12th Five-Year Plan preparation

	Make everyone offer good	Collect ideas	Extensive consultation	Collegial decision	Inform the public
Research on 'Basic ideas'	Subject research, sectoral and local worskshops	Draft 'Basic ideas'	Regional meetings, expert committee meetings	Party and State Leadership	Investigation, provincial and ministerial level study classes
Compile 'Suggestions'	Subject research, departmental thematic research, advice from the NPC and CPPCC, research by the drafting group	Listen to reports, collective learning, compile opinions, discuss, draft	Solicit opinions, seven times of extensive consultation	Politburo Standing Committee, Politburo Meetings, Plenary Sessions of the Central Committee of the Communist	Preaching sessions, local and departmental party committee meetings, publicity and mobilisation
Compile 'Outline'	Public suggestions research, seminars	Drafting internal discussions	Premier's Symposium Vice-Premier's Symposium Expert Committee Meetings, Solicit local opinions	State Council executive meetings, State Council plenary meetings, Politburo standing committees, Politburo meetings, National	Publicity and mobilisation

Source: Wang Shaoguang, Yan Yilong, 2015, 'Big Wisdom for a Prosperous Nation: How China Makes Five-Year Plans', Renmin University of China Press, p. 93.

It can be seen from the above table that the formulation of China's five-year plan (planning) is a continuous process from democracy to centralisation and from democracy to centralisation again, which condenses the will and wisdom of the whole party and the whole society. Finally, it elevates to law and becomes a programme and goal for the nation to strive for in unison.

4. Characteristics of collective wisdom decision-making model

The 'Collective wisdom' decision-making model of the five-year plan reflects several characteristics of China's decision-making process:

First, pay attention to research. Emphasis on research is a prominent feature of the five-year plan formulation. Systematic and specialised investigation and research have been carried out in all previous five-year plans in China. During the '12th Five-Year Plan' formulation, China has formed different levels and types of research, including research conducted by top decision-makers. The planning drafting groups, the National People's Congress, the Chinese People's Political Consultative Conference, and think tanks participating in decision-making consultation have conducted a large number of studies. 'The research on the preparation of the 13th Five-Year Plan was innovative in that President Xi Jinping held seminars for the heads of different provinces and regions in Zhejiang, Guizhou and Jilin to exchange views directly with the heads of the provinces, regions and cities on the preparation for the 13th Five-Year Plan.

It is precisely through extensive research that decision-makers are able to grasp first-hand information and make the formulation of the five-year plan realistic. At the same time, the research process is also a process of mutual communication and consultation.

The second is mass participation. This is different from public participation, in which the public participates not as an individual or a small group, but as a whole. The process of participation brings about the greatest and broadest representation, enabling the interests of different groups and parties to be reflected, so that policies can reflect the overall, fundamental and long-term interests of the people. Unlike public participation, mass participation requires decision-makers to proactively engage in the reverse direction, reaching out to the general public and encouraging the general public to fully express their views in order to understand their needs. In addition to carrying out activities specifically for the whole society, it also listens to and absorbs public opinions by conducting research, holding symposiums, and listening to public opinions expressed through formal and informal channels. From the 16 to the 29 of August 2020, the 14th Five-Year Plan preparation work was launched online for comments. The broad masses of the people actively participated and left more than 1 million messages, from which relevant parties sorted out more than 1,000 suggestions.[3]

The third is deliberative democracy centred on the aggregation of ideas. Carry out different forms of consultation at all levels and on an ongoing basis. Planning was prepared through repeated exchanges, comparisons and consultations before its scientific nature was gradually realised. This kind of consultation and concentration is a vivid example of the practice of deliberative democracy in China. The introduction of the plan must be subject to repeated discussions and deliberation, and multiple decision-making meetings at different levels should have been held. In this process, the National People's Congress and the Chinese People's Political Consultative Conference played an important advisory role, with a large number of experts and scholars participating, and the general public also put forward their opinions. Another important feature of China's deliberative democracy is that it is an aggregation of ideas rather than preferences. Preference Aggregation Theory is a very important theory formed after the rise of Western deliberative democracy theory in the 1990s. That is, why is it necessary to negotiate? Because people who prefer different positions can change their preferences after negotiation. However, preference change has proved difficult in practice. China's consultative democracy is an aggregation of ideas, not preferences, where various opinions and wisdom from all sides can be effectively pooled. This policy process is also like cooking a hot pot, where different participating subjects keep adding ingredients to it, making a soup with a mixed taste.

The fourth is democracy and centralisation. We emphasise not only democracy but also centralisation, basing a high degree of centralisation on full democracy so as to ensure both the democratic nature and the efficiency of decision-making. The political logic behind the collective wisdom decision-making system is democratic centralism. As Professor Hu Angang outlined, the logic of decision-making in the Five-Year Plan is 'democratic first, then centralised, and then democratic, then centralised'.[4] Only through a high degree of democracy can decision-makers with bounded rationality deal with massive amounts of scattered and insufficient information and coordinate the diverse interests of the participants. Making everyone offer good ideas is a round of democracy, and collecting ideas a is round of centralisation, while extensive consultation is another round of democracy, and collegial decision-making is another round of centralisation.

The fifth is to integrate science into democracy. The organic combination of science and democracy is the core feature of the collective wisdom decision-making system. It is a process of integrating science with democracy, through the mechanism of 'Make everyone offer good ideas' to collect scattered information and overcome information asymmetry; through the mechanism of 'collegial decision-making' to reach political consensus; through the mechanism of 'extensive consultation 'to overcome the one-sidedness and subjectivity of individual decision-making.

Thomas Friedman compares the decision-making process in China to that in the United States, saying: The United States is no longer a democracy, it has become vetocracy, a system designed to prevent anyone from doing anything.[5] The decision-making process in the United States is full of veto players, and the main goal of many policy players is not to improve policies, but to overturn them. What is democracy in China's decision-making? Participants are not vetoes, but opinion inputters. Democracy is to maximise the input of opinions from all parties, and centralisation is to limit the power of vetoes.

We have seen that the five-year plans are voted on by the National People's Congress with a high number of votes. This reflects a feature of China's decision-making process, which is to 'incorporate checks and balances afterwards through adequate consultation beforehand'(通过'事前充分协商吸纳事后制衡'). In the year or so before the five-year plan was submitted to the NPC for a vote, the NPC participated extensively in the preparation of the plan through special studies, suggestions and advice, and early intervention in the review. While repeatedly consulting the NPC at different stages of preparation and carefully incorporating relevant opinions to amend the document. Therefore, the high pass rate of the NPC votes reflects a high degree of policy consensus.

Fukuyama made an assessment of the Chinese political system in 2011, saying: 'The most important strength of the Chinese political system is its ability to make large, complex decisions quickly, and to make them relatively well, at least in economic policy'.[6]

In turn, what is his assessment of the United States? He says: 'It is easy for different branches of government to move against each other. Combined with the judicialisation of politics and the widespread penetration of interest groups, the US political system ultimately shapes the structure of government in a way that undermines the basis for collective action, creating what is called 'veto politics'. The separation of powers and checks and balances in the US political system is stricter than in other countries, or rather, there are more so-called 'veto points', leading to higher costs of collective action and even difficulty in moving forward.[7]

China has innovated a new model of state decision-making, which we call the collective wisdom decision-making model. It goes beyond both the so-called authoritarian and pluralist democratic decision-making models, and is able to combine democracy with centralisation, and democracy with science, to produce high-quality planning by pooling the wisdom of all parties.

---

1 Zhuge Liang, 'Giving instruction to subordinates', quoted from *Chen Shou: Three Kingdoms*, Shu Zhi, Dong He Biography. [诸葛亮：《与群下教》，引自陈寿：《三国志·蜀志·董和传》]
2 This was originally called 'Broadly accepted the ideas', but was revised to 'Extensive consultation' on the advice of Professor Lan Zhiyong from the School of Public Administration, Tsinghua University. 此环节原为"广纳言"，根据清华大学公共管理学院蓝志勇教授的建议修改为"广征询"，特此致谢。
3 President Xi Jinping's note on the 'Proposal of the Central Committee of the Communist Party of China on the Formulation of the 14th Five-Year Plan for National Economic and Social Development and the the Long-Range Objectives Through the Year 2035'. [习近平总书记关于《中共中央关于制定国民经济和社会发展第十四个五年规划和二〇三五年远景目标的建议》的说明]
4 Hu Angang, 2010, 'Democratisation of Public Decision-making with Chinese Characteristics: The Making of the 12th Five-Year Plan as an Example', China Study, No. 30. [胡鞍钢：《中国特色的公共决策民主化：以制定"十二五"规划为例》，《国情报告》2010年第30期]
5 Thomas L. Friedman, 2012, 'Down With Everything', *The New York Times*, 21 April 2021, <http://www.nytimes.com/2012/04/22/opinion/sunday/friedman-down-with-everything.html?ref=opinion#>, [4 May 2021]
6 Francis Fukuyama, 2011, 'US Democracy Has Little to Teach China', *Financial Times*, 17 Jan, <http://www.ft.com/intl/cms/s/0/cb6af6e8-2272-11e0-b6a2-00144feab49a.html#axzz33fKEP4uL>, [4 May 2021]
7 Francis Fukuyama, 2011, 'Oh for a Democratic Dictatorship and Not a Vetocracy', *Financial Times*, 22 Nov, <http://www.ft.com/intl/cms/s/0/d82776c6-14fd-11e1-a2a6-00144feabdco.html#axzz28PC8kNpJ>, [4 May 2021]

PART 5
CHINESE GOVERNANCE MODEL

The foundation of our governance of the country, is the leadership of the Communist Party of China and the socialist mode. We must be very clear that promoting the modernisation of the national governance mode and capacity is by no means Westernisation and capitalisation!

– Xi Jinping's speech at the seminar on the study and implementation of the gist of the Third Plenary Session of the Eighteenth CPC Central Committee to comprehensively deepen reform (17 February 2014)

CHAPTER 9
The World is Equally Shared by All – Traditional Concept of Good Governance

(* the article is based on the speech given by the author in the third conference of Chinese Studies in Central Research Institute of Culture and History on 15 Dec, 2016. Subsequently it is revised and published in Vol. 3, *Chinese Political Science* on 3 Sept, 2019) [footnote with *]

The Third Plenary Session of the Eighteenth Central Committee and the Fourth Plenary Session of the Nineteenth Central Committee of the CPC proposed to realise the modernisation of the national governance mode and capacity. The modernisation of Chinese governance is not Westernisation, but the self-improvement of China's governance mode and capacity. The existing good governance literature were mostly introduced from the West in the 1990s. Meanwhile, China has nurtured various good governance theories in its long history, nevertheless they have not been fully discussed. This session tries to illustrate the traditional concepts and practices of good governance in China.

In the long history of China, an abundance of governance ideas and practices have been formed. Confucianism as the main body of various schools of thought has various governance ideals. Among them, *Book of Rites: The Conveyance of Rites* (《礼记·礼运》) can be described as the prime principle of traditional good governance thought. Because it does not only propose the concept of 'the world is for the public', but also puts forward a whole set of governance ideas, such as selecting the meritocracy, promoting trustworthiness and cultivating harmony. That is to say:

> 'those who were good at governing in ancient times must first seek to understand their virtues, and govern the world for the sake of all families, not for the sake of one particular family. One must put people first, make prefectures and counties as the system, appoint the talented, use virtue as the guide and courtesy as the covenant. One also needs to realise everyone's happiness with good fortune, with good governance as the order, law as the rule, the army as the

defence, and the state as the co-ordination. Therefore the oceans and rivers can be as tranquil as the central area enjoys happiness and the world achieves peace.'

1. The paradigm of 'The World is Equally Shared by All'

In the research trend on *governance* and *good governance* that has formed since the 1990s, *governance* and *good governance* are often assigned specific meanings. Governance is considered to be a new paradigm that is different from management or rule; it is a multi-subject governance method that weakens the authority of the established, and tends to be anarchic. Good governance, on the other hand, is considered to be 'the return of the power from the state to the society', and 'the foundation of good governance does not lie so much in the government or the state, but instead in its citizens and civil society.'[1]

Some important international organizations try to construct a general theory of good governance, and this concept of good governance is also endowed with a specific Western-centric tendency. The 1992 World Bank report 'Governance and Development' saw good governance as creating and maintaining an environment that fosters strong and equitable growth.[2] In order to measure good governance, the World Bank has also constructed a set of Worldwide Governance Indicators, which are measured from six aspects: Voice and Accountability; Political stability and Absence of Violence/Terrorism; Government Effectiveness; Regulatory Quality; Rule of Law; and Control of Corruption.[3] In 1957, the United Nations Development Programme (UNDP) summarised good governance is measured by eight factors: Participation; Rule of Law; Transparency; Responsiveness; Consensus Oriented; Equity and Inclusiveness; Effectiveness and Efficiency; Accountability.

The term *governance* (治理 Zhi Li) in Chinese tradition refers to governing the country. 'Zhi' (治) originally refers to flood control, 'Yu the Great used to control floods';[4] 'Li' (理) originally refers to the treatment of jade, 'to analyse the patterns of jade'.[5] The meaning of the two-character-jointed word has been extended to governing a country, and governance refers to governing and administering a country. For example, in *Xunzi: The Way to Be a Lord* (《荀子·君道》), 'Then the division of duties, the order of careers, materials, skills and faculties are clearly established. If one does not govern, then justice is not clear and cannot be achieved, while private affairs will violate the collective deeds.' The ancients referred good governance and policies to good management. For instance, in *Tao Te Ching* (《道德经》), it refers to 'just and good governance' (正善治); in *Book of Documents: Counsels of Great Yu* (《尚书·大禹谟》), it is called 'Virtue is based on good governance, and governance is about nourishing the people'; in *Guanzi: Pivot* (管子·枢言), it is explained 'Those who do not have good deeds but have good governance have never been experienced since ancient times.' Although the ancients did not further develop the theory of good governance, they have formed traditional good governance standards and practices in their governance theories and long-standing governance practices.

China has had the standard of good governance since ancient times, and good governance refers to ideal models. The Western idea of good governance also falls into this category, and the concept remains the same when we talk about traditional Chinese good governance. *Book of Rites: The Conveyance of Rites* posits that 'the world is for the public' (天下为公) itself is a description of the ideal society in ancient times, just as China has not been able to get out the state that 'The Great Principle of the World is hidden, therefore the Public World has been privatised by the Ruling Family' for thousands of years, and can only pursue a 'moderately prosperous' (小康) society. In this case, the governance practice in history is far from reaching the rule of 'The World is Equally Shared by All '. Although the Chinese traditional good governance refers to the ideal model, it is by no means a false statement or a utopian notion, on the contrary, it is rich in classics and historical facts, with at least three evidences. One is the 'Rule of Three Dynasties' (三代之治), which in the eyes of the ancients was the golden age, the rule of sages, and became a model of governance for later generations. The second is the 'Rule of Prosperous Times' (盛世之治). In China's long history, there have been several periods of relatively good governance, such as 'the rule of Zhenguan', 'the rule of Wenjing', 'the prosperous age of Kaiyuan', and 'the prosperous age of Kang and Qian', which are respected by many. The third is the theories of ideal governance discussed by Confucianism, Legalism, Taoism, and other different schools, among which Confucian theories turned into the mainstream. Each school has different ideas, but there are also similarities.

What is 'The World is Equally Shared by All'? (公天下) The meaning of the word can be clearly defined, in terms of public (公) and private

(私) opposition. One definition can be found in *Han Feizi* (《韩非子》): 'In ancient times, Cangjie invented writing characters, and the one who writes circles around oneself is called '厶', and the one who is against '厶' is called '公'.'[6] Another way of interpreting it is that the self-centric ones hold the rice with their hands, expressing the monopoly of interests, while the ones who care about public interest, on the contrary, 'divide equally into the public', therefore the character of public is '公' (*Equality* or *Justice*). Either way, *Equality* or *Justice* refers to collective ownership, not private ownership by a few.

The concept of state sovereignty can be used as a rough analogy. In ancient China, the sovereignty neither belonged to the people, nor the monarch, or to the state or the almighty/sky (天),[7] instead, the sovereignty belongs to the public, under the commonly shared sky (天下).

In traditional politics and governance, the monarch is not the supreme sovereign, and the monarch is always restricted by various factors such as the laws of the ancestors. Moreover, the monarch is only authorised by the almighty (天) to govern the country and become the executor of the destiny, and the monarch has no power to surpass the destiny (天命). Therefore, some scholars believe that 'heaven/sky' (天) is the supreme sovereign, and sovereignty of China belongs to 'heaven/sky'.[8]

The problem is that the heaven that the Chinese believe in is not a personalised god, therefore there is no substance of the almighty at all. In many cases, the attitude is expressed by these quotes: 'God's will is always high and difficult to ask, and human feelings are sad and difficult to tell'; 'four seasons come and go, and all things live accordingly'. The destiny runs naturally regardless of human interference, or it can only be revealed in divination and various omens. In practice these representations of destiny are only for reference. For example, in *Book of Documents: Great Plan* (洪范九畴) puts forward the principle of decision-making when encountering difficulties, and it is necessary to 'first advice with one's heart, then with dignitaries and common people, then with divination'. In this case, divination's opinion is only one aspect of reference.[9] Precisely because the mandate of heaven is hidden and not revealed, the destiny of the ruler becomes mandate of heaven. Many tyrants in history are unscrupulous and omnipotent because they believed the doctrine of 'L'état, c'est moi'. In the past dynasties, the usurpation behaviours were mostly falsely entrusting the transfer of destiny to carry out their own desires.

In traditional politics, sovereignty cannot be said to belong to the almighty, but to the world and to the public. That means 'The world is equally shared by all', and the sovereignty is shared by all the people of the world. That is as what *Master Lü's Spring and Autumn Annals* (《吕氏春秋》) said: 'The world is not the world of one person, but the world of all people.' Confucianism also shared a view similar to that of Western Enlightenment scholars on the 'state of nature', which is 'the beginning of human life'. At the beginning of life, human beings were in the 'natural state' of living in caves, eating herbs and trees, drinking blood, clothing with animal skins and feathers.[10] In the period of ignorance, relying on almighty's long-term support to survive, this is the almighty virtue of good life, the world is of course shared by all, and no one can have it privately. Heaven's virtue is selfless, and heaven will not favour 'one person', and honour the selfishness of 'one person' with the greatness of the world. Although the world belongs to everyone, it is also a 'state of war' among selfish individuals. That is to say, 'at the beginning of life, people have their own personal interests, meanwhile, the world has public interests, and if there are public harms, they might be eliminated.'[11] Human beings have neither the benefit of sharp teeth and claws nor the ability to bite; to survive, 'one must use external objects', and 'external objects' at one's disposal are limited, therefore this will lead to competition.[12]

Different from the analytical approaches of Western scholars such as Thomas Hobbes, this 'state of war' is not guided by the strict and terrible Leviathan, but the rule of merit that can promote public interests, eliminate public harm, and do justice. Here are some ancient quotes: 'Nothing is more beneficial to the people of the world than governance, and governance is more important than the establishment of a ruler' and 'Those who can give right judgement and follow principles, are wise and clear, therefore they will convince the crowd to obey. If they know what is wrong and one does not mend it, they will make the rogue fear with painful punishment'.[13] In order to maintain good governance, people started to make rites and music 'to set rules between the ruler and ministers, to maintain the harmonious relationship between fathers, sons and brothers. It is also for making the upper and lower classes get along, husbands and wives live happily'.[14] Then the ruler, rites, music, punishment, government are all in the right place, well prepared, in order to receive grace of god. In this case, people would stop fighting and be moderate, thus the society could evolve from the 'state of nature' to the state of civilisation.

'To make a ruler is for the benefit of the world, not for the sake of one person', this is a natural inference. Whether the destiny favoured the ruler or not, all depends on whether the ruler can benefit the world. 'The World is equally shared by all', rather than 'possessed by a ruler'. If the ruler can perform justice, he will be the king with whom the people would like to be, and the ruler would not lose his people, because he has the moral sense (德). With the moral virtue, the king will be supported by the people, otherwise, he will be abandoned.[15] This idea has been shared by all great Confucians over thousands of years. For example, Mencius said, 'The people are the most precious, while the ruler is the least important.' That is to say, the world can choose the ruler, but the ruler cannot choose the world. In addition, Huang Zongxi said: 'The world is the master, whilst the ruler is only a guest', that means, as a guest, the ruler only serves and works for the world. Furthermore, Gu Yanwu believes that the destruction of a country is not the same as the destruction of the world: 'It is easy to change dynastic name, which can be regarded as the destruction of the country. When the benevolence and righteousness are not in function, subsequently beasts start to eat people, and people begin to eat each other, that is called the destruction of the world.' The ones who protect the country are merely meat-eaters (aristocracy) who hatch plots; while the rise and fall of the world is the responsibility of every man (common folks).[16]

The fundamental purpose of politics is to 'promote public interests and eliminate public nuisances', and good governance must be the governance of *Great Equity* (大公). 'In the past, when the sage kings ruled the world, they must first serve the public. Putting the public first will make the world peaceful.' 'Trying to examine the ambitions of the ruling class, one can tell that there are many rulers who have won the world by taking the public interests seriously and not biased, otherwise they will lose the world.'[17] The sky, earth, sun and moon are selflessly operating, and the *Great Equity* is like the sky, earth, sun and moon, serve the world selflessly.[18] The 'Three Guidelines' and 'Eight Objectives' of Confucianism proposed by *Great Learning* (《大学》) can be traced back to their origins and cannot be separated from 'The World is Equally Shared by All'.[19] The root of self-cultivation lies in the *Great Equity*, and for those who 'takes care of the destiny of the heavens', if justice is not served, then those people cannot be sincere and upright. The root of having a harmonious family lies in self-cultivation, 'If one doesn't know the evil of his son, then one cannot be sure of the greatness of his seedlings'. That is to say, if one does not have a sense of justice, one cannot have a harmonious family. The essence of governing a country is to serve the country and families. 'As a ruler, one cannot indulge one's own relatives and sons', because one 'must treat the people as one's own children' and 'like what the people prefer and dislike what the people hate'. That is to say, the way of cultivating oneself, keeping family happy and governing with peace lies in refraining from selfishness and serving the public, treating one's family as one's own, treating the country as one's family, and treating the world as one's own country. In a word, rulers should share their worries and joys with the people of the world.

The original intention of the governance of 'The World is Equally Shared by All' is to respect the ruler, making the virtuous ruler the highest symbol of public will and the unity of the country. In addition, respecting the ruler and the people must be carried out simultaneously, in a sense that, the world is the master, and the ruler is only the guest. Since sovereignty is shared by all, the monarch cannot share the nation only with his relatives. The essence of having prefectures and counties (郡县) is for the sake of *Great Equity*, but they must be supplemented by the meaning of feudalism (封建) in order to achieve good governance. The monarch also needs to share the regime and govern it jointly with the wise men and officials, and this is also the principle of electing meritocracy. The governance of 'The World is Equally Shared by All' requires the utilisation of rituals, music, and punishments as governance tools. Virtue is the main principle whilst punishment is auxiliary. That is to say, ritual and law are combined to govern. Virtue promotes good, punishment punishes evil; etiquette gives principles, and law brings justice. The central realm (中国) is the root, and the provincial areas are its branches and leaves. If the world is not peaceful, then the nation cannot operate properly. Only by regarding the central realm as the base and placing the world at the bottom of heart, can we achieve the governance of 'The World is Equally Shared by All'.

2. The world is the master, the ruler is the guest

The foremost principle of 'The World is Equally Shared by All' is that the ruler and the people are equally respected, in the sense that, the people are more important and the ruler is less; that is to say the world is the master, and the ruler is the guest. The idea has two folds. On the one hand, the ruler needs to be respected, because the highest political power needs to be concentrated on the prince, so that the public interest can be realised through the highest symbolic meaning. On the other hand, the people are the foundation of the world, which requires the political leader to govern with full respect of the populace.

'People are born with their own personal interests', and it is necessary to establish officials to promote public interests and eliminate harm to the public. The officials also have their own interests, which requires the highest official – the prince, as the incarnation of 'selflessness' (大公无私), suppressing individual, factionary and regional bias. This is the so called: 'If the people's private desires are not governed by a ruler, the world will become chaotic',[20] 'The worst chaos is no greater than the absence of the Son of Heaven. Without the Son of Heaven, the strong will prevail over the weak, the majority will become violent and the minor will be destroyed by armies, and there will be no peace.'[21]

In a big country like China with a vast territory and great population, in her long history, the Son of Heaven (天子), or the Emperor (皇帝), was regarded as the premise for the maintenance of the national community – the Son of Heaven is the leader of all the people, thereafter the world has a master, just like the human body has a head. The Son of Heaven is the premise for the unity of the world. Everyone has ideas and interests. 'Ten people have ten kinds of justices, and a hundred people have a hundred kinds of righteousness'; and if that is the case, the country will be in chaos and nothing can be accomplished. 'The Son of Heaven is the only one who can unify and enlighten the meaning of the world, governing the world in a good way.'[22] This governance has an analogy: the Son of Heaven represents the Heaven, and quintessentially, the ruler is required to represent the public interest. In the feudal period of the Zhou Dynasty, if the world were to achieve a great governance state, it is necessary to 'have a great moral sense in the world, and all ritual, music and wars must be decided by the Son of Heaven.' Otherwise, all rules will collapse and the world will be in chaos. For thousands of years, later generations have implemented Qin's politics and laws, and they all needed an emperor who assumes the power of the world. Without this premise, if there is no ruler, there will be chaos, the country will fall apart, and the people's lives will not be guaranteed, let alone other things.

At the same time, the prince must govern according to the politics of the people, which is revealed by the Pi (否 ䷋) and Tai (泰 ䷊) hexagrams of *Book of Changes* (《易经》). The Qian (乾 ☰) hexagram is used to describe the king, and Kun (坤 ☷) is used to describe the people. Qian is on the top, Kun is on the bottom, such a symbol means the world cannot run properly. Meanwhile, if Qian is at the bottom, Kun is at the top, it is the Tai hexagram, meaning 'the upper and lower classes are like-minded.' This is also revealed by the Qian hexagram, according to *Book of Changes*, that means after the honour of the ruler, there are regrets of the dragon, and it is necessary to assert the ruler, confronting the situation that the group of dragons are not principled by a dragon lord, only then the rules of heaven can be revealed. Despite the honour of the prince, the people must firstly be respected, in order to achieve the governance of 'The World is Equally Shared by All'.

The monarch is not the supreme, but the bearer of the greater will, the executor of the will of heaven. Destiny of Heaven is always changing, 'The greater will has no relatives, therefore only by virtue, world shall be ruled'.[23] King Wen of Zhou (周文王) conquered Li State, a subsidiary state of Shang, and the kingdom of Shang was terrified. King Zhou of Shang (商纣王) was still saying: 'Alas! Am I not born in the god's will?' While, minister Zuyi (祖伊) told him that God had abandoned him long ago because of his sins.[24]

When a monarch serves God, he must follow the way of heaven, respect rituals, and the laws of nature, not to be arrogant or fall into hubris, 'Heaven honour the people, and whatever the people want, God will allow.'[25] The most important thing for a monarch to serve God is to respect God and protect the people. The wills of heaven and the heart of the people are connected, and the heaven will be able to listen, look, be smart as well as being terrified according to the will of the people.[26] Those who respect the heaven and protect the people will be favoured by the heaven, 'When the heaven is in power, seeking democracy, the great destiny rests on King Tang, demanding him to punish the evil Xia Dynasty.'[27] 'If God did not will it, how come our small state such as Zhou can be the master of the world?'[28] Only when the ruler's virtue is in line with 'regarding the will of the people as his own', with less selfishness and few desires, taking the world as justice in his own way of governance, can he receive the grace of God for a long time. The ruler should be one with the people, 'The Son of Heaven must consider himself the parent of the people, only then he can truly be the king of the world'[29] 'Like protecting children', the prince shares the joys and sorrows with the people, 'loving what the people love, and hating what the people hate'.[30] 'Removing the troubles of the people is like removing the disease of the heart'.

If the monarch tyrannises the people, God will punish him 'for the crime of King Jie of Xia, the almighty will bring him down.'[31] This kind of monarch is nothing more than what Mencius called 'a thief and tyrant', and to vanquish him is 'to obey the will of heaven', not an act of usurpation. That is so called: 'the revolutions led by Tang and Wu obeyed the God's will and responded to the people.' (汤武革命，顺乎天而应乎人)[32] 'Water can carry a boat while can also capsize it' (Water refers to the people, and boat refers to the ruler) Wise rulers always take the will of the people in great care. From an individual and short-term perspective, of course, the monarchy is powerful and the common people are insignificant, but in a collective and long-term perspective, people's power is dominant. That's why the Great Yu said that if the tyrant bent the will of the people, it is like pulling rotten reins and driving six horses.[33] 'The people are the foundation of the state, and if the foundation is solid, the state will be peaceful.' Mencius said, 'The people are the most valuable, the society is the second, and the ruler is the least significant.'[34] This order is based on the essentialism of politics. Without the people, the government has no meaning, and without the government, the monarch is of no use. The legitimacy of a monarch can only be based on the needs of the people. That is why Xunzi said, 'Heaven offers lives of the people, not for the ruler, instead the heaven invests the ruler for the people.' Huang Zongxi said: 'In ancient times, the world was the master, the ruler was the guest, and the ruler's life-long management was for the world.'

The foundation of the people-based politics (民本政治) is the self-sufficient state of the agricultural society of – 'ploughing the fields for food, digging the fields for drinking, what is the God's will to me?' The people-based politics is to maintain this state of self-sufficiency, 'to make the people live according to how time changes, and relieve the people of the other kinds of burdens.'[35] To avoid those can make people's homes ruined, such as wars, robbers, disasters, mergers of tyrannical powers, etc., so that people can be happy and keep their homes, only then the foundation of a country will not be shaken. From the perspective of the reality of state governance, the people are the foundation of the state, and the main class is the farmers (the other classes are officials, craftsmen and merchants). The farmers are responsible for taxation and other corvée duties to the state. But at the same time, the country cannot shake the people's foundation, and well-governed dynasties often demand less tax and duties from the people. For example, in the Han dynasty, the land rent rate was 3.3% of the income, and in the Tang dynasty, the rent was regulated and simplified in forms of grains, paid corvée and textiles (租庸调), that means the rulers measure the people's strength then decide taxation. To relieve people's burden, the ruling group needs to be streamlined and economical. The major drawbacks of the Song dynasty were caused by redundant soldiers, officials, and expenses, which made the whole society overwhelmed. At the same time, national construction cannot exceed the power of the people, and it is necessary to carry out major projects without exploiting the actual bearing capacity of the people. The first Emperor of Qin (秦始皇) and Emperor Yang of Sui dynasty (隋炀帝) made the same mistake.

The challenge of both respecting the monarch and the people is that the power of the monarchy can often be opposed to the guest (反客为主). The ideal politics is 'the world is the master, and the ruler is the guest', while the real practice often tends to be 'the world is the guest, and the ruler is the master'. The greatness of the world, only serves the selfish desires of one person. The monarch takes the world as his property, just like Liu Bang (刘邦), the first Emperor of the Han dynasty, boasted to his father: 'you used to think that I was a rogue, because I would not be able to buy property, and I was not as good as my younger brother. Then look at my property now. Who dare say they possess more property than I, the Emperor?' Those kind of rulers regard the exploitation of the people as the interest of investment in the property.[36]

The premise that both respecting the monarch and the people is that it is a virtuous person who occupies the high position, in which case, respecting the monarch is respecting virtue. Regarding the succession of the ruling position, the legendary Chinese ruler Yao (尧) did not let his son Dan Zhu inherit the throne, because Dan Zhu was 'selfish and not suitable'. After recommendation, and actual investigation of Shun (舜) in terms of virtue, ability, performance, etc., Yao asked 'Shun to be the regent', and finally confirmed Shun as his heir to the throne.[37] After the Xia dynasty, the position of rulers had always been inherited by relatives (brothers or sons according to a patriarchal succession order) and not the ones with virtue. In the Qing dynasty, the policy of 'establishing heirs in secret' (秘密建储)

meant choosing the best among the sons, but the range of choices was very limited. The change of dynasties is not dependant on the assumption that the leadership is assumed by the virtuous, but more related to the tendency or inertia of power. Since the monarch possesses the whole world, it is ridiculous that he prefers to work as a prisoner. 'The world does not serve one person, while it takes one person to rule the world', this is also against human nature. Even though when the Emperor was still an heir, he was 'surrounded by all kinds of teachers' and 'being taught all kinds of virtues'; after he came to power, there were ministers who gave suggestions and criticisms, and historians to record his behaviours and speeches. That is to say, the prince was supported and confined by constitutions, nevertheless, in history, there are still very few good rulers who maintained a good government and loved the people.

3. Integrate feudalism in the system of prefectures and counties

The second principle of the 'The World is Equally Shared by All' rule is to 'integrate the meaning of feudalism in the prefectures and counties'.[38] China has a vast territory, great population, and different areas with cultural diversity, managing China is a difficult task. Two profound traditions in ancient China have jointly shaped the governance model of later generations. One is the governance tradition of feudalism (封建) during the Zhou dynasty. The second is the governing convention of the Qin dynasty implementing the system of prefectures and counties (郡县). And the dispute of the two modes runs through Chinese history, mainly because, feudalism is out of necessity due to the tendency or inheritance of power, meanwhile the system of prefectures guarantees long-term stability and the public interest. Even so, with the unified laws and centralised power, the system of prefectures may cause faults of despotism, therefore Gu Yanwu believed only by 'Integrating the meaning of feudalism in the prefectures and counties', a good and stable governance can form.

Zhou dynasty organised the kingdom with feudalism, and made a large number of feudal principalities, distributed to relatives and heroes, 'Seventy-one countries were established, and the direct relative of Zhou got fifty-three of them.'[39] Then they divided the world by constructing the order of concentric feudal patriarchal rule: 'The Son of Heaven established countries (国), the feudal lords made households (家), the ministers set up side chambers, the consultants made two branches in family, and the gentlemen had their disciples'.[40] The feudal system enabled Zhou, a former sub-state to divide and rule the vast land and people after conquering their former suzerain Shang dynasty. The order of etiquette had been maintained for hundreds of years preventing the king's lineage from failing. With the feudal system, the world was divided and shared by nobles, forming a limited democracy. Although each country was privately owned, the Son of Heaven hoped all of them could respect morality and protect the people, so that collectively, the dynasty can be handed down for a long time. Kings of Zhou invested feudal lords as the branches protecting the main trunk.[41] Those feudal countries were like stars all over the sky, guarding the central realm, and to collectively maintain long-term peace and order.

The disadvantages of the feudal system of Zhou are also obvious. The authority of the Son of Heaven was gradually weakened, and the feudal lords ruled independently. When King Li of Zhou (周厉王) had quarrels with his people, the king was forced to flee the capital, and then feudal lords decided not to pay tribute to the king anymore. When King You of Zhou (周幽王) conscripted troops from the feudal lords, the princes ignored it, resulting the king being killed by the nomadic tribes under Mount Li. After King Ping of Zhou (周平王) moved eastward, the Zhou dynasty declined, subsequently the stronger states annexed the weaker states, the strong overlords became de facto leaders among the lords.[42] Thereafter, ritual, music and wars were decided by the princes, and the king's order was shattered into ashes. During the Warring States Period (战国), rituals and music were broken, and the feudal lords fought each other chaotically.

The failure of feudalism lies in the private interest tarnishing the public order, endless arguments eventually led to wars. Feudal lords implement a hereditary system, dividing the power of the monarch, as each feudal country has its own fiefs, government, and army. With the absence of a strong centralised control, only relying on the ritual order can't curb the selfish desires of the princes. Feudalism is a hereditary system, so that the ruling position was inherited by close relatives instead of wise people. If the heir is unworthy, the central government cannot intervene. That is to say 'the princes shall not change the established policies, and the Son of Heaven shall not change the rulers', for example, King Xuan of Zhou (周宣王) could not decide the heir of the Dukedom of Lu.[43] As the power of the princes increased, their ambitions expanded accordingly. Then the feudal lords had the desire to covet, and then acted on winning the crown, meanwhile the Son of Heaven felt the lords suspicious, and made moves of cutting down the vassal. Under the feudal system, when the trunk is weak and the branches are strong, then the conflicts are hard to avoid. The game for the throne began with suspicion and resulted in war. This is why the feudal system of Zhou was in trouble, and same can be said about feudalism in later generations. At the beginning of the Han dynasty, the founding heroes were appointed by the Emperor, Liu Bang, as kings, which was the last resort to maintain the loyalty of the abled retainers. Later, the Emperor made the blood alliance with the lords, swearing 'anyone without the family name Liu cannot be a king'. The Emperor invested 'nine kingdoms of the same family name', but unfortunately, those kingdoms equally caused huge conflicts and nearly overthrew the Empire. The Jin dynasty also made feudal lords, and the original intention was to defend the imperial power, but it led to the 'eight princes rebellion', a series of family bloodshed. The system of setting up vassal towns in the Tang dynasty was originally to expand border defences, but later the vassal towns became stronger and resulted in a trend of separatism. It finally led to the 'An Shi Rebellion' (安史之乱); after the chaos, the tigers' were vanquished at the front door while 'the wolves' entered at the back door, therefore the turmoil among the feudal towns is endless.

Qin dynasty changed from feudalism to prefectures, which is one of the most momentous points in Chinese history. The First Emperor (秦始皇) adopted Li Si's suggestion: 'sons of the Emperor are not made to be kings, and retainers and heroes are not made to be feudal lords, so that the Empire is not divided', instead 'former kingdoms are unified, and the world is governed through prefectures and counties.'[44] The Qin Empire was divided into thirty-six prefectures, and under the prefectures are counties, towns, districts and neighbourhoods. The later Chinese governments had followed the politics and laws of Qin, and the system of prefectures became a compulsory policy since the Han dynasty. Qin built the prefectures out of selfishness, however it did create the system for 'The World is Equally Shared by All'. The realisation of the public world begins with Qin, because in ancient times, the ruling position was passed through the system of Shanrang (禅让), a legendary way of inheriting the throne from the former ruler to a recommended champion nominated by leaders of tribes. Later on, the world was ruled by families, and each family had its private interest, why not let the world be ruled by one single family, it would seem fair to all. Emperor Yongzheng (雍正帝) put in this way: 'after the Qin and Han dynasties, the land belonged to the emperor, and if feudal system were to be applied, there would be conflicts among the lords, conversely the system of prefectures is fair'(with a single Emperor as the mediator).[45] The prefectures are governed together as one, which stops disputes, quells and wars among different areas, and the peace is realised under a centralised governance. At the same time, it unifies the standards of writing, weights and measures, laws, and markets. It has made China as a vast national community, which is more than 2,000 years ahead of the West. The great unification of the Qin dynasty combined the countries of the central areas as one; the great unification of the Yuan, Ming and Qing dynasties, integrated the inside and outside of the Great Wall. Those achievements are due to the system of prefectures, laying an inalienable territorial foundation for China.

'The system of prefectures may cause faults of despotism', Sovereignty is concentrated in the centre, and provincial officials only have the right to govern. In addition, due the frequent change of the post, the officials do not have a long term plan for their governing area. They tended to be irresponsible, some even exploit the people, and some would introduce harsh policies for getting the credibility of being a so-called good governor. The central government had strengthened supervision through various means, and officials had been overwhelmed by self-preservation having no will to govern positively. Moreover, while the governors were appointed by the central government, the local clerks, who helped the governors in daily political practices, took the posts via a system with feudal tendency. The real power of local governance often falls into the hands of subordinate officials. These problems are the institutional costs of the prefecture system, and the way to make up for it should lie in governance (治), not in rule (制). The rule is dominated by hegemony (霸道), and the governance relies on harmonious way (王道). That is to say under the general framework of the prefecture system, the factors of decentralisation of the feudal system can be incorporated, so that the enthusiasm and autonomy of local governance can be improved, thereafter, the talented can be selected, and the principles of morality implemented. Gu Yanwu proposed to implement a hereditary feudal system for county magistrates under the framework of the county system, because in this case, the magistrates can be professional due to the specific local interest, while they would not betray the central government because they are not powerful enough.[46] Huang Zongxi proposed that there should be feudal towns as a supplement to the prefecture system in the frontier areas.[47] In fact, China has always been supplemented by semi-feudal entities such as feudal towns, chieftains, and vassals in the mainframe of the prefecture system.

4. Selecting and appointing the talented

Selecting and appointing the talented is the third principle of the 'The World is Equally Shared by All'. 'When the talented are in charge, the people will follow gladly.'[48] 'Appointing virtuous persons in charge is the foundation of good governance, benefitting the gods and the common people.'[49] Both Confucianism and Mohism regard the use of the talented as the key to governing the country, meanwhile the Daoist idea of 'not honouring the virtuous, so that the people will not contend' is very difficult to practice.

Since having a monarch is for making sure the world operates in order, the world cannot be ruled by the monarch alone, but must be ruled together with worthy persons. It is said 'By seeking the great heroes and working together with wills and forces accorded, the world can be operated by great governance.'[50] That means the monarch and the minister are integrated in one body of government, the monarch is the head of state, and the ministers are the arms, ears, and eyes.[51] The head cannot play a good role if without the ears, eyes, femoral and brachial muscles. 'The officials are like arms and legs; and everyone knows if one went missing, the person is not a whole. All body parts must act as one.'[52] The rulers and ministers are all positions established to govern the world. Governing the country is like lifting a big tree. The monarch sings in the front, and the ministers echo in the back. The two have an orderly and different division of labour, but there is no absolute boundary between the superior and inferior as regarded by the later generations.[53] The power of the civil official group is a supplement to the monarchy, and it is also a constraint on the monarchy, so as to create a system that conforms to the general will of the world.

China is a country that opened its ruling power to the common people very early in the world, and the principle of selecting officials to govern the country is ' honouring the virtuous and appointing the talented'.[54] The talented rule the country, 'regardless whether ones upbringing is noble or not, because the only standard is morality......even if one is poor and of humble upbringing, as long as one is just and honest, he/she can lead the people.'⁵⁵ 'The grandsons of princes, scholars and officials, if they do not belong to the gentle and honest group, they shall no longer be regarded as noblemen......even the grandsons of the commentors, as long as they are gentle and honest, they should be regarded as the ones in the ruling class.'⁵⁶ 'Therefore, officials are impermanently noble and the people are impermanently common, as long as one is capable, they will get promoted, and incompetent ones would become inferior.'⁵⁷ Yao chose Shun instead of his son Danzhu, because he wanted to give the throne to the talented instead of the relative. King Tang (汤) chose Yi Yin (伊尹) among the cooks, King Wuding (武丁) chose Fu Yue (傅说) among the prisoners, and Duke Mu of Qin (秦穆公) chose Baili Xi (百里奚) among the servants, these are famous examples of meritocracy, regardless of one's original class.

In China, the system of electing the talented has a long history. In *Book of Documents*, it is recorded that Yao and Shun asked ministers to recommend the talented to govern the country. In the Zhou dynasty, there was a system for selecting virtuous people. Through the three-year competition of 'virtues and arts' worthy people were elected, and 'officials were asked to present books of virtuousness to the king'.⁵⁸ After inspection and selection at various levels, the township selects the talented, which are called the *candidates* (选士). The Administrator of Land selects *handsome scholars* (俊士) from the *candidates*, and the Administrator of Music selects *advanced scholars* (进士) from them, and then judges the ranks, titles, and peerage, only after then could the talented start to work, receiving salary accordingly.⁵⁹ Of course, in the feudal era of Zhou, hereditary succession was the main system, and elections were mainly carried out for lower-level positions, while upper-level positions were still monopolised by aristocrats. 'The scholars (士大夫) and above are all gentry, so there is no need for them to be in the elections.'⁶⁰

During the Warring States Period, the aristocracy collapsed, and the civilian forces rose through military exploits, lobbying, etc., becoming a precedent for the large-scale employment of ordinary people. After the Han dynasty, the selection of the talented from the whole society to govern the country became a custom, and there were many changes in the system, but the spirit of 'selecting and appointing the talented' remained the same.⁶¹

Historically, there have been various ways to select the talented from the whole society, but there are two major approaches. The first is through recommendation (荐举), that is, the rulers widely select the talented through recruitment, inspection, talent appraisal and other channels, and there are specific projects such as *recruitment, exploration, filial piety, virtuous founder, literature* (征、辟、孝廉、贤良方正、文学) and so forth. The second is the imperial examination, in which case, the talented are selected through the civil servant examination. The difference between the recommendation and the imperial examination is that through the latter, talented people take the initiative to participate in the examination and enter the political system. During the Han, Wei and Jin dynasties (汉、魏、晋), the recommendation was the main path, whilst after the Sui and Tang dynasties (隋唐), the imperial examination became the major method.

The first Emperor of Han dynasty (刘邦) made decrees, seeking virtuous people to share the power of ruling the world. 'If there are wise men and scholars who are willing to take the journey with me, I will make them honourable and famous.' He asked all regions to recommend the talented. Emperor Wen of the Han dynasty issued an edict to search for virtuous people; later on Emperor Wu of the Han dynasty adopted Dong Zhongshu's suggestion and then formally established the inspection system (察举制). The inspection system was the main method for recruiting talents from the society during the Han dynasty. It was a system arrangement in which the talented were recommended by various regions to serve in the central government. The annual elections included *Xiaolian* (the filial and incorrupt) and *Maocai* (talented scholars). Xiaolian were elected by each county (郡), and the number of candidates was adjusted according to the county's population. Maocai was elected by the state (州). The specially tested subjects include virtue, literature, the classics, laws, art of war, yin/yang and other subjects, which shows the wide range of outstanding people recruited.[62] The nine-rank system (九品中正制) implemented in the Wei and Jin dynasties demonstrates the development of the inspection system. In order to avoid the randomness of recommending, the government appointed 'the virtuous and knowledgeable' people as the judges who were specially responsible for appreciating the talented, writing comments, and classifying them into nine ranks, on which basis, the Ministry of Personnel decide their appointment.

The advertising job system (征辟) is also an important channel for recruiting the talented. It is a system in which the rulers actively invite outstanding scholars to serve. The appointment by the emperor is called Zheng (征). The state and county select and appoint vassal officials called Pi (辟).[63]

The inspection, the nine-rank, and the advertising job systems broke the monopoly of power, allowing the government to select the talented widely in the whole society. However, the shortcomings are also obvious. Direct employment is limited by information, and most of them rely on recommendation. Both the inspection and the nine-rank systems institutionalise recommendation. However, not all judges were selfless, and they would also use their power for personal gain, so that the actual power of employing people was still controlled by the high ranking families (门阀). The premise of the effective inspection system in townships is that the social atmosphere is relatively just. By the end of the Eastern Han dynasty, the society had become corrupted. It appeared that 'the so-called talented people, did not read books; the filial people forced their fathers to live separate; the so-called pure ones are as dirty as mud, and the so-called good generals are as cowardly as chickens.'[64] The nine-rank system was originally intended to correct the corrupt atmosphere of employing people at that time, and implement the measures of 'only the talented can be selected'. However, after a period, due to the concentration of the power of assignment in judges, they were also corrupted, and 'do not care about the actual abilities of the candidates, only recommend due to the factional benefits; weighing the ruler unevenly, according to personal affection, whoever's in his faction, even without actual talent, would still be celebrated, and whoever is not in the faction, will be nit-picked.'[65] The judges colluded with the powerful, and corrupted the system. Subsequently most of the positions fell into the hands of noble families. 'High-ranking excludes poor families, and no one of gentry would be judged as the low-ranking'. It became an important reason for the formation of the clan politics (门阀制度) in the Jin dynasty.

With the corruption of the inspection and the nine-rank systems, the imperial examination system began to rise and became the main channel for selecting the talented. Emperor Yang of the Sui dynasty established the *advanced scholar* degree (进士科) to set a precedent for the imperial examination system, and the Tang dynasty began to institutionalise the imperial examination system. There were many subjects, but the main ones were *advanced scholar* and *classics*. The advanced scholar degree required the candidates to be talented at writing poems and essays, while the other tested the ability of reciting and interpreting the classical texts. In the Song dynasty imperial examination, in addition to the *advanced scholar* and *classics*, there were also military arts, policy system and lyrics examinations. Moreover, a three-level examination system has been formed, namely the tests consist of the township, the provincial and the imperial palace examinations. At the same time, in order to ensure the fairness of the examination, the system of anonymous name, transcription, locking-down the exam room, and other examinations had been formulated. The government also revised the exam content, so that in the Song dynasty, the imperial examination had become a better functioning system with 'rules, compliance and feasibility', and the scale and fairness of the selection far greater than those of the Tang dynasty.[66] The imperial examination system flourished in the Ming and Qing dynasties, and a complete imperial examination system was formed. In addition to the three-level examinations of the township, provincial and the palace examination, candidate exam (科考) and the *men of virtue* degree (庶吉士) were added. It formed a system of fame and ranks from low to high, including *new students* (生员), *advanced students* (贡生), *supervisors* (监生), *candidates* (举人), *advanced scholar* (进士), *high rank scholar* (进士及第) and *men of virtue*. The format of the exam is standardised, the subject of the exam includes classics, policy theory, etc. The exam writing format follows the standard eight-part essay (八股). With these introduced, the method of preventing cheating in the exam became stricter.

The imperial examination is different from the recommendation system. The talented can 'represent themselves' and take the initiative to apply for the examination, so that they can participate in the selection, which reduces the chance of corruption of the referees. The imperial examination is more fair than the recommendation system, and the standards are more objective. The design of the examination system and the rules of examination supervision have become stricter, so that talented people from humble backgrounds can also stand out and participate in the governance of the country. Ouyang Xiu praised the fairness of the imperial examination, 'as objective as the creator, as fair as the balanced scale'.[67] The imperial examination has become the main path for attracting the talented in the whole society. When Emperor Taizong of Tang (唐太宗) inspected privately, he was delighted to see the new scholars entering in a row: 'The heroes of the world have entered my quiver!' The imperial examination provided an opportunity for rising social ranks for the intellectual elites.

The imperial examination system established the literati class, making the 'scholar' the highest among the four social classes (scholars, farmers, craftsmen and merchants') of the country. The intellectual class in Chinese society provided a thinking tank for national governance, and at the same time, it has become an important force for social autonomy. The country gentry became the backbone of maintaining the order of rituals and customs in the countryside, meanwhile the literati became active participants in the country's political life by becoming officials or civil servants. At the same time, the literati accepted Confucianism and became the backbone of maintaining the Confucian order through schools and political discussions.

The disadvantage of the imperial examination is that the contents are not empirical. It is difficult to mark morality with scores. The philosophical studies are 'neither enough nor practical for governing the world'.[68] Historically, the subjects and methods of examinations have been reformed many times, but these problems have not been solved. Although there were many subjects to be tested in the Tang dynasty, they mainly examined poetry, and *classics* with a focus on reciting selected books. Wang Anshi sighed in the poem 'Reading the Examination Paper for the *advanced scholars*': 'literature as a tested subject began in the Sui and Tang dynasties, and the standard is about rhymes and rhythms. How could such *advanced scholars* possibly know the way to solve actual problems?' In view of this, he pushed forward reforms. Instead of poetry, essays of politics were introduced. Instead of dictating the classical scriptures, it examined the understanding of classics, preventing people from memorising the canons dogmatically. During the Ming and Qing dynasties, the format of the test essays was further clarified, and the main format was regulated in eight-part essays, but this reform could not solve the problem of 'what's tested is not practical'. The eight-part essay format has become a set of answering strategy. People who have no real talent can pass the exam because they knew how to employ those formalist strategies. Therefore, Huang Zongxi went so far as to say, it is better to draw lots, because it might offer a higher chance to select virtuous and capable people.[69]

Another major drawback of the imperial examination system is that it imprisons the scholars. On the one hand, it provides a way for scholars to enter the ruling class, but it also limited what they could have learnt, since they only focused on the textbooks. 'Everything is inferior, only reading those about *advanced scholar* matters' refers to the situation. Only passing the imperial examinations is the right path in life. The scholars were like the fish striving for leaping over the Dragon Gate, hoping to turn from ordinary fish to the powerful dragons. Others are either to be a celebrity in poetry, or to become a secretary serving the officials, or to open a library and become a teacher, all of which are helpless choices. The imperial examination was a prison for the intellectual class, and it could be said that there was no escape in such a society. The entire intellectual class wasted their entire lives on this, which was a great waste of knowledge. This was also an important reason for the slow scientific development in ancient China.

The imperial examination system is of course a system that cooperates with feudalism, and because of which, the path is narrow, and those who can pass the imperial examination are extremely limited. Although the monopoly power of the aristocracy was shaken on the whole, hereditary succession and nepotism were prevalent. In some cases, by donating rice if not cash, posts can be bought. At the same time, due to the small number of officials, local power is often entrenched in the hands of the local subordinate class. They colluded with the local gentry, forming a situation where the imperial appointed officials had to succumb to local feudal force. Ye Shi said that the literati class was busy seeking promoting ranks and cared less about helping the people to solve problems. The officials in administrating only followed the suggestions by the local secretaries, and the local power became indulgent.[70] Gu Yanwu said: 'There are three kinds of groups harming the people: they are called gentry, *new students*, subordinate officials.'[71] The three colluded with each other and became an underworld force that dominated the provincial areas and harmed the local villages.

5. Morality is the mainstay, while punishment is auxiliary; Ruling with rituals and laws combined.

The fourth principle for 'The World is Equally Shared by All' is 'Morality is the mainstay, while punishment is auxiliary; Ruling with rituals and laws combined.' The order of governance is to lead by virtue, covenant by courtesy, manage by governance, and judge by law. Virtue is the foundation, whilst politics and law are the last straw of governance. 'The priority is to promote morality, if it is time to punish, the ruler must act cautiously.'[72] 'If guiding the subjects with politics, aligning them with punishment, the people will not feel too shamed, while guiding them with virtue, and aligning them with propriety, they will know what is shame and improve themselves.'[73]

Morality denotes internal canons, courtesy is a set of soft principles, while politics and law are a set of hard regulations. This is not only a way to maintain long-term stability, but also a systematic governance method that minimises governance costs.

Virtue is the root of the rule, a key to Confucian resolution. *Book of Documents: Counsels of Gao Yao* said that governing a country must start with self-cultivation, 'be careful with one's behaviour and cultivate one's mind constantly', so that 'the rule can be everlasting'. Confucius said, 'regarding listening to a lawsuit, I am just as useless as the other people. My solution will be preventing all lawsuits from happening.' The state of having no lawsuits can only rely on the rule of virtue, not the rule of law. This is the fundamentalist knowledge in *Great Learning* (大学). In the Confucian governance system, it is not that there is no need for law and punishment, but the rule of virtue is given priority, 'disrespecting the father and the king' is the doom of the world. 'Propriety, righteousness, integrity and shame, are the four principles of the country, if the four are not widespread, the country will perish.'[74] Destroying family ethics is tantamount to destroying the foundation that maintains the entire national order. Those who want to govern their country must first organise their families well. Governing by virtue means expanding the family's ethical relationship. A leader should focus on the ethics of the five constants (father's righteousness, mother's kindness, elder brother's friendliness, younger brother's respect, son's filial piety), then expand those to governing the country, employing filial piety to serve the ruler with loyalty, the elder with respect, and the public with kindness.[75]

Governing a country requires the combination of kindness and harshness, the simultaneous use of morality and punishment, and the combination of etiquette and law. But it is also necessary to distinguish the mainstay and the auxiliary, the root and the branches, so that the governance of the country is fortified against nepotism. That is to say, 'to use etiquette to nurture people's hearts, music to echo people's voices, governance to regulate the behaviours, and punishment to prevent selfishness.'[76] Ritual is a soft line of defence, while punishment and law are rigid; and the cost of rule of ritual is less than rule of law. 'The teaching of propriety is also subconscious, and it can stop evil invisibly, causing people to move away from the evil day by day, without even realising it.'[77]

The earliest ritual may be a sacrificial ceremony. 'Ritual is a performance;

it is also a blessing to serve God.'[78] Later it evolved into a flexible norm covering all aspects of personal life and national governance, including 'Funeral, sacrifice, shooting, chariot mounting, coronation, marriage, courtly greetings and betrothal'. As long as there is a social life, there is no lack of ritual. In Confucianism, it can be said that the great use of propriety is extremely high, because ritual is the rule of action, the great handle of governing the country. The rule of etiquette will keep things in order, while the disorder of etiquette will make things chaotic. If you don't know the ritual, you would be as if you were in a secluded room in the eternal night, being blind and deaf. Thereafter, you cannot act properly. If you don't know the ritual, you will fail to distinguish civilisation from barbarism, as if living with animals. In this case, what's the point of living?[79]

The reason why Confucianism attaches so much importance to the rule of etiquette is that etiquette is the realisation of the idealistic moral and ethical order. 'Moral benevolence and righteousness cannot be realised without rituals.'[80] Virtue is the incorporeal ritual, and ritual is the corporeal virtue, which makes moral ethics externalise rules. Thereafter rituals, symbols and behaviours, can become the key factors in the rule of law. The form of the rule of etiquette has changed from time to time and is ever-changing, but its inner spirit is the basic ethics that Confucianism advocates: one needs to respect their kins and elders, and know the distinction between men and women, which cannot be changed.[81] Ritual mediates between private desires and collective principles. Humanitarian sense is bound with ritual, and ritual can be changed according to customs. Meanwhile ritual could also protect the good from evil, and revise customs, providing guidelines for human nature. Ritual supports the three ways of the universe, namely those of heaven, earth and people, to rectify the country and the world. In this sense, ritual has become the guideline for maintaining the order of equality advocated by Confucianism. It can help the people distinguish between high and low, superiors and inferiors, the closed and alienated ones, the suspicious and the problematic, the similarities and differences, the right and wrong.[82]

One should govern the country with rituals rather than strength. That is why the Zhou royal family could still maintain the royal line for hundreds of years, despite that the authority of the king was weakened. Society can operate on its own with the order of ritual and music, in this case, the monarch can be at ease. To make rituals and music is to establish national order, to maintain the rule of rituals is to maintain national order, and the collapse of rituals and music is the collapse of national order. Therefore, there is no trivial matter in the rule of etiquette. When the Ji family (季,a petit branch of the Duke of Lu, by extension the minor branch of the King of Zhou) violated the etiquette system by having 'the royal exclusive six-four-person-dance in the courtyard', Confucius said: 'if it is bearable, what else can be unbearable?'[83] When Zhongshu Yuxi had meritorious deeds to the state of Wei, he refused to accept the rewarded city, instead asked for a ostentatiously decorated horse to come to court, and the Lord of Wei agreed. When Confucius heard this, he said: 'It is better to give more towns, because the ritual tools and the titles are more important and should not be offered to the inferior ranked.'[84] The traditional imperial power does not extend beneath the county, and the governmental order does not apply to the countryside, the local order relies on the system of etiquette. Fei Xiaotong called the rural society at the grassroot-level a 'rule of rites' society, which had an autonomous order even though there was a hierarchy among the people.[85] The rule of etiquette is a kind of governance method that manage things silently, and it is also a governance method with relatively low cost.

The rule of etiquette does not mean that the rule of law is not necessary, and neither two should be neglected. Etiquette and law are not two things, they are both the essential rules of governance. Etiquette is a soft criterion, law is a hard regulation. In a sense, propriety is a customary law, while law is a written ceremony; they must work together. The rule of law is also about preventing selfishness and extending the public justice, restraining the selfish desires of people's hearts. 'Law is for asserting the standard and to correct the wrong.'[86] The legalists believed that the law is the tool for achieving the greater justice, and private feelings should not meddle in the law. Shang Yang (商鞅) promoted the rule of law in Qin state, and the important starting point was precisely to change the unfairness of the rule of man. 'If the heir to the throne broke the law, he will be punished as a commoner.' When the crown prince broke the law, Shang Yang severely punished the teacher of the prince. China is a country with a long tradition of rule of law. At the time of Shun, there were 'five punishments'(墨、劓、刖、宮、大辟). In the Xia and Shang dynasties, China had law dictating punishment. The *Commentary of Zuo* records that 'When the king of the Xia ruled the world, the five punishments extended to three thousand clauses, and the Shang and Zhou dynasties revised them while still maintaining key principles.'[87] Under the Qin's rule 'laws and decrees were made clear', which had initially formed a legal system. By the time of the Sui and Tang dynasties, China already had a complete system of written law, which was very advanced at that time. In the seventh century, Japan sent students to China to study the legal system. Under the direct influence of the 'Chinese legal system', the Taihō Code (大宝律令) was promulgated, which led Japan into the era of the legal system (律令制Ritsuryōsei).

A very characteristic feature in the Chinese tradition of rule of law is the educational function of punishment. In the legal system of the Tang Dynasty, 'is based on the ritual', as punishment is not only revenge, but also the continuation of the function of ritual education. That is to say, education precedes punishment. 'It is abusive, if one is killed without having the chance to be educated.'[88] 'If the ruler does not educate the people, then the people should not be responsible for breaking the law. If in that case, the people are judged and punished, the ruler should be condemned as low as the scoundrel.'[89] 'The ruler must be patient to guide the people, teaching them the right way, and correcting their bad behaviours.'[90] Punishments are employed only when education did not work. 'The punishments are designed for vanquishing the necessity of having punishment.'[91] Punishment is expected to have the function of learning from past and having a better future. It is clear that education is prior to punishment, and the five kinds of punishment assist the five kinds of education. The establishment of the criminal law needs to be in line with humanitarian concerns. 'Punishment and ritual are not two separate things, both of which make people get closer to good and get rid of evil.'[92] The role of indoctrination is reflected in the fact that in addition to the law and facts, the judgment must also consider 'the love between father and son, the righteousness between monarch and ministers'. Punishment should be prudent and merciful. 'When measuring the scale of punishment, the judge must show mercy. If it can be punished lightly, then the judge should give the less severe verdict.' Procedurally, the king grants leniency according to three situations. 'The execution must be in the downtown area, so that everyone can cast aside him. In ancient times, princes did not accommodate criminals, and doctors did not support criminals. When a scholar meets a criminal on the road, he shouldn't talk to him.'[93] It can be said that the punishment system in ancient China was not only about legal judgment, but also concerned with moral education.

6. Regarding the central area as the foundation for taking care of the world

The fifth principle for 'The World is Equally Shared by All' is 'Regarding the central area as the foundation for taking care of the world'. The order of the world is a civilised one, that includes the people living in the marginal areas. The heaven/sky is selfless, and within the four seas, all people of the world would be cared for by the Son of Heaven.[94] According to Confucianism, there are nine methods of governing the world, and taking care of the people living far away from the central areas is the second important one, because 'by taking care of the people far away, the marginal areas will follow the order of the Son of Heaven.' If the governance is great, 'its fame can be heard all over the world'; 'the one who is lively and cares about the people, is worthy of the grace of god.'[95]

Although the order of the world is different between the Central (中国) and the marginal (四方) areas, namely the distinction between Chinese and Aliens (华夷之辩), it is different from the solidified central-periphery hierarchical order, but it is an equivalent order that is accessible and circulated. The meaning of China and its civilisation changed from 'settling in the central land' to 'if the people follow the Chinese moral codes, then they are Chinese, regardless of their origins'. Therefore, China the Central Land is not only a geographical term but a system of civilisational code; 'if people in China abandoned the civil codes, then they succumb to barbarism'.[96] 'If the Chinese feudal states stray to the barbarian ways, then they are no longer regarded as Chinese.'[97] Historically, when the Mongolians and Manchus came to dominate the Central Plains (中原), they both regarded themselves as masters of the world and adopted the Chinese civilisation system and governance methods. The Mongolian dynasty is called the Yuan dynasty (元朝), and the name is derived from *Book of Changes*: 'Qian (乾) and Yuan (元) trigrams are the greatest'. Before the Qing dynasty entered the Shanhai Gate for claiming the central land, the Manchu people hoped that 'the destiny is at their hands, therefore they will conquer world'.[98]

The China–World order is distinguished according to geographic distance, and cultural exchange, but it is also unified. These domestic and international conditions would change based on the priority of governance. In the chaotic times (乱世), China must take care of itself first;

while if China is moving towards peace (升世), then it is happy to help the rest of the world. If China is under great governance (太平世), then it would treat the world equally with all kinds of benefits.[99] Looking at the facts, in the world, of course, people have selfish tendencies, and there are all kinds of people, with differences and boundaries. Fundamentally, after all, the world is shared by all and public justice can be achieved. Even though, in forms of different families and nations, good governance is far from about governing one body, one family, and one country, but organising the world 'no matter how far and near, small and big a place is.' The method could be eclectic: regarding the central area as the foundation for taking care of the world. That is to say, to harmonise the world by concentrating on formulating a good model for all.

The way to pacify the world is to use virtue rather than strength. Although China is armed, it does not rely on establishing a domineering order by force. In the Chinese ideal, humanistic order is 'keeping an army, while trying not to start a war; having weapons, while trying to hide them away.' This is what *Spring and Autumn Annals* said 'the humane ruler is invincible, as he talks about virtue and the rest of the world is convinced to follow.'[100] 'If people from afar are dissatisfied, then try to cultivate them with virtues, so that they are convinced to come (to the central land). Since they have come, they will be at peace (with the people in the central land).'[101] By offering favours, courtesies, and kinship, so that China does not have to use force to maintain the world peace and the marginal people will be happy to come and defend China beyond borders. 'If the Son of Heaven is virtuous, the marginal people will guard the central land; if the feudal lords are virtuous, their neighbours will also defend them.'[102] Among them, what is similar to the feudal meaning of 'being intimate to the vassals' is the 'marriage alliance' foreign policy (和亲), which has been implemented in all dynasties. In the sixteenth year of Zhenguan (642 AD), the Xueyantuo turkic tribe (薛延陀) in the north was prosperous and disobedient, Emperor Taizong (唐太宗) considered making the tribe submit to him by means of marriage. 'The customs of Northern tribes are mostly determined by internal affairs, and if they had children, namely my grandsons, then they will not invade China, so we can definitely keep peace.'[103] The most successful implementation of imperial marriage in the past dynasties is the one between the Qing dynasty rulers and Mongolian tribes. Not only did Mongolia become the Great Wall in the northern part of the Qing dynasty, but also the Manchus and Mongolians were culturally merged under the same set of rules, and finally most of the Mongolians were integrated into China.

China has always insisted on the policy 'no territorial expansion and no invasion to the rest of the world'. In dealing with foreign regimes, China has always employed friendly supporting policies, 'keeping the heritage lines for the fallen regimes'. It seeks to harmonise all nations in order to help them realise autonomy. Only in rare cases, did the central land engulf these places, as the last resort. China had many opportunities to expand its territory in history, but hadn't done so. It is a rare strong and peaceful civilisation in the world. In the fifth year of Zhenguan (631 AD), Kangju (康居), a foreign state in central Asia requested to merge to the Tang dynasty, but Emperor Taizong refused their request, thinking that China cannot 'seek a false glory and harm the people'; military force must be used as a last resort, as the one who abused such a force, would always end up destroying himself.[104] Conquering the poor border lands and deserts, with toiling expeditions, is useless for China, because it would only consume huge human and material resources. As poet Du Fu puts it: 'There are two hundred states in East China, while wars will make thousands of villages wastelands.'[105]

If you are wary you will die, if you forget how to fight you will be in danger. No intension of expansion, does not necessarily mean no military preparation. China has faced severe northern border threats in all dynasties, and strong national defence is the premise of defending the country. 'Those who guard the land are not in danger, and those who prepare to have wars, will not be sieged.'[106] Armament is the main task of the king to govern a country. If you are good at military manoeuvre, you can stop the war. If you know the art of war, you can maintain the order of virtue. In history, the eras of weak military virtues were the weak dynasties in which the people were displaced. 'Ritual, musical and military rules should all come from the Son of Heaven.' To conquer the treacherous, defending the justice of the world, is also regarded as Great Justice. Shun found some tribes guilty and had to punish them to protect the bullied. Military means has never thought to be a good omen, therefore it has to be used as a last resort. In Chinese the character 'military' (武) literally means 'stop the spears' (止戈). That is to say military means is for restoring order, and it is impossible to harmonise and protect all nations without the option of using force.

'China is the root, and overseas are the leaves.' Although the foreigners are not Chinese citizens, they are also people of the world. Compared with the Chinese people, they are regarded by the Son of Heaven as the leaves to the root. It is necessary to be concerned with the world, but not to undermine the roots because of the leaves. During the Zhenguan period, the Turkish tribes were in civil strife and nearly 100,000 surrendered to China. Emperor Taizong can be said to have used the power of the whole China to implement the strategy of softening the conflicts caused by foreign customs. Not only did he set aside a large area to resettle the Turks, but also, the tribal leaders who came to surrender were appointed as military officials. There were more than 100 tribal leaders above the fifth rank, almost accounting for half of the officials in the imperial court. This was not only a waste of national strength, but later became a hardcore issue undermining the foundation of the Tang dynasty. Emperor Taizong later lamented that: 'The Chinese people are the root of the empire, and the foreign people are the leaves. Disturbing the roots, while growing leaves, this kind of method of seeking long-term peace, can never to achieved.'[107]

7. 'The World is Equally Shared by All' and contemporary good governance

To summarise, China's long civilization has nurtured a variety of ideas and practices of good governance. Those who talk about good governance do not have to always use the West as examples, but can cite inexhaustible source from Chinese tradition.

Good governance in China can be summed up as the governance of 'The World is Equally Shared by All'. The principles are: 'The world is the master, the ruler is the guest'; 'Integrate feudalism in the system of prefectures and counties'; 'Selecting and appointing the talented'; 'Morality is the mainstay, while punishment is auxiliary; Ruling with rituals and laws combined', and 'Regarding the central area as the foundation for taking care of the world'. Good governance in contemporary China is rooted in Chinese tradition and combined with modern governance methods to form a modern version of governance.

First, uniting the people's subjectivity and insisting on the Party leadership. The people are the heaven and form the society of the country, and the subjectivity of the people needs to be realised through the leadership of the Party. The Chinese Communist Party played the role of the 'modern prince', as Antonio Gramsci proposed in discussing party organic positioning in modern politcs. The Party is required to integrate fragmented viewpoints and interests, so that the overall interests of the people could be realised. The legitimacy of the Chinese Communist Party's governance lies in the relationship between the Party and the people. The Party itself belongs to the people and is a tool for the people to realise their own interests. The Party members, principles and policies all come from the people and in return they serve the people. What transcends traditional people-based governance is that it not only puts the people first, but also builds a people-centred political and economic order to ensure the realisation of the people's subjectivity from the economic, political, social and cultural levels.

Second, combining the political centralisation and administrative decentralisation. As a unitary country under the leadership of the Communist Party of China, the central government has the unquestionable political authority. At the same time, China is a country with administrative decentralisation. In recent years, the proportion of local fiscal expenditures has reached more than 85%. The central government conducts macro-guidance through objectives, standards and policies, and 'contracts' specific tasks to the sub-levels of government, then the local governments can flexibly implement them according to the actual situation. This allows the country to maintain its diverse flexibility while maintaining its strong national capabilities.

Third, the system of selecting and appointing the talented is different from the Western competitive election system. China has a competitive selection system, which can more effectively select people with experience and ability. And it is also different from the traditional political meritocracy, which was only controlled by a group of civil servants, and the highest power was hereditary. Contemporary meritocracy in China is a process of competitive selection from the bottom to the top, which largely avoids the 'bad emperor' problem in traditional politics. This is also an important reason why contemporary politics can break the dynastic vicious circle in the imperial period. The contemporary selection and appointment system, covering all levels of civil servants, the scope of which is much wider than the traditional imperial examination, which does not predominantly rely on the form of examinations. The examination only solves the problem of basic qualifications for entry. While the current system primarily values the actual performance, which is more reasonable than the traditional way.

Fourth, ruling the country by law and virtue. There is no doubt that governing the country according to law is one of the basic principles of contemporary Chinese governance, but 'law alone is not sufficient', and good governance in contemporary China also needs to emphasise morality, harmonising the society with both etiquette and law. Compared with the traditional good governance, the rule of etiquette has become a shortcoming. To implement the rule of virtue, it is necessary to embody morality and etiquette, and actively build a modern system of etiquette and rule of law that takes socialist core values as the connotation and adapts to the living environment of modern society.

Fifth, regarding China as the foundation, then taking responsibly of keeping the world peace. Good governance in contemporary China should also consider the good governance in the world, and China should actively participate in global governance. As pointed out by President Xi Jinping, the Communist Party of China not only seeks the well-being of the Chinese people, but also seeks great harmony for the world. Those who cherish the greatness of the country, would actively promote the construction of a 'community with a shared future for mankind'. At the same time, 'China is the root, and overseas are the leaves', and we must know what is the priority. Foreign aid and international responsibilities must be based on the premise of not exceeding the country's development stage and national strength. We must adhere to peaceful development, promote inclusive development, and refrain from military expansion. At the same time, we must strengthen national defence and actively respond to various international struggles. We endeavour to promote a people-centred security concept that emphasises universal security, a concept of cultural exchange and mutual learning; then to form extensive partnerships, and new communal world order that develops political-economic communities based on geopolitics.

---

1 Yu Keping, 1999, 'On Governance and Good Governance', *Marxism and Reality*, Vol. 5. Yu Keping, 'On Global Governance', *Marxism and Reality*, 2002, Vol. 1. [俞可平：《治理和善治引论》，《马克思主义与现实》1999年第5期。俞可平：《全球治理引论》，《马克思主义与现实》2002年第1期。]
2 World Bank, 1992, 'Governance and Development', Washington, D. C.: World Bank.
3 <http://info.worldbank.org/governance/wgi>, [4 May 2021].
4 Li Daoyuan, *Commentary on the Water Classic*, Northern Wei Dynasty (386–534 AD) [郦道元《水经注》]

5 Xu Shen, Discussing writing and explaining characters, Han Dynasty, 100 BC [《说文解字》]
6 *Han Feizi: Five Poisonous beings* [韩非子·五蠹]
7 Kang Youwei asserted that the sovereignty belongs to the state, see Zhang Yongle, 2014, 'Sovereignty belongs to the state: the reconstruction of a theoretical theme', *Historicism of Modern Chinese Ideas*, Vol. 2, Shanghai People's Press. [章永乐：《清末民初的"主权在国论"：一理论命题的重构》，《现代中国思想史》（下册）,上海人民出版社2014年]
8 Jiang Qing, 2016, 'The legitimisation of Confucianism is "sovereignty belongs to heaven" instead of "sovereignty belongs to the people"', *Confucians Post*, Vol. 268, 4th Nov. [蒋庆：《儒学的最高合法性是"主权在天"而非"主权在民"：——"政治儒学"对自由主义学理的回应之二：以白彤东教授为例》，《儒家邮报》第 268 期，2016 年 11 月 4 日]
9 Book of Documents: Great Plan
10 Book of Rites: The Conveyance of Rites
11 Huang Zongxi, *Waiting for the Dawn*, Ming dynasty, early 17th century [黄宗羲：《明夷待访录·原君》]
12 Liu Zongyuan, *On Feudal System*, Tang dynasty, early 9th century [柳宗元：《封建论》]
13 *The Book of Lord Shang*, 3rd century BC [《商君书·开塞》]
14 Book of Rites: The Conveyance of Rites
15 Dong Zhongshu, *Luxuriant Dew of the Spring and Autumn Annals*, Han dynasty, 2nd century BC. [董仲舒：《春秋繁露》]
16 Gu Yanwu, *Daily Study Book*, Ming dynasty, 17th century [顾炎武：《日知录·正始》，《日知录校注》，安徽大学出版社 2007 年版，第 722—723 页]
17 *Master Lü's Spring and Autumn Annals* [《吕氏春秋·贵公》]
18 Book of Rites: Confucius at Home at Ease
19 Zhu Xi referred to the three points proposed by *Great Learning* as 'Understanding and Promoting Virtue', 'Closeness to the People' and 'Stopping on Perfection' as 'the guidelines of Great Learning'. He also regard eight points: 'checking things', 'getting knowledge', 'sincerity', 'righteousness', 'cultivating one's body', 'aligning the family', 'governing the country' and 'pacifying the world' as the 'the objectives of Great Learning'. Later generations called those points as 'the three guidelines and eight objectives'. [朱熹将《大学》提出的"明明德""亲民""止于至善"三者称为"大学之纲领",把"格物""致知""诚意""正心""修身""齐家""治国""平天下"八项称为"大学之条目",后人称之为"三纲领八条目",简称"三纲八目"]
20 Book of Documents: Announcement of Zhonghui [《尚书·仲虺之诰》]
21 *Master Lü's Spring and Autumn Annals* [《吕氏春秋·谨听》]
22 *Mozi* [《墨子·尚同》]
23 Book of Documents: Charge to Cai Zhong [《尚书·蔡仲之命》]
24 Book of Documents: Chief of the West [King Wen]'s Conquest of [the State of] Li [《尚书·西伯戡黎》]
25 Book of Documents: Great Speeches [《尚书·泰誓》]
26 Book of Documents: Counsels of Gao Yao [《尚书·皋陶谟》]
27 Book of Documents: Numerous regions [《尚书·多方》]
28 Book of Documents: Great Announcement [《尚书·大诰》]
29 Book of Documents: Great Plan [《尚书·洪范》]
30 Book of Documents: Announcement to Prince Kang [《尚书·康诰》]
31 Book of Documents: Speech of King Tang [《尚书·汤誓》]
32 *The Annotation of Book of Changes* [《易传》]
33 Book of Documents: Songs of the Five Sons [《尚书·五子之歌》]
34 Ibid.
35 *Tsinghua Bamboo Slips: The Way of Governance* [《清华简·治政之道》。转引自陈民镇：《清华简<治政之道><治邦之道>思想性质初探》，《清华大学学报》2020年第1期]
36 Huang Zongxi, *Waiting for the Dawn*

37　*Records of the Grand Historian; Book of Documents* [《史记·五帝本纪》，《尚书·尧典》]
38　*Gu Yanwu: On Feudalism* [顾炎武：《郡县论》]
39　*Xunzi* [《荀子·儒效》]
40　*The Commentary of Zuo* [《左传·桓公二年》]
41　*The Commentary of Zuo* [《左传·僖公二十四年》]
42　*Records of the Grand Historian* [《史记·周本纪》]
43　Liu Zongyuan, *On Feudal System*, Tang dynasty, early 9th century [柳宗元：《封建论》]
44　*Records of the Grand Historian* [《史记·李斯列传》]
45　*Emperor Yongzheng's decree* [（清）爱新觉罗·允禄(爱新觉罗·胤禄)编(官修)，《世宗宪皇帝上谕内》(卷八十二)]
46　*Gu Yanwu: On Prefecture System* [顾炎武：《郡县论》]
47　Huang Zongxi, *Waiting for the Dawn*, Ming dynasty, early 17th century [黄宗羲：《明夷待访录·方镇》]
48　*Tsinghua Bamboo Slips: The Way of Governance* [《清华简·治政之道》。转引自陈民镇：《清华简<治政之道><治邦之道>思想性质初探》，《清华大学学报》2020年第1期。]
49　*Mozi* [《墨子·尚贤》]
50　*Mozi cites Book of Documents: Speech of King Tang* [《墨子·尚贤》所引《汤誓》]
51　*Book of Documents: Counsels of Gao Yao*
52　*Tsinghua Bamboo Slips: The Way of Governance* [《清华简·治政之道》转引自李守奎:《清华简﹤治政之道﹥的治政理念与文本的几个问题》，《文物》2013 年第 9 期。]
53　Huang Zongxi, *Waiting for the Dawn*, Ming dynasty, early 17th century [黄宗羲：《明夷待访录·原君》]
54　*Mozi* [《墨子·尚贤》]
55　*Tsinghua Bamboo Slips: The Way of Governing the Country* [《清华简·治邦之道》]
56　*Xunzi* [《荀子·王制》]
57　*Mozi* [《墨子·尚贤》]
58　*Rites of Zhou: Offices of Earth* [《周礼·地官·乡大夫》]
59　*Book of Rites: Royal Regulations* [《礼记·王制》]
60　Yu Zhengxie, *A Scholar's Notes* [（清）俞正燮：《癸巳类稿·乡兴贤能论》]
61　Lü Simian, 2011, *A History of China*, Phoenix Press, pp. 109-125. [吕思勉：《中国通史·选举》，凤凰出版社2011年版，第109-125页]
62　Xue Deshu and Xu Jie, 2016, 'The significance of the recommendation system in the Han dyansty', *China Post University Journal*, No. 3. [薛德枢、 徐杰：《汉代察举征辟制度评析及其借鉴意义》，《中国石油大学胜利学院学报》2016年第3期]
63　Luo Tianye and Zhao Meng, 2014, 'Studies of civil servants selecting system', Examination Studies, Vol. 45, No. 4. [罗田野、 赵萌：《汉代选官征辟制度考述》，《考试研究》 2014 年第 4 期(总第 45 期)]
64　*Baopuzi*, 3rd century AD [《抱朴子外篇·审举》]
65　*Book of Jin* [《晋书·刘毅传》]
66　Yu Caofan, 2016, 'General summary of the imperial examination system in the Song dynasty', *Studies of Laws*, No. 5; Zhang Xiqing, 1987, 'On redundant officials caused by the imperial examination system', *Peking University Newspaper*, No. 5. [于凡超：《宋代科举制度研究综述》，《法学研究》 2016 年第 5 期；张希清：《论宋代科举取士之多与冗官问题》，《北京大学学报》（哲学社会科学版)1987 年第 5 期]
67　Ouyang Xiu, *New Book of Tang*, 1060 [欧阳修：《新唐书·选举四》]
68　Wang Anshi, *Petition to Emperor Renzong*, 11th century [王安石：《上仁宗皇帝言事书》]
69　Huang Zongxi, *Waiting for the Dawn*, Ming dynasty, early 17th century [黄宗羲：《明夷待访录·取士下》]

70 Huang Zongxi, *Waiting for the Dawn*, Ming dynasty, early 17th century [黄宗羲：《明夷待访录·取士下》]
71 Gu Yanwu, *On Feudalism* [顾炎武：《封建论》]
72 *Book of Documents: Announcement to Prince Kang* [《尚书·康诰》]
73 *Analects of Confucius* [《论语·为政》]
74 *Guanzi* [《管子·牧民·四维》]
75 *Book of Rites: Great Learning* [《礼记·大学》]
76 *Book of Rites: Record on the Subject of Music* [《礼记·乐记》]
77 *Book of Rites: Different Teaching of the Different Kings* [《礼记·经解》]
78 Xu Shen, *Discussing writing and explaining characters*, Han Dynasty, 100 BC [《说文解字》]
79 *Book of Rites* [《礼记·礼运》，《礼记·仲尼燕居》]
80 *Book of Rites* [《礼记》]
81 *Book of Rites: Great Treatise* [《礼记·大传》]
82 *Book of Rites: Summary of the Rules of Propriety* [《礼记·曲礼》]
83 *Analects of Confucius* [《论语·八佾》]
84 *The Commentary of Zuo* [《左传·成公·成公二年》]
85 Fei Xiaotong, 1998, *The rural area in China*, Peking University Press, p. 9 [费孝通：《乡土中国》，北京大学出版社1998年版，第9页]
86 *Four Canons of the Yellow Emperor* [《黄帝四经·经法·道法》]
87 *The Commentary of Zuo* [《左传·昭公七年》]
88 *Analects of Confucius* [《论语·尧曰》]
89 *Tsinghua Bamboo Slips: The Way of Governance* [《清华简·治政之道》 转引自李守奎：《清华简＜治政之道＞的治政理念与文本的几个问题》，《文物》2019年第9期]
90 *Family Sayings of Confucius; Book of Rites* [《孔子家语·刑政第三十一》，《礼记·王制》]
91 *Book of Documents: Counsels of Great Yu* [《尚书·大禹谟》]
92 Lü Kun, *Groaning Words*, 16th century [吕坤：《呻吟语》]
93 *Family Sayings of Confucius; Book of Rites* [《孔子家语·刑政第三十一》，《礼记·王制》]
94 *Classic of Poetry: Sacrificial Odes of Shang* [《诗经·商颂·玄鸟》]
95 *Doctrine of the Mean* [《中庸》]
96 Liang Qichao: *On Chinese Concept in Spring and Autumn Period* [梁启超：《春秋中国华夷辨》序]
97 Han Yu, *How to be a Lord* [韩愈：《原君》]
98 Zhao Tingyang, 2003, 'The Chinese concept: The Empire and the World', *World Philosophy*, No. 5. [赵汀阳：《"天下体系"：帝国与世界制度》，《世界哲学》2003年第5期]
99 He Xiu and Xu Yan, 2014, *Commentary on Gongyang Zhuan* [何休、徐彦：《春秋公羊传注疏》(上)，上海古籍出版社2014年出版，第38页。据乱世、升世、太平世的"三世说"经康有为、梁启超等人发挥]
100 *Discourses on Salt and Iron*, 81 BC [《盐铁论·世务第四十七》]
101 *Analects of Confucius* [《论语·季氏》]
102 Jia Yi, *New Books*, 2nd century BC; *Huainanzi*, 139 BC [贾谊：《新书·春秋》，《淮南子·泰族训》]
103 *Policy Hightlights in Zhenguan Period*, 7th century AD [《贞观政要·议征伐第三十五》
104 Ibid.
105 Du Fu, *The Army Wagons: A Ballad* [杜甫：《兵车行》]
106 *Wei Liaozi* [《尉缭子·战威》]
107 *Policy Hightlights in Zhenguan Period*, 7th century AD [《贞观政要·议征伐第三十六》]

CHAPTER 10

The Leadership of the Communist Party of China and the Chinese Version of Good Governance

(*This article is based on the speech delivered to the conference 'National Developmen and Modernisation of Governing' in China Studies Department, Tsing Hua University on 21st Sept, 2019, and subsequently published on Administration Reform, No.1, 2020)

The leadership of the Communist Party of China (CPC) is the most essential feature of socialism with Chinese characteristics. The national governance system and governance capacity are the concentrated expression of the socialist system with Chinese characteristics and its ability to implement it. The modernisation of the national governance system and governance capacity refers not only to the modernisation of government, but also to the modernisation of governing the market and society.

1. The diamond model of the Chinese version of good governance

As discussed in the previous chapter, the disenchantment of the Western dogma of governance and good governance, allows us to return to our roots, the actual social conditions in China. Only under this condition, can we look at China's own governance system and good governance model more realistically. Many scholars have pointed out that China's governance system is different from that of the West. For example, Justin Yifu Lin (林毅夫) believes that in addition to an efficient market, China also has a well-functioning government (有为政府).[1] Li Ling and Jiang Yu further proposed that in addition to a well-functioning government and an efficient market, an organic society is also needed.[2]

However, without the crucial key, the CPC, the door to understanding the 'Governance of China' will not truly be opened. Whether it is the 'government-market' dichotomy or the 'government-market-society' trichotomy, the key variable of the CPC needs to be added.[3] Some scholars have proposed the 'party-government-society' trichotomy,[4] while others believe that market governance can be separated from social governance to form the 'party-government-society-market' quadrant.[5] In his speech at the 2018 National Situation Forum, Professor Li Junru said that our national governance system is dominated by the ruling party the CPC, with political institutions (including the People's Congress and the government), the market (including state-owned enterprises and private enterprises), and the society (including social organisations).[6] Here he clearly puts forward the four-element theory of the Chinese governance system.

On the basis of previous research, this book proposes a diamond model, for the Chinese version of good governance. The foundation of good governance lies in realising the subjectivity of the people (人民主体) to the greatest extent, fully ensuring that the people are the masters of the country, and giving full power to the enthusiasm, initiative and creativity of the people. The four elements of the avant-garde party, the well-functioning government, the public market and the organic society jointly ensure the realisation of the people's subjectivity. The leadership of an avant-garde party (先锋政党) is the key and fundamental advantage of China's good governance. It determines that China has a well-functioning government (有为政府) rather than a limited government, a market economy for mutual benefit (共益市场) rather than a free market economy, and an organic society (有机社会) rather than a 'civil society'. (Fig. 1)

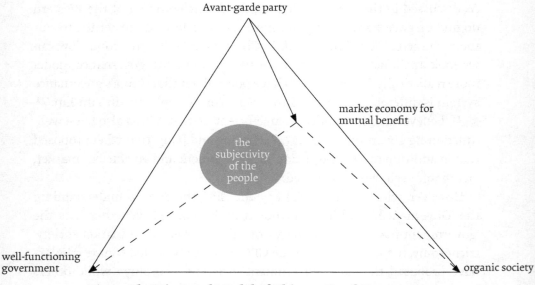

Fig. 1: The Diamond Model of Chinese Good Governance

2. The Avant-Garde Party

To understand the Chinese version of good governance, we must first understand the nature of the CPC, avoid cognitive bias, and we cannot apply the Western electoral party thinking to view the CPC and China's party system. New thinking is required in the typology of political parties and party systems. Comparing the two-party system in the United States with the CPC, one finds that: The two parties in the United States are the so-called 'Three-No' parties: there are no loyal party members, only party affiliation, no party platform, only election platform, no strict organisation, only loose coordination.[7] The Communist Party of China is a political party with 'three heights': highly loyal party members, high sense of political program, highly strict organisational discipline (Table 1). Why do these political parties take such different shapes?

It is because that the two are fundamentally different in nature. The two parties in the United States are electoral parties, while the CPC is an organisational party. The party system in the United States is designed around elections, and the Founding Fathers of the United States hated party politics. George Washington, in his *Farewell Address*, repeatedly warned against party politics, which 'serves always to distract the public councils and enfeeble the public administration. It agitates the community with ill-founded jealousies and false alarms, kindles the animosity of one party against another, occasionally foments riot and insurrection.'[8] Thomas Jefferson once said that if one has to be in a political party to go to heaven, he would rather not go there.[9] The United States later chose party politics because the operation of electoral politics requires parties to organise elections, mobilise voters, and coordinate political operations.

Different from the electoral political parties in the United States, the CPC has played the role of an organisational political party since its inception. The modern China is a scattered China, how can one organise the people to jointly deal with the internal and external crises faced by the Chinese nation? The CPC came into being, with a mission being the organiser of the people. Because of the leadership of the CPC, the Chinese people have been shaped into a solid collective form, from piles of loose sand. With collective will, objectives, and actions, the people have mastered the power to change their own destiny, "from passive to active in spirit",[10] and become an invincible organism.

Table 1 Communist Party of China in comparison with the two-party system in the United States

	CPC	Two Parties in the US
Nature	Organisational	Electoral
Definition	A political party that realises the national strategic mission by leading, organising and and mobilising party members and the people	A party that wins elections by mobilising voters for their own party's candidates
Function	Making decisions, integration, organisation and ideology	Organising elections, uniting voters, coordinating political operations and policy expression
Relationship with the Nation	Integrated in the Nation (State-Party)	Independent from the Nation, but participating in state governance
Representative	The interests of all the people, the main representative mechanism is democratic centralism	The interests of some groups, the main representative mechanism is election
Party Programmes	Mission-based programme	Election platform
Party Members	Highly loyal and disciplined	Party Affiliation
Organisation	Strict organisational system	Loose union
Party System	Collaborative party system (Chinese Communist Party + democratic parties)	Competitive party system (two-party system)

The CPC is an organisational party that realises the national strategic mission by leading, organising and mobilising party members and the people. The reason why the CPC can play an organisational force lies in the dual attributes of it as a super-powerful state agency and a super-political organisation.[11] (Table 2)

Table 2 The Dual Attributes of the CPC

Nature	Characteristics	Main Organisational Form	Authority Type	Institutional Characteristics
National leaders and organisers	Hardcore State Power Organs (Super Power State Institutions)	Party committees and groups at all levels	Official	The national political system with seven divisions of powers
Social leaders and organisers	Avant-Garde Organisation (Super Political Organisation)	The party's grass-roots organisation system	Non-Official	Network-based social governance system

On the one hand, the CPC committees at all levels, as super-powerful state institutions, are embedded in the state and become the organisers and leaders of state power. The Party committees at all levels, as the hardcore organs of state power, exercise public power and are constrained by written and unwritten constitutional structures.[12] In this sense, the party's power is inherent in the state, and it is the 'nation-party' (国党) rather than the 'party-state' (党国).[13] At the level of state power, it has established top-down organisational channels, with party organisations set up from the provincial level all the way down to the village level (table 3).

Table 3 The coverage of party organisations at all levels of political power in China (2017)

	Administrative	Party organisation	Coverage (%)
Provincial	31	31	100.00
Municipal	334	397	118.9
Minor-Municipal	2,851	2,780	97.5
District	8,243	8,439	102.4
Township	31,647	31,726	100.2
Community	10,600	100,602	94.9
Village	554,000	547,152	98.8

Source of data: *2017 CPC Intra-Party Statistical Bulletin* by Organisation Department of the Central Committee of the Communist Party of China.
2017 Social Service Development Statistical Bulletin by National Civil Affairs Bureau
2018 China Statistical Summary, by National Bureau of Statistics

On the other hand, the Communist Party of China, as a super political organisation, is embedded in the society and becomes its organiser and leader. The Party is both internal and external to the state, and it exists widely in society, and grass-roots party organisations have been established in different forms.

The avant-garde nature of the CPC is the premise of realising its organisational function. The CPC is not an elite party or an electoral party but an avant-garde party. The basis of the party's authority lies in the credibility of the party organisation, its avant-garde nature and exemplary role of party members. The CPC is the only one that can always be a pioneer and advanced organism in the tide of human historical progress. Only then can it realistically undertake the mission of representing, leading and organising the people. The avant-garde nature of the party is not a given attribute, but a characteristic that needs to be obtained through continuous struggle in the specific historical process. In the face of real and endless severe tests, the Party needs to maintain its own avant-garde nature through continuous 'self-revolution' and party building, so as to become the hardcore force for promoting the modernisation of national governance. 'The enemy exists and destroys, while the calamity could keep everyone alert.' The CPC is the centre of power in the entire economy and society. If it lacks competitors and does not promote self-revolution, the nature of the regime can easily change. The CPC is the largest political party in the world, with more than 91 million members, accounting for 6.4% of the country's total population, but a large number of people does not mean it is truly powerful. In fact, in 1988, on the eve of the disintegration of the Soviet Union and the drastic changes in Eastern Europe, the proportion of Communist Party members in the Soviet Union reached 6.8%, while the proportion of Communist Party members in Romania was as high as 16.1%.[14] To maintain the party's long-term governance, it is fundamentally necessary for the party to maintain its avant-garde nature and vitality through continuous self-revolution. The Fourth Plenary Session of the Nineteenth Central Committee of the CPC proposed to establish a system arrangement that does not forget the original intention and keeps the mission in mind. The CPC has always attached great importance to organising the party and kept a strict management. Since the eighteenth National Congress of the CPC, it has carried out rapid self-revolution, turning the blade inward, scraping the bones to cure poison, and carrying out self-improvement. The reason why the CPC has always been at the forefront and has become the backbone of the Chinese people and nation is that: 'fundamentally our party has always maintained the spirit of self-revolution, maintained the courage to admit and correct its mistakes, and took up the scalpel again and again to get rid of illness. It has solved its own problems time and time again. This ability is not only a distinguishing mark of our party from other political parties in the world, but also an important reason for our party's longevity.'[15]

3. Party leadership and the well-functioning government

Many scholars have pointed out that the Chinese government is not a limited government, but a well-functioning or facilitating state.[16] The characteristics of China's well-functioning government are mainly manifested in that it can show higher efficiency in national governance, and can use the 'visible hand' to promote development, social equity, environmental optimisation and so forth. As Wang Shaoguang said, the leadership of the party solves the problem of national governance capacity,[17] and the fundamental reason why the Chinese government can become a well-functioning government lies in the leadership of the Party.

A. The leadership of the Party has made the division of labour in China's political power system undivided and it has become an organic whole. The fundamental reason why China's political system is a division of labour system rather than a separation of powers system is due to the integration of the leadership of the Party Central Committee, which makes the operating principles of China's political system fundamentally different from that of the United States. The core principle of the operation of the U.S. political system is the separation of powers and system of checks and balances. In China, the principle is about the division of labour and cooperation, the operation of a democratic centralised system is more efficient.

The national leaders of the U.S. are mainly elected through competitive *elections*, empowering politicians who are good at 'election battles'. China's national leaders are mainly selected through competitive *selections*, and the empowered politicians are practical and professional politicians. Corruption of power is avoided mainly through power supervision rather than through separation of powers and system of checks and balances. As pointed out by the Fourth Plenary Session of the Nineteenth Central Committee of the Communist Party of China, 'The supervision system of the Party and the state is an important institutional guarantee for the Party to achieve self-purification, self-improvement, and self-innovation under the conditions of long-term governance.'

B. The Party's leadership enables China to achieve an organic combination of a high degree of political centralised unity and a of administrative decentralisation. China is a unitary country with unbalanced regional development and huge differences, with a high degree of administrative decentralisation. The local governments have a high level of autonomy in local development. The central government mainly formulates macro objectives and overall policy framework, and distributes contracts at different levels, allowing the local government to implement the objectives according to its specific situation. The proportion of Chinese local fiscal expenditures reached 50.2% in the 'Sixth Five-Year Plan' period in the early reform time, and has continued to rise since then, reaching over 85.2% since the 'Twelfth Five-Year Plan' period. On the contrary, the United States, as a federal country, the proportion of local fiscal expenditures in 2014-2018 was only between 52% and 53%. (Table 4 & 5)

Table 4 The Chinese central and local general public budget revenue and expenditure

Period	General public budget revenue	Proportion of the Central	Proportion of the Local	General public budget expenditure	Proportion of the Central	Proportion of the Local
Sixth Five Year Plan (FYP)	740.28 billion CNY	34.9%	65.1%	748.32 billion CNY	49.8%	50.2%
Seventh FYP	1228.06 billion CNY	33.4%	66.6%	1286.57 billion CNY	34.4%	65.6%
Eighth FYP	2244.21 billion CNY	40.3%	59.7%	2438.75 billion CNY	30.0%	70.0%

Period	General public budget revenue	Proportion of the Central	Proportion of the Local	General public budget expenditure	Proportion of the Central	Proportion of the Local
Ninth (FYP)	5077.44 billion CNY	50.5%	49.5%	5704.35 billion CNY	30.6%	69.4%
Tenth FYP	11505.07 billion CNY	53.8%	46.2%	12802.29 billion CNY	28.6%	71.4%
Eleventh FYP	30303.21 billion CNY	52.6%	47.4%	31897.08 billion CNY	20.7%	79.3%
Twelfth (FYP)	64297.69 billion CNY	46.9%	53.1%	70307.62 billion CNY	14.8%	85.2%
2016	15955.21 billion CNY	45.4%	54.6%	18784.11 billion CNY	14.6%	85.4%
2017	17259.277 billion CNY	47.0%	53.0%	20308.549 billion CNY	14.7%	85.3%
2018	18335.184 billion CNY	46.6%	53.4%	22090.607 billion CNY	14.8%	85.2%

Source of data: National Bureau of Statistics: *China Statistical Abstract 2018*.

Table 5 The U.S. government spending at all levels (2014–2018)

Year	Federal government spending	Inter-governmental transfer	State government spending	Local government spending	Total spending	Proportion of the Central	Proportion of the Local
2014	3.5 trillion USD	0.6 trillion USD	1.6 trillion USD	1.7 trillion USD	6.2 trillion USD	46.8%	53.2%
2015	3.7 trillion USD	0.6 trillion USD	1.6 trillion USD	1.8 trillion USD	6.5 trillion USD	47.7%	52.3%
2016	3.9 trillion USD	0.7 trillion USD	1.7 trillion USD	1.8 trillion USD	6.7 trillion USD	47.8%	52.2%
2017	4.0 trillion USD	0.7 trillion USD	1.8 trillion USD	1.8 trillion USD	6.9 trillion USD	47.8%	52.2%
2018 (estimate)	4.1 trillion USD	0.7 trillion USD	1.8 trillion USD	1.9 trillion USD	7.1 trillion USD	47.9%	52.1%

Note: federal spending = federal government spending + federal transfers to states and local governments

Total spending = federal spending – intergovernmental transfers + state spending + local government spending

Source of calculation data: US Government Spending Network <https://www.usgovernmentspending.com/>, [4 May 2021].

At the same time, China is highly centralised and unified politically, which is a prerequisite for the effective implementation of national objectives. Taking the national five-year plan as an example, 75% of the local targets in the Twelfth Five-Year Plan are the same or consistent with the national five-year plan. As long as local governments complete their own plans, they can largely implement the central government's objectives. It is mainly achieved through political guidance. China has taken a path that is different from the dichotomy of politics and administration in the United States. The Chinese government is an organic combination of politics and administration. Local officials are first and foremost Party cadres, and implementing the principles and policies of the Party Central Committee is their primary task. Therefore, China can realise the unity of political centralisation and administrative decentralisation, and the organic combination of flexibility and unity of governance.

During the fight against the Covid-19 pandemic, China has dealt with the problem using a total national plan across the country, while in the United States, local governments did not have a consistent plan, resulting in the local people fighting the virus on their own. China's way of dealing with Covid-19 reflects two overall situations. The first overall situation is that the heroic city of Wuhan blocked the passage from the city to stop the virus spreading. This unusually hard-core decision and unprecedented measure curbed the spread and protected the people of the whole country. The second overall situation is that the whole country launched a national rescue with vast resources committed to Wuhan and other areas in the Hubei Province. The government sent 346 medical teams and more than 42,000 medical staff to support Hubei, which enabled Wuhan to avoid the collapse of the medical system and protected the people of Wuhan. This is also the application of the mutual aid governance system between China's counterpart support and the places in need during emergency situations.

The prevention and control of the pandemic in the United States mainly relies on the local people. The main function of the federal government is to prevent the import of foreign cases, prevent transmission between states, and provide assistance to states. The states were fighting each other, the federal government was not well coordinated, and states and hospitals needed to bid for critical medical supplies and equipment. In terms of testing, treatment, isolation, social distancing, resumption of work and other policies, the policies of the states are inconsistent and uncoordinated. On the surface, they are 'united states', but in essence, the U.S is a 'bulk-packaged' country.

C. The mass line (群众路线) is embedded in the process of government governance, which makes government management and people's demands form a close interactive relationship. The Chinese government is not a government with limited liability, but a well-functioning government that always responds to the needs of the people and provides services to the people. This is the inherent requirement of the Party's mass line. Embedding the mass line into government governance helps to break the bureaucratic issue of government management. The mass line requires government officials to maintain a close interactive relationship with the people, ensuring that Party members and cadres 'always serve the masses, trust the masses, rely on the masses, lead the masses, go deep into the masses, and go deep into the grassroots', and require government management to come from the people, take root in the people, and serve the people. 'From the people' means that the Party's will and proposition must come from the people, consolidating the scattered wisdom of the people into the Party's will and proposition. At the same time, Party cadres also come from the people, maintaining the openness of the public power system. 'Rooted in the people' means that the people are the main body of history. The Party's will and proposition are realised through the enthusiasm, initiative, and creativity of the people. The Party should play its vanguard function, organise and mobilise the people, and be with the people as well as work together with the people. 'To serve the people' means that the Party cannot have selfish interests and always aims to serve the people wholeheartedly.

4. The Party's leadership and the beneficial market

Many scholars have pointed out that China's market economy is an efficient market, but in addition to being effective, the market economy must also distinguish between serving the few and benefiting the people as a whole, which determines the basic nature of the market economy. China's socialist market economy is a market economy of mutual benefit, which means that China's economy is people-centred rather than capital-centred, and serves to maximise the people's well-being rather than the maximisation of capital interests. This is the fundamental advantage of the socialist system.[18]

A. *The organic integration of socialism and market economy forms compound advantages.*

First of all, China has taken a path that is different from both free competition and welfare states, emphasising that people's livelihood issues cannot be solved solely by the market and individual forces, but must be solved by force, combining the individuals, collectives and the state, preventing private interests from obstructing collective benefits in the market economy.

Second, the state holds a large amount of public assets that can be used to further public welfare. In addition to the state-owned economy, key public means of production, urban and rural land, mines, forests and other public assets are in the hands of the state and collectives, enabling people not only to have a good private life, but also to enjoy a higher level of public welfare. This is crucial to realise people's happiness and maintain social justice. Taking Chinese high-speed rail as an example; it could be a non-profitable project for the China Railway Corporation, nevertheless it is crucial to the national economy and the well-being of society as a whole. The construction of high-speed rail has stimulated regional economic development and greatly improved the convenience of people's travel.

Third, China has a national plan that can compensate for market failures and promote a higher level of equilibrium in development. After the reform and opening up, China abolished the planned economy, but there are still national plans in-place. Market equilibrium has strict premise. When factors such as time variables, social equity, natural environment, and external uncertainties are added, the market is often unbalanced. New national planning can compensate for market failures and promote a higher level of national development. It mainly includes the following five equilibriums: 1. The supply and demand balance. The market cannot spontaneously achieve equilibrium between aggregate supply and aggregate demand, which is also the root cause of cyclical crises in capitalist economies. Planning can promote the balance between total supply and total demand through the choice of development strategies, stimulate economic growth, and reduce its volatility. 2. The time balance. What is rational in the short term may not be rational in the long term, and vice versa. Short-term maximisation of consumer benefit is not equivalent to the long term maximisation of societal well-being. Unlike the market that only focuses on the short-term, planning can take into account both the short-term and long-term, and achieve time balance. The planning system enables Chinese policies to plan and deploy in the long-term. 3. The space balance. For a long time, national planning has needed to consider the balance of population, industrial layout and spatial distribution of resources, while the planning of main functional areas considers the balance of the spatial distribution of population, industry, resources, ecology and other elements on a larger scale. Then it divides land and space, knowing the difference among the optimised, focused, restricted and prohibited developments. 4. The ecological balance. The balance of natural ecosystems is often disrupted. This is mainly due to the exploitative activities of human beings, but it is also effected by natural factors. In restoring the ecological balance, the market mechanism is incapable of maintaining order and needs to be actively guided through planning. 5. The internal and external balance. Development is not only a small cycle of the domestic market, but also a large cycle of domestic-international markets. It is necessary to consider the balance of supply and demand on a global scale. External macro conditions are often uncertain. We cannot rely only on the free market, but need to form forward-thinking plans.

B. *The Party's control over capital enables it to steer the motive of maximising profits to the direction of maximising people's well-being.*

Under the conditions of a market economy, the power of capital is what Marx asserted 'the power of irresistible purchase', which can dominate other types of power. The power of capital can manipulate political, media and social organisational influence. Capital power can be transformed into various appearances, expressed as beauty, authority, care and many other benign things in the world. Capital power is omnipresent and pervasive. As long as there is commodity trading, it would keep functioning, and the power of capital continues to grow with its accumulation.

The primary stage of socialism needs to protect the rights of capital. The report of the Nineteenth National Congress of the CPC further emphasised that the market plays a decisive role in the allocation of resources, and clearly required that the reform of the property rights system should be promoted. It is to improve the modern property rights system with 'clear ownership, clear rights and responsibilities, strict protection, and smooth circulation', the core of which is property rights protection.[19]

At the same time, it is necessary to restrain the power of capital, to prevent the contemporary bourgeoisie from being transformed, from free to selfish. Such a control is for ensuring that our system cannot be manipulated by capital, so it is truly people-centred. To do this, The Party leadership is a must. The report of the Nineteenth National Congress pointed out that 'No matter its whereabouts in China, and regardless whether it is the Party, government, military and civilian affairs or education, the Party leads everything'. The leadership of the Party is also a total power, it is the power of the superstructure, and only the total power can control the general power. What determines the fundamental direction of China's future lies in the overall power game of the Party's leadership and capital power. For example, the real estate industry, if it only considered the interests of capital, then the housing prices would soar, and the government also has a share of it. However, to truly represent the interests of the people, it is necessary to implement the fundamental positioning of 'houses are for living, not for marketing'.

The Party organises the people to follow the path of common prosperity. The rural revitalisation strategy marks the third leap of the rural socialist approach since the founding of New China. How to achieve an appropriate scale of operation? How to achieve common prosperity? At present, there are about 200 million farm households with land management area of less than 10 acres (亩) in China, accounting for more than 80% of the country's farm households.[20] Farmers have serious concerns about land transfer, and many local cooperatives are just empty shells. The essence of the problem lies in who will organise farmers to carry out large-scale operations. Is it led by capital, or is it organised by the Party and the government?

In September 2019, the author conducted research in Yantai (烟台), Shandong Province. In Yantai, the local Party branch guided the cooperative, the branch members register and establish the cooperative on behalf of the village collective, then the land was transferred to the collective cooperative for large-scale operation. A community of interests of collectives, masses, and enterprises is formed. The villages invested in collective funds, assets and resources, as well as organised the masses to invest in forms of capital, lands, infrastructure, labour, and so forth. Thus agricultural enterprises participate in business activities. This is a vivid practice of the 'political economy of party building': On the one hand, due to the prestige and credibility of the Party, it can effectively concentrate and disperse resources, promote large-scale operation, guide petite farmers to enter the track of modern agricultural development, and effectively promote the development of collective economy. At present, there are 1,470 village Party branches in Yantai City leading cooperatives. Which account for 22.8% of the total number of administrative villages, with an increase of 380 million CNY in collective income and 490 million CNY in individual incomes. It effectively increased the income of farmers, who can not only have guaranteed income from land transfer and dividends from cooperatives, but also get paid for working in cooperatives.[21] On the other hand, due to the fact that the Party has organised Party members and farmers, through real economic activities, the prestige of the Party as well as the village Party secretary have been established. Thereafter the Party's grass-roots organisation has been consolidated. The common people in this case, see that the Communist Party helped them tremendously. The cadre team has been tempered, and the selecting orientation of 'good people + capable people' has been formed. The enthusiasm of the masses has become high, and the spirit of the masses to get rich together is rejuvenated. The villages have been reshaped into a better form.

5. Party leadership and organic society

On the one hand, modern society certainly has, what Émile Durkheim called, solidarity based on the division of labour that maintains individual differences and at the same time depends on each other.[22] But this kind of solidarity may not necessarily be called 'organic solidarity'. Modern society has not only destroyed the 'real and organic community'[23] based on kinship, geography and spiritual belonging in traditional society, but also enables the power of capital to atomise the individual in organising the society, as a result individuals become isolated and fight individually for survival. The relationship between people has been separated into the relationships of profit competition and exchange. After entering the Information Age, individual lifestyles are further abstracted, and the relationship between people is more alienated.

To truly achieve organic solidarity in a modern society, at such a large-scale, mobilised and alienated mass, for it to work together, it is necessary to maintain its diversity while running through it with commonality. The premise for China to become an organic society lies in the fact that the leadership of the Party plays the role of social glue and catalyst, making society an organic whole that maintains a high degree of diversity and also has a high degree of cohesion.

The basic feature of modern society is organisation. The organisational system of the CPC is embedded in different types of institutions. Whether it is a government unit, a public institution, national enterprise, private cooperation, or social community, grassroots Party organisations can be established. At the same time, the Party 'connects base units' organically (See table 6). This strengthens the organisation within, enhances the cohesion of members, and the organisational power of the grassroots. At the same time, social, market and state organisations could achieve organic connections through the Party's organisational mechanism, making the entire society form a network structure.

Table 6 Coverage of Party Organisations in Different Types in China (2017)

	Number of organisations (thousand people)	Number of Party organisations (thousand people)	Coverage (%)
Institutional Units	233	232	99.7
Government-affiliated Institutions	542	516	95.2
National Enterprise	203	185	91.2
Non-Public Enterprise	2568	1877	73.1
Social Organisation	491	303	61.7

Source of data: Organisation Department of the Central Committee of the Communist Party of China: *2017 Communist Party Intra-Party Statistical Bulletin*, State Civil Affairs Bureau: *2017 Social Service Development Statistical Bulletin*.

The Party organisation is not only embedded in the production unit, but also in the community and other living units, so it is possible to reconstruct the 'corporeal and organic' community of the traditional society among the alienated individuals. For instance, in our research in Haiyang Community, Yantai City in September 2019, we saw a typical example of building the community into a 'big family' through the Party's organisation of the masses. The Party branch solved the problems faced by the masses by organising Party members, 'circle leaders', and the masses, including running canteens for the elderly, temporary child care centres, mediation centres, maintenance teams, dog breeding associations, and other various interest groups. While helping the masses to solve problems, it also mobilised the enthusiasm of the masses and lifted the community spirit. At the same time, Yantai was also promoting the 'integration of the two social organisations', connecting the service functions of social organisations to the needs of community services.

In December 2020, the author went to Fengqiao, Zhejiang Province for research. An important aspect of the 'Fengqiao Experience' in the new era, is to lead the 'one core and multi-subject' joint governance through Party building, and to organise and mobilise the masses, for facilitating them to solve their own problems and rebuild the rural organic society. The judicial and other governance methods are embedded in the grassroots organic society, focusing on the source of complaints: service, mediation, and case filing. It employed the method of 'educating first, with early warning mechanisms; mediation mechanisms first, then litigation; forming hierarchical filtering'. The local Party branch is required to pay attention to the mediation of conflicts and disputes, with comprehensive management, so we can achieve 'small things do not leave the village, big things do not leave the town, and contradictions are not turned over to high-ups'.

Durkheim's equating of 'common consciousness' with 'consistency' in his early writings is too mechanical. Common consciousness does not mean the extinction of diversity. The common consciousness, based on cultural traditions, not only provides social solidarity, but also nutritious soil for the creativity of social individuals. Solidarity based on shared consciousness has not degenerated as he predicted, but is increasingly important in modern society. Without a common cause, not only is it impossible to work together, but even living together is extremely difficult. Under the leadership of the CPC, through the shaping of common ideals and values, the people have not only individual dreams, but also common pursuits and aspirations. The guidance has mobilised the enthusiasm of the people and enhanced social cohesion.

One consequence of the unbalanced diversity of modern society is the conflict and antagonism between the individuals and the collective, as well as between the collective and the nation. This is what is called 'negative solidarity'. In China, the leadership of the Party has played the role of attenuator and coordinator of social conflicts. It emphasises the collective consciousness and cooperation of individuals. It also asserts that the rights and freedoms of individuals must be consistent with the common rights and freedoms of the community. It articulates that the cooperative relationship among different strata, groups, the society and the state, rather than a confrontational relationship.

In terms of 'active solidarity', we not only have various social organisations that are highly active, but also a well-structured community system, with industry and volunteer associations. They are the bridges and links between the state and society, between different social organisations. The system gives full play to the functions of the Communist Youth League, the Women's Federation, the trade unions, the workers' congress and other organisations as a bridge for the expression of workers' rights and interests. These are the glue for workers' self-organisation, forming a familial atmosphere where workers are the masters.

The Party organisation is the core force of an organised society. By encouraging and regulating the development of various types of social communities, mobile internet exchange, and multiple online-offline activities, the mode not only has the self-organising skills but also a overall guidance. It will form a new type of information sharing and organic governance. This is a new model of social governance in which the people form small units, then centralise forming national unity. In so doing, China can promote a modern co-operative community, proposed by the Fourth Plenary Session of the Nineteenth CPC Central Committee, in which 'everyone is responsible, and everyone enjoys'.

In short, China's good governance system is composed of vanguard political parties, well-functioning governments, a market for mutual benefit, and an organic society to ensure the subjectivity of the people. It differs from Western governance systems of electoral parties, limited government, free markets, and civil society.

The essence of the Chinese version of good governance is to safeguard the subjectivity of the people. The Fourth Plenary Session of the Nineteenth Central Committee of the CPC clearly pointed out that it is necessary to adhere to the main body of the people and ensure that the people manage state affairs, economic and cultural undertakings and social affairs through various channels and forms in accordance with the law.

Party leadership is the key to achieving Chinese governance. The Fourth Plenary Session of the Nineteenth Central Committee of the CPC clearly pointed out that it is necessary to adhere to and improve the Party's leadership system and improve the Party's scientific, democratic and law-based governance. The Chinese governance system is neither a single-centre nor a multi-centre governance system, but an attempt to organically combine the advantages of the two. It is a governance system that not only divides labour but also connects productivity, giving full play to the enthusiasm of all parties, and becoming an organic and unified whole, which is both lively, consistent and efficient. We might call it a '1+N' central governance system.

---

1 'An dialogue with Justin Yifu Lin: "A well-functioning government and a efficient market"', 2013, *Economic Guide*, No. 4. [《对话北京大学国家发展研究院荣誉院长林毅夫:"有为的政府和有效的市场"》，《21世纪经济报道》，2013年7月22日]
2 Li Ling and Jiang Yu, 2014, 'A Well-functioning Government, an efficient market and an organic society', *Economic Guide*, No. 4. [李玲、江宇:《有为政府、有效市场、有机社会——中国道路与国家治理现代化》，《经济导刊》2014年第4期]
3 Jin Yuejing, 2019, 'The CPC must be considered in reflecting and reconstructing the relationship between the nation and the society', *Exploration and Free Views*, No. 8. [景跃进:《将政党带进来——国家与社会关系范畴的反思与重构》，《探索与争鸣》2019年第8期。]
4 Jin Yuejing, 2005, 'Party, Nation and Society: The relationship of the three', *Journal of the Middle China Normal University*, No. 3. [景跃进:《党、国家与社会:三者维度的关系——从基层实践看中国政治的特点》，《华中师范大学学报》(人文社会科学版) 2005 年第 3 期]
5 Yan Xiaolong, 2014, 'Quadrant in Modernisation of Governing the Nation', *Marxism and Reality*, No. 6. [严小龙:《国家治理现代化的四维结构特征》，《马克思主义与现实》2014 年第 6 期。]
6 Li Junru, 2018, *The Eighteenth Speech*, 4 December. [李君如:《不忘改革初心，牢记历史使命》，清华大学国情研究院"国情讲坛"第18讲，2018年12月4日]
7 Wang Shaoguang, 2014, 'How to understand the current party politics in the United States', Renmin University Press. [见王绍光:《如何理解当前的美国政党政治?》，赵忆宁:《探访美国政党政治:美国两党精英访谈》一书序言，中国人民大学出版社 2014 年版]
8 George Washington, 2012, *Farewell Address*, translated and published by the Commercial Press, p. 303. [华盛顿:《告别演说》，《华盛顿选集》商务印书馆 2012 年版，第 303 页]
9 James MacGregor Burns and J.W. Peltason, 2007, *Government by the People*, translated and published by Renmin University Press, p. 169, Originally published in 1952, Prentice-Hall. [转引自伯恩斯等:《民治的政府——美国政府与政治》，中国人民大学出版社 2007 年版，第 169 页]
10 Xi Jinping, 2017, *Building a Well-Being Society: Report on the nineteenth national congress of CPC*, Renmin Press, p. 13. [习近平:《决胜全面建成小康社会 夺取新时代中国特色社会主义伟大胜利——在中国共产党第十九次全国代表大会上的报告》，人民出版社 2017 年版，第 13 页]
11 Yan Yilong et. al., 2015, *A Great Path – The Communist Party of China and Chinese Socialism*, Renmin University Press, p. 2. [鄢一龙等:《大道之行:中国共产党与中国社会主义》，中国人民大学出版社 2015年版，第2页]
12 Qiang Shigong, 2009, 'The Unwritten Constitution in the Chinese Constitution – A New Perspective for Understanding the Chinese Constitution", *The Open Era*, No. 12. [参见强世功:《中国宪法中的不成文宪法——理解中国宪法的新视角》，《开放时代》2009年第12期]
13 *Ideal Political Order: An Exploration of Chinese, Western, Ancient and Modern*, 2012, ed by Wang Shaoguang, Sanlian Publishing, pp. 307-330. [参见王绍光主编:《理想政治秩序:中西古今的探求》，三联书店 2012 年版，第 307—330 页]
14 Wang Shaoguang, 2011, 'The party needs to reduce the body, while maintaining its avant-garde-ness, instead of being elitist', *National Studies Report*, ed by Hu Angang, Social Science Documentary Press, p. 322. [王绍光:《要瘦身，不要虚胖，要先锋队，不要精英党》，胡鞍钢主编:《国情报告》(第 14 卷)，社会科学文献出版社 2011 年版，第 322 页]
15 Xi Jinping, 2018, *On Adhering to Comprehensively Deepening Reform*, Central Literature Publishing House, p. 326. [习近平:《论坚持全面深化改革》，中央文献出版社 2018 年版，第 326 页]
16 For example see in, Justin Yifu Lin, 2014, 'A Transforming Country requires an efficient market and well-functioning government', *Chinese Economy Weekly*, 17 Feb. [林毅夫:《转型国家需要有

效市场和有为政府》，《中国经济周刊》 2014年2月17日] Neo-Structuralist economics defines *facilitating state* as in various economic developing stages, it could adjust and accommodate the societal situation, nursing, protecting and supplementing the market, as well as promoting social fairness, benefiting people of all strata when market fails. Also in, Wang Yong and Hua Xiuping, 2017, 'On the content of facilitating state in Neo-Structuralist economics', *Comments on Economics*, No. 3. [王勇、华秀萍：《详论新结构经济学中"有为政府"的内涵———兼对田国强教授批评的回复》，《经济评论》2017 年第 3 期] This article has different views about the well-functioning government

17 Wang Shaoguang, 2014, 'National Governance and National Capability – China's Governance Concept and Institutional Choice', *Economic Tribune*, No. 6. [王绍光：《国家治理与国家能力——中国的治理理念与制度选择》，《经济导刊》2014 年第 6 期]

18 Yan Yilong, 2015, 'Socialism on the neck of Capitalism', *The Great Way: The Communist Party of China and Chinese Socialism*, Renmin University Press Chapter 5. [参见鄢一龙：《骑在资本头上的社会主义》，《大道之行: 中国共产党与中国社会主义》，中国人民大学出版社 2015 年版，第 5 章]

19 Mu Hong, 2017, 'Accelerating the socialist market system', *Guideline of the Report of the Nineteenth National Congress*, Renmin Press, p. 230-235. [穆虹：《加快完善社会主义市场经济体制》，《党的十九大报告辅导读本》，人民出版社 2017 年版，第 230-235 页]

20 Wang Yaping and Su Yiqing, 2018, *Institutions, Mechanisms and Policy Systems to Promote Urban-Rural Integration Development*, Dec. [王亚华、 苏毅清：《促进城乡融合发展的体制机制和政策体系》，2018 年 12 月]

21 'The Party Branch of Yantai Promotion Village leads the cooperative to explore a new path for common prosperity', 2019, provided by the Organisation Department of Yantai City, Sept. [《烟台市推行村党支部领办合作社趟出共同富裕新路子》，烟台市组织部提供，2019年9月]

22 Émile Durkheim, 2000, *On The Division of Labour*, Vol. 1, translated and published by Three-Link Press, Originally published as *De la division du travail social*, 1893, Félix Alcan. [涂尔干：《社会分工论》（第一卷），三联书店 2000 年版。]

23 Ferdinand Tönnies, 1999, *Community and Society*, translated and published by the Commercial Press, Originally published as *Gemeinschaft und Gesellschaft*, 1887. [滕尼斯：《共同体与社会》，商务印书馆 1999 年版。]

PART 5
CHINA AND THE WORLD

People across the world should be guided by the vision that all the people under the heaven are of one family, embrace each other with open arms, enhance mutual understanding, and seek common ground while setting aside differences. Together, we should endeavor to build a community with a shared future for mankind.

– Xi Jinping's Keynote Speech at the CPC in Dialogue With World Political Parties High-Level Meeting (1 December 2017)

CHAPTER 11

Where the World Is Going: The New Order of 'contact of two extremes'*

(*The first draft of this article is the speech of the 'One Belt, One Road' Initiative from an Interdisciplinary Perspective on October 28, 2015—the second session of the Academic Salon for Young Experts and Scholars in Humanities and Social Sciences held by the National School Communist Youth League Research Centre. The second draft was published as Yan Yilong and Cui Jing: 'On the New Global Order of "contact of two extremes"', Explore, 2017, No. 1. There were revisions during the writing of this book.) [本文初稿系 2015 年 10 月 28 日 '跨学科视野中的 '一带一路' 倡议' ———全国学 校共青团研究中心第二期人文社科青年专家学者学术沙龙活动的发言稿第二稿刊发于鄢 一龙、 崔京：'试论 '两极相联' 全球新秩序'，'探索' 2017 年第 1 期。本书写作过程中有修订。]

In the 1850s, Karl Marx wrote a set of articles on China's issues for the *New-York Daily Tribune*. This is a set of commentary articles about major historical events that affected the global landscape, such as the Opium War. Marx pointed out that the global situation at that time was an order in which the Western world and China underwent the 'contact of two extremes', and pointed out that the Chinese revolution would have a profound impact on the changes in the European order.[1] In this series of essays Marx once again demonstrated his genius for seeing the profound historical significance of contemporary events.

Today, we seem to have reached another important historical moment. At present, with the new round of 'de-globalisation', major changes have taken place in the political landscape of the United States and Europe. The problem of the failure of the old global order has become increasingly prominent. The new global order is in the process of being shaped. The international situation is highly uncertain. Many people have asked the question: Where is the world going?

The rise of China as a great power is a historical event on par with the British Industrial Revolution and the French Revolution. It marks the collective revival and collective rise of other countries outside the Western world, thereby reshaping the world pattern of 'centre-periphery' or 'centre—semi-periphery—periphery' since the Industrial Revolution, making the global order emerge from Western dominance to the historical normality of pluralistic coexistence.

Marx's wisdom is still instructive today, and we can use Marx's insights to predict the new global order that is emerging.

1. The debate on the changing trend of the international pattern after the Cold War

For more than 20 years since the end of the Cold War, Globalisation and Regional Integration has been accompanied by the acceleration of 'the rise and fall of great powers',[2] and triggered a profound change in the way of 'international production activities'.[3] However, the trajectory of the international pattern was not clear with the differentiation and reorganisation of the power centres, which caused extensive debate. In these debates, whether from the perspective of power hierarchy and power comparison, or from the perspective of international public goods supply, the international pattern is defined from the perspective of international power centres and power relations between major powers, with the number of 'poles' as the main factor. Therefore, the theoretical viewpoints of 'unipolar', 'bipolar', 'multipolar' and even 'non-polarisation' are derived.

The theory of 'unipolar world' posits that in the foreseeable future, the United States will remain the only global power centre with the most powerful strength and international influence in the world, and will not be completely surpassed by any country or region. The disintegration of the Soviet Union marked the arrival of the 'unipolar moment' of the United States, which will gradually evolve into a 'unipolar world', and despite the periodic self-confidence crisis, the United States will not decline and will always be the 'world's Hyperpower'.[4] This view was also accepted by the Obama administration to some extent. In his State of the Union Address, Obama repeatedly declared that he would not accept the United States as second and allow China to set the rules. The view of a 'unipolar world' is still the mainstream view in the United States. An article published on 'Foreign Affairs' in the United States in 2016 still insists that China cannot become a superpower like the United States, and the future world will still be a 'unipolar world' dominated by the U.S.[5] The 'unipolar' theory also describes the United States as a 'benign hegemony', and after the end of the Cold War, the United States will dominate and build a stable and peaceful 'unipolar world' as 'the only major power capable of global action'.[6] It will maintain the international peace and public order provided by the United States as a long time hegemonic, that is, 'Pax Americana'.[7] This is also accepted by some Chinese scholars, who believe that in economic, military, political and cultural terms, the United States is the undisputed and unchallenged 'pole' of the world, and the changes in the international power structure brought about by the rise of China should not be over-exaggerated. It is a challenge for us to handle external relations well in the 'unipolar world' and realise the peaceful development of China as a rising country.[8]

The view of a 'unipolar world' deviates from the historical trend of the declining relative strength of the United States, the collective rise of developing countries, and the general convergence of development levels across all countries in the world since World War II. It has been widely questioned. In fact, since the 1970s, with the collapse of the world colonial structure and the rise of Europe and Japan, there has been a trend towards diversification of the global power centre. The Nixon administration of the United States once proposed that there are five power centres in the world: the United States, the Soviet Union, Western Europe, Japan and China. After the Cold War, global power has been changing, the Soviet Union has disintegrated, the relative power of the United States and Japan has declined, China's power has risen, and other power centres have also emerged.[9] Some proposed 'the ternary structure of the United States, the European Union and the 'BRICS' under the dominance of the United States'.[10] Some posit the coexistence of three super economic circles.[11] These all reflect the shifting of polycentric forces. Therefore, many scholars also believe that 'multi-polarisation' is the basic feature of the current international pattern and the inevitable trend of future development.[12] And 'multi-polarisation' is an open policy proposition of the Chinese government, and believes that 'the international political landscape is developing toward a balanced power structure'.[13]

The limitation of the 'multipolar' view is that, the relative decline of U.S. power and the formation of multiple power centres, does not mean that these power centres are all qualified to become 'poles' like the United States, namely a global energy force. Therefore, many people advocate the middle ground of these two viewpoints, and believe that the world pattern is evolving towards 'one supreme-multipolarities' or 'one hyperpower and many superpowers'.[14] Although the pattern of 'one hyperpower and many superpowers' is only a transitional stage, it will last for a long time.[15] There are also people who advocate the parallel construction of 'unipolar world' and 'multipolar world'.[16]

Whether it is 'unipolarisation' and 'multipolarisation', or the 'polarisation' theoretical system, with sovereign states as the main international participant and powerful countries as centres, with the development of multinational corporations, new media, terrorist organisations, international and non-governmental entities as well as other non-traditional global forces, many scholars believe that the international pattern will develop towards a 'non-polarisation' trend without a true core force.[17]

The view of 'non-polarisation' exaggerates the role of non-traditional forces to a certain extent. On the international stage, sovereign states are still the only participant capable of comprehensively applying economic, political, military, and cultural resources and participating in the governance of global affairs. The protagonists are still sovereign states, and this does not tend to change in the foreseeable future, until the advent of the so-called 'world governments'.

The 'unipolar', 'multi-polar' and 'non-polar' views all underestimate China's potential to grow into a global dynamic power. Since the beginning of the twenty-first century, China's status has become more and more prominent, and 'China has gradually moved to the centre of the transformation of the international system.'[18] While the power gap between other countries and China-U.S. has widened, China has begun to break away from the power centre of the 'second tier' and become a member of the 'first tier'. Some scholars lean towards the bipolar view of China and the United States, the most typical of which is the idea of 'G2' (Group 2). American economist Fred Bergsten believes that the global economic governance system has fallen behind the times. Therefore, 'only this G2 model can accurately position China's new role and make Chinese people feel that China is a global economic giant, the legitimate maker and defender of the international order'.[19]

Although there have been some doubts about the G2 view in recent years, it more accurately captures the basic trend of changes in the pattern of international power and the central role of global powers in shaping the global order than other views. The biggest problem with the G2 view is that it is a miniature version of the G7. It is hoped that China and the United States will cooperate on the basis of the G2 to govern the global economy and even more other international affairs. This concept is in conflict with the international order of 'American Hegemony – Western Centre'. China is not a traditional Western country, and the United States cannot accept China as a global ruler in the same way that it accepts traditional allies. That is why this is a short-lived concept.

In recent years, Chinese international relations scholars such as Yan Xuetong and Jin Canrong have tried to propose that the 'bipolar' pattern is a more likely world order in the twenty-first century than the unipolar and multipolar pattern.[20] Different from the concept of G2, most Chinese scholars advocate that China should play the role of a new pole, that does not only participate in the power-shift within the established order, but will also have an important impact on existing international norms.

These ideas are further than the G2 view, but lack empirical support. The concept of bipolar pattern is not enough to describe how the global order will be different from the Cold War after China joins as a new pole. In addition, the new features of the G2 are also insufficient to respond to the changes in global economy and politics and the implications of global governance issues for the international order. The concerns about the new hegemonic struggle show exactly that, it is necessary to further clarify the relationship between the emerging and the conservative powers, the connection and changes between the new and the old orders, and finally answer the fundamental question of 'what is the global order in the 21st century'.

2. Introduction of the concept of 'contact of two extremes'

In May 1853, Karl Marx in his article 'Revolution in China and in Europe' utilised Hegel's theory of 'two extremes' to analyse the relationship between the Chinese revolution and the Western world,[21] and explained in depth in a series of articles explaining 'China-Europe Relations'.

Marx first used the concept in the sense of the relationship between the two extremes is mutually influential and promotional. Compared with the Eurocentric world system that had gradually formed since the 16th century, the Chinese Empire was an isolated and closed extreme. He foresaw that when European industrial products flood in, the Chinese imperial system will be crushed. This is the impact of the Western extreme on China, and subsequent historical development has verified his view.

Marx's analysis did not stop there, he believed that China's changes would in turn act on Europe, pushing the European revolution forward. This connection not only implies that the Chinese revolution will inspire the European revolution to move forward, but also serve as a political and economic driving force. If there is no Chinese market, European capitalism cannot develop, meanwhile in turn, the turmoil in the Chinese market will prompt the outbreak of a general crisis of European capitalism.

Although Marx's 'contact of two extremes' refers to the interdependence and mutual promotion of changes between opposites in the international pattern, it is different from the concept of 'extremes' capable of global action in international relations. Marx's view is indeed very insightful. In the non-flat expansion process of the global capitalist system, there is always a reverse force. The formation of the socialist bloc and the disintegration of the world colonial system can be regarded as reverse movements. After the Cold War, the United States' efforts to build a 'unipolar empire' were unsuccessful, regardless the bipolar pattern between the United States and the Soviet Union collapsed and reorganised. Since the capitalist pole overwhelmed the Soviet superpower pole, the Soviet Union and Eastern European countries were expected to be reorganised into the global capitalist system. Russia has regained some power and is ranked as a second-tier country, nevertheless it has not been fully absorbed into this system.[22]

Since the reform and opening up, China has conducted market-oriented reforms and gradually integrated into the global trade and governance system. China's participation has also changed the global industrial division of labour. Therefore, after the international financial crisis of 2008, Han Yuhai used the concept of 'connection of two extremes' to analyse the changes in the global production system after the financial crisis, believing that the rise of China will 'squeeze out' the unbalanced global production-financial system. Once China's huge market and enormous labour resources are activated, it will break the existing capitalist world order from within.[23] Here we try to combine the concept of Marx with the concept of 'pole' in international relations, and further expand the concept of 'contact of two extremes' to describe the interdependent and mutually influential relationship between the two poles, the United States and China, two great powers with global outreach. The 'contact of two extremes' is not limited to two countries, but has global significance, because it shapes the profound global order.

When Marx discussed the impact of 'contact of two extremes' on the global pattern, he discussed it from the perspective of the global production and trade system. The connotation is clearly closer to the concept of global order than international order, which is also instructive for the contemporary era. With the rise of non-traditional forces, the issue of global governance has become increasingly prominent. To be specific, the concept of international order, which mainly focuses on the relationship between states, is increasingly showing its limitations in understanding the changes in global patterns. In the liberal institutionalist theory of international relations, the discussion of globalism has actually gone beyond the scope of traditional international relations to the concept of global order. Although scholars use the concept of global order with different connotations, most of them agree that the concept is not limited to the relationship between countries, but incorporates the concept of global community. That is to say, when debating the issue, not only the international political category, but also the global political and economic structure needs to be considered. In addition, not only the comparison of strengths, but also global value norms required to be viewed.

The concept of 'contact of two extremes' global order can be defined at the levels of participants, international patterns, governance systems, and global economic systems.

Globalisation has increased the role of multinational corporations and non-governmental organisations on the international stage, nevertheless before the advent of world government, sovereign states remained the main actors in this order. Great nations, in particular, are still the most important force driving changes in the global order due to their comprehensive utilisation of resources. The 'contact of two extremes' is based on the international pattern of two poles. It reflects that due to China's growth into a global dynamic power, the United States has gradually lost its status as the sole power centre of the world, and the international pattern has changed from 'one hyperpower, many superpowers' to a 'two poles and multiple strong powers' pattern.

The 'contact of two extremes' refers to the unity of opposites between the two poles, which is not only the competition and cooperation between countries, but also the mutual competition and interdependence in the global economic and political system. The 'contact of two extremes' is different from the concept of the bipolar pattern in that it emphasises the significance of the 'two poles' in shaping international principles, rules and norms. China's entry as an emerging pole will not promote the subversion of existing international norms and governance change, but will contribute to a more just, reasonable and relatively stable global community order.

As Robert Keohane and Joseph Nye suggested, under the conditions of globalisation, global governance issues such as cross-border capital flow, global allocation of production factors, and climate change have increasingly become critical issues, and major power relations have become complex dependencies. The 'contact of two extremes' focuses on global economic development and non-traditional security issues governed by this order.

3. The long-term weakening of U.S. hegemony and the formation of the international pattern of 'two poles and multiple powers'

The U.S. hegemony is different from the global colonial empire built by Great Britain. Its essence is to use its dominant position to control the lifeline of global production, the global political agenda, and occupy the commanding heights of global discourse in order to maximize its own national strategic interests. Western countries headed by the United States are at the centre of the global order and are the dynamic force, while other countries are at the periphery position and are passive subjects.

The U.S. population accounts for only 4% of the world's population and 22% of the world's total economy, yet it controls the world. Therefore, U.S. hegemony is a strategic art of 'winning more with less'. Essentially it competes with the other countries by controlling strategic factors at different levels of the global system. It establishes a complete system of hegemony, which includes five aspects:

First, the hegemony of 'manufacturing-military'. The United States serves the global investment and trade of the U.S. and its allies by building a global military system. As Niall Ferguson, the author of the book *Empire: How Britain Made the Modern World*, pointed out, if you compare the military bases of the United States with the coal ports of British imperialism, you will find that the two are highly overlapped.[24]

Second, the hegemony of 'petrol-dollar'. After the USD was decoupled from gold, the U.S. used its ability to control global oil production to make the USD the standard currency for oil, thus maintaining the world's confidence in the USD as a world currency and the 'U.S. Dollar Standard'. A considerable part of the dollar circulates abroad, which is equivalent to the seigniorage imposed by the United States on other countries.

Third, the hegemony of 'technology-standards'. The United States takes advantage of its first-mover advantage and its cutting-edge technology to lead the formulation of standards, thereby grabbing higher added value. Especially after entering the Internet Era, a new round of virtual world hegemony characterised by the internet, big data, intelligent manufacturing, and biotechnology is being laid out.

Fourth, the hegemony of 'rules-agenda'. The United States uses its founding and discourse advantages in international organisations to lead the formulation of international interaction rules and agenda setting to achieve its dominance over global politics.

Fifth, the hegemony of 'English-ideology'. The United States takes advantage of the status of English as a world language, occupying the commanding heights of the global discourse system and realising the output of its ideology. Thus it constructs global value norms, and finally realises the dominance of the global value system.

On the one hand, the deep order of 'American hegemony-Western-centred' is transformed into multilateral action by leading the dominant global order of multilateral co-determination. On the other hand, it provides a stable mechanism for the dominant global order of multilateral co-determination, to a certain extent, it has solved the 'Prisoner's Dilemma' of the multilateral mechanism.

The decline of American hegemony is due to its internal crises. Just as Mao Zedong commented on the United States that 'it extends its hands too far' and 'a big country has bigger problems',[25] America's global presence has outstripped its national capacity.

The decline of American hegemony is due to three major crises that are difficult to overcome: first, the crisis of separation of the real economic centre and the virtual economic centre; second, the crisis of global military hegemony and its cost mismatch; third, excessive consumption and debt crisis.

The U.S.'s share of global GDP is in a long-term decline, while China's economic power continues to rise and there is a tendency of surpassing that of the U.S. in the future. In purchasing power parity terms, in 1950 the share of the United States in world GDP peaked at 27.3%, while China was at historical low of 4.6%. At present, regarding GDP by purchasing power parity, China has surpassed the U.S., and ranked the first in the world. Moreover, if calculated by the exchange rate method, China's GDP in 2019 is equivalent to 67.2% of the United States. And under the impact of the Covid-19 pandemic, it rose to 70.4% in 2020.

A more meaningful indicator is production capacity. The strongest period of American manufacturing was right after World War II, when manufacturing output peaked in 1953, where the U.S. accounted for 44.7% of the world. Subsequently, the global production centre shifted from the United States to East Asia, and the proportion of Japan's manufacturing industry in the world increased from the Post-War 2.6% to 14.9% in 1980. Then it was transferred to China. By 2009, China's manufacturing output value had accounted for 25.9% of the world, which was 1.6 times that of the United States.

With the transfer of production centres, the United States continues to maintain its status as a global enterprise innovation centre by utilising its global production resource allocation capabilities of multinational corporations. But since 1980, the number of Fortune 500 companies in the United States has dropped from 217 to 121 in 2020; while China started from scratch, by 2020, it has reached 124 (including Hong Kong, and excluding Taiwan), surpassing the United States. At the same time, China's international patent (PCT) has reached 59,000 in 2019, surpassing the United States and ranking first in the world. In 2014, Huawei was already the global company with the largest number of international patent applications. As Chinese companies enter the oversea market with a more active stance, they will play a key role in setting global standards.

In the more than ten-year period, since the beginning of the 21st century, China's innovation capability has grown rapidly. It has become one of the leaders of global innovation from an insignificant role in the global innovation landscape, and has also challenged the dominant position of the United States. In 2000, China's Research and Development (R&D) investment accounted for only 3.3% of the world's total, the number of invention patent applications accounted for 3.8%, and the number of scientific and technological papers was less than 3%. However, by 2019,

China's R&D investment became close to that of the United States, and the proportion of R&D investment in GDP reached 2.23%, which exceeded that of the EU. In 2011, the number of invention patent applications in China surpassed that of the United States, and in 2019, it accounted for 38% of the world, which was already 1.7 times that of the United States. In 2019, the number of PCT patent applications in China surpassed that of the United States, ranking first in the world, and the gap in the number of scientific papers is also shrinking rapidly. China is the second largest country in the world in the production of international scientific papers and highly cited papers, second only to the United States.

At the same time, China's huge human resources give it a greater chance of innovation. In 2000, China's total human resources was equivalent to 2.8 times that of the United States, and now it has reached 3.84 times. In 2014, the number of scientific and technological workers in China reached 81.14 million,[26] which is equivalent to the population of Germany. At the same time, by encouraging innovation and development, China's economic prosperity and preferential policies will also attract more global innovative talents to serve China's development.

China's development is a long-term catch-up process in competing with the United States. We surpassed the United States in indicators such as total human resources, grain output, and urban population during the early construction period (1949-1978), and surpassed it in steel production in 1993. Entering the new century, the aggregates related to modern factors such as the number of mobile phones, the number of the internet users, the value of export goods, industrial added value, power generation and highway mileage have all surpassed that of the United States. In 2014, the GDP according to the purchasing power parity method also surpassed that of the United States. In addition, it can be conservatively estimated that the GDP will surpass the United States before 2030. The only important aggregate indicator that we cannot and need not surpass the United States is total military spending.

The long-term hegemony of the United States lies in its financial sector dominance. The status quo of the separation of the financial centre of the United States from the global production centre is the crucial reason for the predicament of the American hegemony. The foundation of the U.S. dollar's financial hegemony lies in its military hegemony, the world's largest trading body, its control over global oil, grain and other strategic resources, and the world's strong confidence in the United States. This state of separation has been going on for decades, and there are great doubts about it sustainability in the long run. As analysed by scholar Wang Xiangsui, the international financial crisis is largely a crisis of the USD standard. If China integrates with Europe, it will form a huge non-dollar currency circle, which will become a nightmare for the United States.[27]

China has replaced the US as the world's largest trading nation. The importance of the CNY in global payments is rising. According to the data provided by the Society for Worldwide Interbank Financial Telecommunication (SWIFT), the proportion of CNY in international payments jumped from the 35th global currency in October 2010 to the fourth largest currency in the world in August 2015, with a market share of 2.79 %. In October 2016, the CNY was added to the Special Drawing Rights (SDR), becoming the fifth currency in the 'basket', after the USD, the euro, the Japanese yen and the U.K. pound sterling. China established the CNY cross-border payment system in 2015, and as of July 2020, 984 financial institutions from 97 countries and regions have participated.[28]

On the contrary, American hegemony faces debt crisis. The U.S. general government debt as a proportion of gross national product increased from 54.7% in 2001 to 76.1% in 2008 during George W. Bush's term, an increase of 21.4%. After Trump took the White House, the U.S. government debt has continued to rise, reaching $23.7 trillion in 2019, which has exceeded the U.S. GDP and has risen sharply since 2020.[29]

From the perspective of the U.S. military hegemony, it is neither feasible nor economical to maintain its huge military expenditure, which will inevitably lead to the contraction of its military power. In 2005, the US military expenditure accounted for 44.9% of the world's military expenditure, equivalent to 1.6 times the US's GDP and 5.2 times the world's share of US exports.

The cultural hegemony of the United States is largely based on its leading advantages over other countries in terms of economy, technology, and institutions. The global centre of cultural creation and production will increasingly shift from the United States, and even from the Western world, to other countries.

In fact, the hegemonic crisis of the United States shows that the United States' national strength is no longer sufficient to maintain the existing global order and governance model. On the one hand, the United

States' hegemony provides the international community with certain 'public goods' and suppresses wars and conflicts within a certain range. On the other hand, these strategies and ideas themselves have become the source of international wars and conflicts. Not only has the United States itself become a 'source of war' in a sense, the wave of terrorism and democratisation crisis, it has made the whole world, including the United States, deeply affected. Paul Kennedy pointed out that the U.S. military presence all over the world has actually exhausted the basis of its national strength, and the best outcome of U.S. hegemony is a smooth contraction.[30]

When the Obama administration took office, it made a series of strategic adjustments, including shrinking intervention in the global military. The global share of military spending fell by 10% compared with 2005. During the Trump administration, military spending rose again. In 2019, military spending accounted for 38% of the world's total, which is the sum of the military spending of the following 12 countries.[31] He promoted the 'remanufacturing industry' and actively promoted the growth of U.S. exports; he implemented the 'return to the Asia-Pacific' strategy, more respect for the diversity of global cultures and systems, and emphasized the use of 'smart power'. This can be seen as a sensible response to the inherent crisis of American hegemony, but it does not change its ability to control the global situation and its long-term decline in global hegemony.

During the Trump administration, the United States turned to a domestic focused strategy, seeking to maximise the benefits of its global hegemony while reducing its commitment to global responsibilities. This adjustment makes the so-called 'benign hegemony' further manifest its essence. In the short term, it will help to enhance the national interests of the United States. In the long run, it will cause harm to the soft power of the United States, and may also further exacerbate its debt crisis, accelerating the decline of American hegemony. The Biden administration proposes that the United States should re-affirm its leading position in the world. But the Biden administration has to face the crisis of the Covid-19 pandemic and the crisis of domestic racial and class division; internationally, it has to face the unilateralism of the Trump administration as well as issues of Covid-19. U.S. hegemony is inevitably going from decline to end.

Of course, the decline of American hegemony is not the same as the decline of the United States. Although it will inevitably have an impact on the nation, the decline of American hegemony refers to the decline of its relative strength, not its absolute strength. During this period, it will still be the 'one pole' of the world.

China will grow into a global power like the United States. In addition to the rapid rise in comprehensive national strength, China is the country with the largest population (4 times the population of the United States), with a rich human resource base, a vast territory, long coastline (18,000 km) and land borders (2.2 10,000 kilometres), these are the basic conditions for becoming a global power.

Contrary to the judgments of Western international strategists such as Zbigniew Brzezinski, China's political system is not a weakness in great power competition, but an advantage. Due to the strong leadership of the CPC, China's efficiency in resource integration, decision-making, strategic implementation and adjustment is not matched by that of the United States, which puts China in a more advantageous position in the great power competition. China's political system determines that China can have a stronger strategic capability and resilience to deal with external challenges. Brzezinski regards China's political system as a shortcoming of great power competition in his book *The Grand Chessboard*, which is a misjudgement. On the contrary, China's political system determines that it can more effectively mobilise and concentrate domestic resources to deal with international competition than the United States. Whether it is a short-term high-intensity confrontation or a protracted war, it will show a higher level of performance.

Likewise, Western international strategy scholars often underestimate the ability of traditional Chinese culture and socialist core values to provide global norms. After thousands of years of civilisation and profound cultural accumulation in China, after modern transformation, the life style and value norms that China can provide for reference are incomparable to a country like the United States that lacks its own historical roots. At the same time, after the reform and opening up, the socialist system model and socialist values have reappeared with vitality, which has universal global significance.

Looking around the world, other major countries in the world do not have the conditions to grow into global countries like China and the United States in the twenty-first century. As the largest country in the world measured by territory, Russia accounts for only 2% of the world's total population and only one-fifth of the United States' total economic output. Moreover, its economic structure is highly dependent on resources.

Although Japan is a big economic power, it is also a small country, in the process of long-term decline, and is firmly bound to the global strategic carriage of the United States. India will become the most populous country in the world and has the most potential to become a world power like China and the United States, but its economy is less than one-third of that of China, and it does not have the ability to provide new value norms. Although the EU alongside other countries and regions are competitive in terms of population, economy and culture, they are not sovereign powers, and it is difficult for them to integrate into a community and compete with the world. (See Table 1)

The rise and fall of the power of great powers reflects the changes in the global pattern of the collective rise of non-Western countries. Since the Industrial Revolution, countries have first experienced a process of great divergence. The share of southern countries in global GDP dropped from 70.3% to 39.5% in 1950, and then went through a process of great convergence, rising to 52.4% in 2010, and we estimate that it will further rise to 67% by 2030.[32]

Table 1 Proportion of several indicators of major countries (organisations) in the world compared to the United States

Unit: U.S. Power=100

Countries (organisations)	Population (2015)	GDP (2017, purchasing power parity)	Territory size	Export (2015)	Import (2015)	Military Expenditure (2016)
The U.S.	100.0	100.0	100.0	100.0	100.0	100.0
China	427.2	108.6	97.7	142.1	68.0	35.59
Russia	44.4	19.3	174.0	21.1	8.4	13.29
Japan	39.7	25.9	3.8	39.0	26.6	7.07
India	391.3	44.7	33.5	18.0	18.4	10.02
The EU	160.6	106.7	44.0	141.4	95.6	40.56
Brazil	63.8	17.6	86.7	11.8	7.4	4.23
Mexico	37.8	12.4	20.0	27.0	18.5	1.04
Indonesia	79.7	15.8	19.4	9.5	5.9	1.39

Notes: Data Source: CIA. The World Factbook, <www.cia.gov/library/publications/resources/the-world-factbook/rankorder/rankorderguide.html>, [4 May 2021].

With the collective rise of non-Western countries, the current US system of global hegemony and the global order in the centre of the West and the periphery of the non-Western world are unsustainable. With the development of China, the gap between the comprehensive national strength of China and the United States and the global strategic layout will gradually narrow, while the gap between other international forces and China-United States will become larger and larger. China has grown into another global power besides the United States, and other major developing countries have also grown into power centres other than developed countries, thus promoting the formation of an international pattern of 'two poles and multiple powers'.

4. China's dual role in the existing global order

The international order is manifested from the explicit level of the system arrangements and value norms shared by the international community, while the deep order is the struggle between the great powers revealed by the realism theory. The existing international political order was gradually formed after the Second World War, and it has the characteristics of duality. From the explicit level, it is expressed as the interactive norms and sytem arrangements that are accepted by members of the international community. It is the result of the victory of the anti-fascist war of mankind, and it is also a system accepted by most countries. Chu Shulong, an international strategist, believes that 'the existing global order not only reflects Western values, but also reflects the interests of most countries in the world, including China.'[33] Politically, this system affirms principles of: equality of national sovereignty and national self-determination, while economically establishing the principles of free trade and multilateralism; it has its progressive side.

At the same time, the system is inherently unequal. The deep global order is the competition between major powers for dominance, which reflects the power comparison between them. The deep order dominates the rules and interaction methods of the dominant order, and is more decisive. After the Second World War, the deep global order was a Cold War pattern in which the United States and the Soviet Union competed for hegemony. The Yalta Conference (February 1945) was an arrangement for the United States and the Soviet Union to rule by demarcation and to control the world's two major blocs. With the disintegration of the Soviet Union, the United States became the only superpower, and 'American hegemony – Western centre' became the global dominant order.

As a victorious country in the Second World War, China participated in the construction of the existing global order, and has been an active participant in and beneficiary of such a global order for the past few decades. Since the reform and opening up, the rapid development of China's economy is inseparable from the external environment of overall peace, free trade and investment provided by this international system. In the more than 40 years of reform and opening up, China has generally integrated into the global financial and trade system, and has followed an export-driven development path. The current account and capital account have been in a state of double surplus for a long time. Under the Bretton Woods system, China's export-oriented economy and the U.S. debt-consumption economy formed the 'two poles' of global economic interdependence.

Mao Zedong and other first-generation leaders of the socialist regime made a major decision to restore diplomatic relations with the United States. Based on this particular starting point, China gradually integrated into the existing international system dominated by the United States. After China regained its seat at the United Nations in 1971, it also joined the World Health Organization, and then gradually joined the International Olympic Committee, the World Bank, the International Monetary Fund, the International Atomic Energy Agency, and the Asia-Pacific Economic Cooperation. A landmark event is it entering the World Trade Organization in 2001. So far, China has joined almost all major international organisations in the world. At the same time, as a founding country of the United Nations, a member of the Security Council, a founding country and a member of the Executive Committee of the World Health Organization, a founding member and the third largest shareholder of the World Bank, and a designated member of the International Atomic Energy Agency, China plays a pivotal role in these international organisations. China is no longer in the marginal position of the international system, instead it is a core force in the system.

China will not challenge the existing international order in a confrontational way like the emerging powers of the past. In addition to that, China as a 'vested interest' of the existing international order, as Chu Shulong said, its historical traditions and the interdependence of the contemporary world due to globalisation and networking also determine this.[34]

At the same time, due to the existence of multiple factors, China is a transformative force in the existing global order, and it is impossible to fully integrate into such a 'centre-periphery' global system. First, as a socialist country, China is surrounded by the economic, political, and ideological circles of global capitalism. In such a global system characterised by capital globalisation, it is relatively isolated and excluded. Second, China, as a developing country, is unwilling to join the dominant and dominated world governance order led by developed countries due to historical memory and practical considerations. An example is that after the G7 group was expanded to the G8, some countries proposed to invite China to join this 'elite club', but China, as a developing country, is more willing to participate in the framework of the G20. Exercising its international influence with the U.N. architecture, rather than entering a central club of an unequal order. Third, Chinese cultural legacy prevents China from fully acknowledging the existing unjust global order. Fourth, as a big country with similar scale to that of the United States in terms of territory, population, and economics, such a big entity will not be completely absorbed by the 'centre-periphery' order.

As a newly added global power, China will not overwhelm the existing global order, nor will it enter the centre of the world stage to play the role of a disruptor, but a 'conservative reformer' of the global order. On the one hand, it seeks its own further development within the framework, and on the other hand, it promotes the gradual change of the global order. There are two main strategies for China to 'crowd into' the existing global order. One strategy is to continue to integrate into the existing global order and push for its reforms in a more just and rational direction. Another strategy is to start anew and build a self-led international cooperation mechanism to complement the existing global order.

5. The long-term grand strategic competition between China and the United States

Shortly after taking office in 2017, the Trump administration defined China as a strategic competitor. On the 20 May, 2020, the White House released the strategic approach to the People's Republic of China, abandoning the previous policy of engagement with China created over the past 40 years, and adopted a competitive approach to China. The Trump administration's approach to long-term strategic competition with China is not a new Cold War, but rather the goal of containing China and achieving 'America First', based on strong comprehensive national strength and global hegemony, backed by military deterrence. It is characterised by the integration of peace and war time approaches, fighting while talking. It is a 'borderless total war' in which wars of trade, industry, finance, technology, information, public opinion and other fronts are coordinated.

Although the world has experienced 'borderless total war' from the United States against China, it is still worth observing whether this containment strategy can continue. At the same time, this 'borderless total war' is not a new Cold War. It differs from the Cold War in the following aspects:

First, the integration of interests between China and the United States is much wider than that between the United States and the Soviet Union at the time, and it is difficult for China and the United States to completely decouple. In recent years, the Trump administration promoted the comprehensive decoupling of China and the United States. Economically, it encouraged the return of industries to the United States, and imposed high tariffs on products imported from China. Technologically, it tightened control over technology exports to China and imposed sanctions on Chinese high-tech companies on the Entity List. Regarding the talented people, it imposed various restrictions on Chinese students, diplomats, and journalists visiting the United States. However, due to the huge complementarity and interdependence between China and the United States, it is difficult for American politicians to completely decouple the two countries. The huge scale of Sino-US trade is difficult to completely decouple. In 2019, the trade volume of goods between China and the United States decreased by 14.6% year-on-year, still reaching 541.223 billion US dollars. In the first half of 2020, the total value of Sino-US trade was about 240 billion US dollars, a year-on-year decrease of 6.6%. It is also difficult to completely separate the interdependence of China and the United States in industry, technology, and finance. According to data from the Chinese Ministry of Commerce, the actual U.S. investment in China in the first half of 2020 did not decline, but increased by 6%. It is also difficult to completely halt the exchange between China and the United States. In the 2018-2019 academic year, the number of Chinese students studying in the United States reached

370,000, accounting for one-third of the international students in the United States.[35] According to estimates, it contributed about $15 billion in revenue to the U.S. economy. Nature Index which tracks 82 high-quality journals, finds Chinese–U.S. research collaborations show resilience amid geopolitical change. The number of collaborative papers increased from 3,413 in 2015 to 4,631 in 2018. China has become the second largest scientific research partner of the United States after the European Union.[36]

Second, it is difficult for the existing multilateral international order to be completely overturned. There is a high probability that China and the United States will not fall into the so-called 'Thucydides Trap'. Different from the history of conflict between major powers in the past, China, as an emerging power, is not expansive or aggressive. China has deeply integrated into the existing global order and is a conservative force and defender of it. As a conservative power, the United States has the characteristics of Realism. As the main founder of the global order, in recent years, although the United States has been 'withdrawing from groups' and disrupting the situation, its purpose is not to subvert the existing international order, but to reshape the international order for achieving greater benefits.

Third, countries in the world will not split into two opposing blocs. During the Cold War, the world was divided into two camps that were opposed to each other economically, politically, militarily and ideologically. Today, the interests of different countries are intertwined, and it is difficult to separate them according to ideology. Western countries are not monolithic, and not many countries are motivated to follow the United States to engage in the so-called 'new cold war'.

The Biden administration criticised the Trump administration not for their hard-line policies toward China, but for not being smart enough in their anti-China tactics. The Biden administration also sees China as the No. 1 threat to the United States and believes that the strategic competition between China and the United States defines the characteristics of the twenty-first century. It will continue its strategy of conducting comprehensive competition with China. What will be changed is the competition strategy, from the so-called 'position of weakness' to a 'position of strength' toward China. The Biden administration aims to achieve this by paying more attention to the exercise of global leadership, winning over allies, using its dominant position in multilateral institutions to force China to submit, and to continue to use the 'whole-of-government response' coordinated and promoted in various fields to conduct strategic competition with China. At the same time, it pays more attention to improving its own competitiveness and rebuilding the future of the United States (build back better).

A just cause attracts much support, an unjust one finds little. China's strategy of having a 'Community with a Shared Future for Mankind' (人类命运共同体) is to embrace the world with an open mind. China is not a country that must have hegemony, but instead wants to be benevolent. It does not hatch petit plots in geopolitical games, but provides the world with a big platform for equal and mutually beneficial cooperation such as the 'One Belt, One Road' ('一带一路'). The rise of China will bring huge development opportunities to the rest of the world. The United States uses its hegemony to suppress and smear China in various ways, which will cause great difficulties to China for a certain period of time, but in the long run, the efforts to contain China are futile. Fundamentally speaking, this is not only a competition of technique (术), but also a competition of way (道). Country first, America first is a domineering way (霸道), and a community with a shared future for mankind is a harmonious way (王道). The Trump administration is tyrannical and a bully. The more domineering, the more difficult it is for it to last. As a political veteran, Biden will more skilfully maintain and apply American hegemony, which means it will only change the means, but not its end. In fact, Trump's need to coerce everywhere has failed to achieve his objectives, which is itself a manifestation of the decline of American hegemony. What Trump can't get through persecution is equally difficult for Biden to get through persuasion. Maybe America is still powerful, but it is like an Indian summer, the heat will soon decline. China's vision of having the 'community with a shared future for mankind' is a better way. It is to convince people with virtue, and provide development opportunities to all countries in the world. It seems to be weak at first, and it will encounter many difficulties, but it is the amiable and agreeable way. As time goes by, it will become stronger.

In the context of the game between China and the United States, the strategic focus of building a community with a shared future for mankind in China can unfold into two fundamentals and two big triangles. Two fundamentals: One is to consolidate the fundamentals among the developing countries. The construction of the 'One Belt One Road' has created huge development opportunities for developing countries and is widely welcomed by countries along the route. The second is to stabilise the fundamentals among neighbouring countries. The United States is pursuing a security Indo-Pacific strategy, trying to contain China and create tension in the region. On the other hand, China is on friendly terms with its neighbours economically, promoting the building of an Indo-Pacific community with a shared future, and developing peace and prosperity within the region. Two big triangles: One is to consolidate Sino-Russian friendly relations in the 'China-US-Russia Big Triangle' relationship. China and Russia will upgrade their relations to a new era of comprehensive strategic partnership of coordination, and the United States will be further isolated. The second is that in the 'China-U.S.-Europe Triangle' relationship, the U.S. alliance system is getting less stable. The traditional alliance between the United States and Europe has become increasingly estranged, while the convergence of interests and cognition between China and Europe is increasing.

'How can floating clouds cover the eyes? The big waves are good for fishing boats.' For the strategic competition and suppression of the United States, China must see both severe challenges and historic opportunities. The right time, the right place and the general trend are on China's side. The United States has the right to choose and right to war, but the initiative is with China. China doesn't have to compromise.

The containment of China by the United States is a hurdle that the great rejuvenation of the Chinese nation needs to face. On the other hand, it can also be seen as a stepping stone for the Chinese Renaissance.

6. 'Connected two poles': The new global order

The pivotal moment we are in today is very similar to what Marx described back then. The global order of 'American hegemony-Western-centred' is in the process of accelerated decline, and the inherent imbalance and unsustainability of the global political and economic order are increasingly prominent. Without the participation of emerging powers, not only will it be impossible to effectively deal with challenges such as global climate change, weak economic growth, and security threats, traditional or non-traditional alike, but also the long-term stability and development of the global order cannot be achieved.

According to China's cultural characteristics, strategic thinking and national nature, once China joins the construction of the global order, it will promote the gradual evolution and make changes in the international pattern and norms, and then gradually form a new global order with 'connected two poles'.

First, in the process of evolving from unipolar hegemony to an order of 'connection of two poles', it means the competition between the two poles. The bipolar order between China and the United States has always been in competition and confrontation, and the competition between the two countries for the dominance of the global order will be a long-term process. China and the United States will carry out long-term competition for dominance in the areas of military control around China, the reform of the global financial system, the discourse right in global economic, political governance, and the moral commanding heights of global principles. After Trump took office, the competition between China and the United States has further intensified, and the structural game based on clear rules in the past has been transformed into an unstructured game. The old order and structure have been broken, and the new structure is in the process of forming. The relationship between the two is uncertain.

Second, 'connected two poles' means that the order of the two poles complements and balances each other. The entry of a new polar order represented by China complements the old order. It makes the global governance system more complete, and promotes its development in a more just and reasonable direction. The order represented by the United States can be said to be a domineering order and the new order is a harmonious way. A global strategy that respects national independence and equality more, rather than based on alliance and control, will undoubtedly promote the multi-polarisation and democratisation of global governance. Economic aid and economic cooperation without political strings attached will undoubtedly inject new momentum into the development of developing countries. The value dissemination method of 'each has its own greatness, and shares with each other' can undoubtedly better adapt to the modernisation and revival of major civilisations around the world. Trump's tactics expose the hegemonic nature of the US-led global order. 'A just cause attracts much support while an unjust cause finds little.' The idea of building a community with a shared future for mankind advocated by China's harmonious order will be accepted by more and more people and become a new global order idea of universal significance. China constitutes a check and balance on the US hegemony, which gives other countries more choices in fighting for global resources, and also makes it more difficult for the US to use 'unilateralism' to intervene, pushing the US to reduce its power extension. Similarly, the US checks and balances constitute an important external condition for China's peaceful and benign rise, and China's neighbouring countries do not need to worry about the return of the so-called 'tribute system'.

Thirdly, 'connected two poles' also means the mutual cooperation of the two poles. China and the United States have extensive global common interests. Globalization has closely linked the two. The two have consistent or similar aims in promoting nuclear non-proliferation, Northeast Asia security, global peace, maintaining trade, investment liberalisation, addressing climate change, energy and food requirements. In global affairs, the two are indispensable, which makes the two not only potential competitors, but also each other's most important partners.

The Trump administration has adopted more selfish policies on global challenges such as climate change, while taking a more aggressive approach to China. Nonetheless this does not change the huge mutual interests between China and the US, and Trump cannot pursue his own objectives without cooperation with China. According to a report released by the National Committee on United States-China Relations on January 10, 2017, the bilateral investment and trade relationship between China and the United States has helped the United States create 2.6 million jobs and contributed 1.2% of its gross domestic product, through which each household saved $850 in expenses.[37] At the same time, the broad issues of 'anti-terrorism' and 'Northeast Asia nuclear security' pursued by the United States are fundamentally inseparable from cooperation with China. After taking office, the Biden administration has clearly proposed to strengthen cooperation with China in the fields of climate change and nuclear non-proliferation.

Fourth, the coexistence of bipolarity and multilateralism. The bipolar order is not a 'two-state bloc', but because China joins as a driving force, it is difficult for any party to bypass the multilateral co-determination mechanism to dominate international affairs. Therefore, the 'connected two poles' will promote the democratisation of global governance and make the United Nations wait for the importance of multilateral mechanisms to rise, not fall.

The existing liberal international order is led and founded by the United

States. It is undoubtedly the biggest beneficiary of the current international order and the most conservative force. However, the Trump administration believes that the United States has taken too much responsibility and too little profit in this system, so it is trying to make major revisions to the existing international order such as free trade. This, to a certain extent, allowed the United States and China to exchange the roles of conservatives and reformers. The United States adopted a more self-interest-oriented policy, which exacerbated the further decline of American hegemony, and created a new era for China and other countries to promote the transformation of the system. The Biden administration has returned to the stance of 'multilateralism', re-joined the various groups that the Trump administration withdrew from, and paid more attention to the role of multilateral institutions, which has also created more opportunities for China and the United States to meet each other in international cooperation.

The 'connected two poles' will promote the development of the dominant global order in a more just and rational direction. The US dollar-based global financial system is gradually shifting to a more balanced and sustainable monetary system that reflects changes in international economic strength, and promotes a more balanced global economic development. In the process of further upgrading of the global trade system, it will further accelerate the cross-border flow of goods, capital, personnel and information, and stimulate global mutual benefit and common prosperity. Global security maintenance will rely more on multilateral mechanisms, rather than unilateral bloc dominance.

In recent years, China has been more active in participating in the construction of the international governance system, which has actually gone through a process of gradual in-depth advancement. From initiating the Shanghai Cooperation Organisation, the Boao Forum for Asia, and the BRICS cooperation mechanism, China now proposes the establishment of the Asian Infrastructure Investment Bank and the 'One Belt, One Road' initiative. The proposal of the 'One Belt One Road' initiative marks the first time that China has formed a global strategy. In January 2017, President Xi Jinping delivered a historic speech 'Jointly Build a Community of Shared Future for Mankind' at the United Nations Office in Geneva,[38] this marks that China will enter the global stage as the leader of a new type of globalisation.

Looking to the future, how will China form a complete global strategy?

The rise of China is not the rise of a new hegemon, but the bellwether of the emerging power to construct the global order. As President Xi Jinping said, China and the rest of the world, especially developing countries, are in a 'community with a shared future' that 'breathes the same way and shares a common destiny.' Starting from this positioning, China's global strategy has the following essentials:

First, take the initiative to act as the bellwether of the southern countries, join forces, and compete with the United States for global development. China's competition is not hegemonic, but aimed at safeguarding its own strategic interests and mutual benefit. Second, manage the differences between China and the United States. Through the construction of the 'new type of major-country relationship' between China and the United States, on the basis of maintaining the 'fighting but not excommunicating' pattern, China will reduce the pressure from the United States. The Chinese government strive to maintain coordination and stability between China and the United States, and actively build cooperation between the two sides, and jointly lead a stably changing international order. Third, the strategy, connecting Latin America and Africa, should be launched in a timely manner to form a complete global strategic layout of 'One Belt, One Road' and 'two continents', thus forming a complete global strategic layout. Fourth, focus on adopting a middle-level breakthrough strategy with development as the core, providing a platform for the world, especially benefiting developing countries, and injecting new development impetus. Fifth, at the bottom of the hard power of the global order, China does not seek to become a global military power. Unlike the United States, who engages in global military expansion, China is content to become a military power capable of safeguarding its core interests and actively undertake responsibilities of maintaining multilateral frameworks. Sixth, China actively participates in the transformation of the global governance system, actively undertakes responsibilities, and vigorously promotes the cooperation and co-construction of the global governance system. Seventh, actively promote the global spread of the Chinese model and Chinese culture, and gradually enter the centre of the world's cultural and ideological system.

Changes in the global order in human history have always been accompanied by wars or huge geopolitical disasters. Countless tragedies in history have shown this, and the rise of China has reminded many of the tragedies caused by the rise of great powers in the past and made many to worry about the recurrence of the 'Thucydides Trap'. Due to the characteristics of the Chinese civilization, the rise of China will not repeat the tragic history of hegemony competition in human history. Instead, it will take the role of a new type of global power on the stage of human history. Not only will it not export bloodshed and turmoil, but it will bring huge opportunities for the common development of mankind, and gradually promote the transformation of the global order to guide it with a more just, development in a more reasonable direction. This strategic choice is undoubtedly full of wisdom, not only conducive to the peaceful development and win-win cooperation of the world, but also fundamentally beneficial to the Chinese nation itself.

---

1 *Selected Works of Marx and Engels*, Vol. 1, 2012 Renmin Press, pp. 778-847. [参见《马克思恩格斯选集》(第1卷), 人民出版社 2012 年版, 第 778—847 页]

2 Men Honghua, 2014, 'The Logic of Regional Order Construction', *World Economics and Politics*, No. 7. [门洪华: 《地区秩序建构的逻辑》, 《世界经济与政治》2014 年第 7 期]3

3 Li Bin, 2005, 'What is the Marxist theory of international relations?', *World Economics and Politics*, No.5. [李滨: 《什么是马克思主义的国际关系理论?》, 《世界经济与政治》2005 年第 5 期]

4 Charles Krauthammer, 2006, 'Don't Believe the Hype. We're Still No.1', *Time*, 5 Feb. <https://content.time.com/time/subscriber/article/0,33009,1156589,00.html>, [2 May 2022]

5 Stephen G. Brooks and William C. Wohlforth, 'The Once and Future Superpower' <www.foreignaffairs.com/articles/united-states/2016-04-13/once-and-future-superpower>, [2 May 2022]

6 William C. Wohlforth, 1999, 'The Stability of a Unipolar World', *International Security*, Vol.24, No.1, Summer, pp. 5–41

7 Robert Gilpin, 1994, *War and Change in World Politics*, translated and published by Renmin University Press, p. 196, Originally published in 1981, Cambridge University Press. [罗伯特·吉尔平: 《世界政治中的战争与变革》, 中国人民大学出版社 1994 年版, 第 196 页]

8 Jia Qingguo, 2007, 'Opportunities and Challenges: A Unipolar World and China's Peaceful Development', *International Politics Research*, No. 4; Zhang Ruizhuang, 2013, 'Changes in the International Pattern and China's Positioning', *Modern International Relations*, No. 4. [贾庆国: 《机遇与挑战: 单极世界与中国的和平发展》, 《国际政治研究》2007 年第 4 期。张睿壮: 《国际格局变化与中国定位》, 《现代国际关系》2013 年第 4 期]

9 For example, Jeffery Sachs, a development economist, argues that the leadership of the US, EU and Asia's G3 can only lead to a common response to global challenges, *The Economic Observer*, 11 July, 2009

10 Qin Yaqing, 2010, 'World Patterns, International Institutions and Global Orders', Celebration Special Issue of *Modern International Relations*. [秦亚青: 《世界格局、国际制度与全球秩序》, 《现代国际关系》2010 年庆典特刊]

11 Xiong Jie, 2007, 'The International Pattern in the 21st Century and the Resurrection of China – Also on the Special Relationship of Northeast Asia', *World Economics and Politics*, No. 12. [熊玠: 《21 世纪国际格局与中国之再起——兼论东北亚特殊关系》, 《世界经济与政治》2007年第12期]

12 Yu Sui, 2004, 'The Problem of World Multiploidisation', *World Economics and Politics*, No.3, p.15. [俞邃: 《世界多极化问题》, 《世界经济与政治》2004 年第 3 期, 第 15 页]

13 Yang Jiechi, 2004, 'The Evolution of the Current International Pattern and my country's Diplomatic Work', *World Economics and Politics*, No. 3, p. 15. [杨洁篪：《当前国际格局的演变和我国外交工作》，《世界经济与政治》2004年第3期，第15页]

14 Liu Jiangyong, 2013, 'Evolution of the International Pattern and China's Peripheral Security', *World Economics and Politics*, No. 6. [刘江永：《国际格局演变与中国周边安全》，《世界经济与政治》2013年第6期]

15 Zhang Liangui, 2002, 'International Pattern and Major Power Relations', *Learning Monthly*, No. 6. [张琏瑰：《国际格局与大国关系》，《学习月刊》2002年第6期]

16 Aleksandr Lilov, 2003, 'The Contrast between the Unipolar World and the Multipolar World: The General Trend of the 21st Century', *Foreign Theoretical Trends*, No. 9. [亚历山大·利洛夫：《单极世界与多极世界的对立——21世纪的大趋势》，《国外理论动态》2003年第9期]

17 Richard N. Haass, 2008, 'The Age of Nonpolarity', *Foreign Affairs*, Vol. 87, No. 3; Liu Jianfei, 2015, 'The Evolution of the International Pattern and the Reshaping of the International Order', *Contemporary World and Socialism*, No. 5. [刘建飞：《国际格局演进与国际秩序重塑》，《当代世界与社会主义》2015年第5期] Liu Jianfei and Qin Zhilai, 2012, 'On the "Depolarisation" of the World Pattern and Its Economic Basis', *International Politics Research*, No. 4. [刘建飞、秦治来：《论世界格局"非极化"及其经济基础》，《国际政治研究》2012年第4期]

18 Men Honghua, 2007, "China: Strategic Adjustment in Interaction with the International System", *Opening Herald*, No. 5. [门洪华：《中国：与国际体系互动中的战略调整》，《开放导报》2007年第5期]

19 Fred Bergsten, 2008, 'A Partnership of Equals: How Washington Should Respond to China's Economic Challenge', *Foreign Affairs*, Vol. 87, No. 4, pp. 57–69

20 Yan Xuetong, 2015, 'Why a Bipolar World Is More Likely Than a Unipolar or Multipolar One', *The Huffington Post*, 22 April; Jin Canrong and Duan Haowen, 2013 'The Pattern and New Trends of Major Power Relations in the Post-Crisis Era', *Journal of Hubei University*, Jan. [金灿荣、段皓文：《后危机时代的大国关系格局与新动向》，《湖北大学学报》2013年1月]

21 *Selected Works of Marx and Engels*, 2012, Vol. 1, Renmin Press, p. 778. [《马克思恩格斯选集》第1卷，人民出版社2012年版，第778页]

22 Giovanni Arrighi, 2009, *Adam Smith in Beijing: Lineages of the Twenty-first Century*, translated and published by Social Sciences Academic Press, Originally published in 2007, Verso. [参见乔万尼·阿里吉：《亚当·斯密在北京: 21世纪的谱系》，社会科学文献出版社2009年版]

23 Han Yuhai, 2012, *Marx's Enterprise – From Brussels to Beijing*, Renmin University of China Press, pp. 112–123. [韩毓海：《马克思的事业——从布鲁塞尔到北京》，中国人民大学出版社2012年版，第112—123页]

24 Niall Ferguson, 2012, *Empire: How Britain Made the Modern World*, translated and published by CITIC Press, p. 320, Originally published in 2003, Allen Lane. [弗格森：《帝国》，中信出版社2012年版，第320页]

25 *The Chronicle of Mao Zedong (1949–1976)*, 2013, Vol. 5, Central Literature Publishing House, p. 262. [《毛泽东年谱（1949–1976）》第5卷，中央文献出版社2013年版，第262页]

26 *Science and Technology Daily*, Beijing, 21 April, 2016. [《科技日报》北京2016年4月21日电]

27 Wang Xiangsui, 2011, 'Monetary Geopolitics Changes and Future of the World Pattern', *World Economics and Politics*, No.4. [王湘穗：《币缘政治: 世界格局的变化与未来》，《世界经济与政治》2011年第4期]

28 'Increased participation in CNY cross-border payment system', 26 Aug, 2020, Nikkei Chinese website: <https://cn.nikkei.com/>, [4 May 2021]

29 CEIC Database

30 Paul Kennedy, 2013, *The Rise and Fall of Great Powers: Economic Change and Military Conflict from 1500 to 2000*, translated and published by CITIC Press, Originally published in 1987, Random House. [保罗·肯尼迪：《大国的兴衰: 1500–2000年的经济变革与军事冲突》，中信出版社2013年版]

31 SIPRI Military Expenditure Database
32 Hu Angang, Yan Yilong, and Wei Xing, 2011, 2030 *China: Towards Common Prosperity*, Renmin University Press, p.30. [胡鞍钢、鄢一龙、魏星：《2030 中国：迈向共同富裕》，中国人民大学出版社2011年版，第30页]
33 Chu Shulong, 2012, 'China's Diplomatic Strategy and Foreign Relations', China.com.cn, 13 Sept, <http://www.china.com.cn/international/txt/2012-09/13/content_26514305.htm>, [4 May 2021]. [楚树龙：《中国的外交战略和对外关系》，中国网]
34 Chu Shulong, 2013, 'Changes and Changes in the International Pattern and China's International Strategy', *Modern International Relations*, No. 4. [楚树龙：《国际格局的变与不变及中国国际战略》，《现代国际关系》2013 年第 4 期]
35 Institute of international education. New OpenDoors Data
36 US-China science weathers political ill wind, NATURE INDEX 20 NOVEMBER 2019, <https://www.nature.com/articles/d41586-019-03541-0>, [4 May 2021]
37 'China-US economic and trade relations support 2.6 million US jobs', *Nanfang Daily*, 12 Jan, 2017 [《中美经贸关系支持美国的260万个就业岗位》，《南方日报》2017年1月12日]
38 Xi Jinping, 2017, 'Building a Community with a Shared Future for Mankind', Xinhua News Agency, Geneva, 18 Jan. [习近平：《构建人类命运共同体，实现共赢共享》，新华社2017年1月18日，日内瓦电]

CHAPTER 12
China's 'Three Circle Theory' and the New Strategic Opportunity Period*

[*The first draft of this article is the author's speech at the 'World Development Trend and Our Strategic Opportunity Period' seminar of the Liaison Department of the CPC Central Committee on 20 Feb, 2019, and relevant forums at Nanjing University and Tongji University on 22 May, 2019 and 15 Nov, 2019 Made a report, published in Theoretical Journal Jan, 2020, and revised by the author for inclusion in this book. The author thanks Men Honghua and many theoriests for their suggestions.]

In the second decade of the twenty-first century, the world has entered a new epoch.

The world situation is undergoing profound changes unseen in a century, with turbulence and turmoil. There have appeared in-depth adjustments in the strategies of major powers, profound reorganisation and reconstruction of the international structure and order.

Since the founding of New China, the nation has experienced three periods of strategic opportunity. At present, the third time has gradually closed, and China needs to actively open up a new strategic opportunity period. And this will mean that the process of China's great rejuvenation is irreversible, and it also means that a new global power is entering the centre of the world stage.

The next thirty years will be the final historical juncture of the great journey of national rejuvenation since modern times, and the decisive juncture in the game of global powers in the twenty-first century. It contains not only huge strategic opportunities, but also great risks.

1. Framework: China's 'Three Circles Theory' of strategic management

How to understand the period of strategic opportunity? Everyone has different analysis, but my view is that a period of strategic opportunity is only constituted from the coupling of the three elements, namely the right time, place and the support of people (天时、地利、人和).

The three-element theory seems to be a well-known saying, but it contains deep conventional wisdom. The *Book of Changes* refers to this as 'the way of the three poles': heaven, earth and human beings. The movement of the hexagram is 'to combine three talents and to know Yin and Yang': 'Qian established the pole of heaven via simple wisdom; Kun establishes the pole of earth via minimal capability; both would attribute to the eclectic pole of people.'

During the Warring States Period, the right time, place and people became an important military strategic thought. According to *Master Pheasant Cap* (鹖冠子): 'Military thinking should have considered the time, place and people……those who are good at commanding always think of the three elements carefully'. Guiguzi (鬼谷子) the master of the School of Diplomacy (纵横家), emphasises the need to analyse the strength of a country according to four aspects: weather, terrain, people, and diplomacy.[1] His pupil Sun Bin (孙膑) further proposed that the three elements of victory in war are the advantages of weather, place, and people. He believes that: 'The time of day, advantage of the place, harmony amongst the people, if these three are not obtained, even victory will bring disaster.'[2]

We can refer to the form of Harvard's 'Three Circles Theory'[3] to modernise and theorise the idea of the right time, place and people, and apply it to the strategic management analysis of countries and organisations. We can take the right time, place and people as the three factors that affect the success or failure of a strategy, it can be called China's 'Three Circle Theory' (Fig. 1).

The first element of strategic management is to adapt to the right time (天时). Unlike Harvard's 'Three Circles Theory', the right time does not refer to the external support, but a current external situation. The right time is the suitable situation of strategic management. As time is constantly changing, it means the correct timing offers opportunity. Situations are intricate, there are big, medium, and small trends, sometimes positive while all of sudden things can change.[4] To grasp the right time is to grasp the general trend and opportunity.

Understanding the current situation is the key to the success or failure of a strategy. As the ancients said: 'Although you have wisdom, it is better to take advantage of the situation. Although you have a foundation, it is better to wait for the right time.'[5] 'When the right time comes, both the heaven and

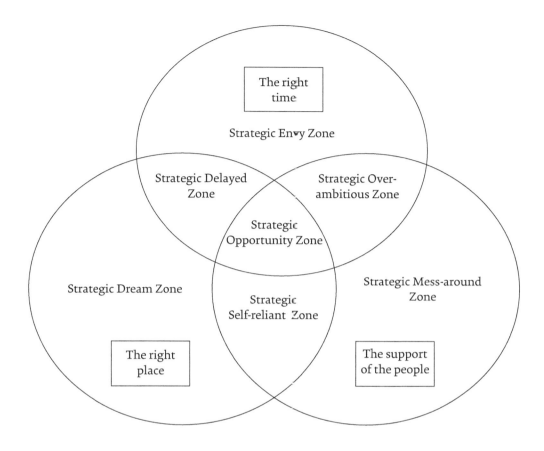

Fig. 1 Strategic Management – China's 'three circles theory'

the earth will lend you strength; when fortune disappears, heroes will no longer be free.'[6] It is also the meaning of the Sui (随) hexagram in the *Book of Changes*, 'only when the world is in accord with the heavenly movement, can the world move happily.' For a country, the right time is the general trend of the world. To grasp the right time is to follow the trend of the world, just as Sun Yat-sen said in the past, 'The trend of the world is mighty, those who follow it will prosper, and those who go against it will perish.'

The fundamental element of strategic management is to identify the correct location. The geographical advantage means the strategic condition, and it does not only refer to ability in the Harvard Three Circles Theory, but also includes strategic conditions such as location and resources. The *Book of Changes* emphasises the role of orientation, and it will affect whether it is superior or inferior, right or wrong.

Geographical factors are the basic conditions for strategic management. This condition constitutes the support for a specific strategy, including both support and constraint factors. Of course, the factors supporting the pros and cons are also dialectical. For example, it is not suitable to grow rice on dry land, but it is suitable to grow wheat.

The dynamic element of strategic management lies in human endeavours. The harmony of the people comes from collaborating efforts, mainly including strategic decision-making and executing capabilities.

People are the active elements of strategic management, and they are also the most critical factors. Mencius believed that 'the right time is not as good as the right location, and the right location is not as good as the right people'.[7] It is the combination of the right people and time with geographical advantages that shapes the period of strategic opportunity. There is no such period of strategic opportunity that 'you can win while lying down'. All of them need to be won through great struggles, especially today.

The right time, place and people, the three elements can form different combinations and constitute different divisions of strategic management (Fig. 1).

There are three situations where there is only one element:

1.1 *Strategic Envy Zone* (战略羡慕区): If there is no right land and people, one can only be envious of the others getting more fish. For example, there was a wave of industrial transfer from the 1950s to the 1970s. In the process of industrial upgrading, the United States, Germany and other western developed countries transferred labour-intensive industries to Japan and emerging Asian countries. These countries seized the opportunity and developed rapidly, while China was in the camp of socialist countries at that time, and neither had the geographical advantage and no people to seize this development opportunity.

1.2 *Strategic Dream Zone* (战略梦想区): It can be a strategic dream if only with geographic advantage without the right time and people. For example, in the 1920s, Sun Yat-sen posited a grand industrialisation plan such as the development of minerals, transportation, commercial ports, and factories.

It can be said to be a great idea of 'making the most of China's vast resources', and is very ahead of its time. But at that time, China was divided and lacked the basic premise of industrialisation. The Western powers regarded China as a source of raw materials, a place for consuming products and semi-colonies, and had little interest in Sun Yat-sen's industrial plan for all countries in the world to jointly invest in China.[8] It can be said that there is not only a lack of support from the people, but also incorrect timing.

1.3 Strategic Mess-around Zone (战略折腾区): There is the support of the people but no right place at the right time, which will only cause unnecessary troubles. This is the situation in the *Book of Changes,* where the Fu hexagram shows it is unwise, lacking in ability, and in a wrong position.[9] It is akin to the situation when people with great bravery and ambition, stepped on the tiger's tail and got reprimanded. A typical example is the 'Great Leap Forward'. The enthusiasm of the whole country to promote the wave of socialist industrialisation was high. It can be said that it had the harmony of the people, but it not only went against the weather, but also surpassed its own development stage and development conditions, resulting in catastrophic consequences.

There are also three cases where there are only two elements:

2.1 Strategic Delayed Zone (战略延误区): When there are the right time and place, yet without the support of the people, strategic opportunities will be missed, which can be called a strategic delayed zone. The 'Hundred Days Reform' in the late Qing Dynasty conformed to the trend of the times and met the needs of China. However, due to the disagreement of the leading groups, after fierce struggles, it ended in miscarriage, which made the nation miss a major historical opportunity.

2.2 Strategic Over-ambitious Zone (战略骛远区): When there are the right time and people's support, but without the geographic advantage, it will turn to be over-ambitious. For example, in the 1960s and 1970s, many foreign policies with strong internationalism were proposed. It can be said to follow the right trend of time, but it disregarded the actual strength of the nation.

2.3 Strategic Self-reliant Zone (战略自力区): When there are people's support and the geographic advantage, but without the suitable timing, it can be self-reliant to achieve certain results. For example, in the 1960s and 1970s, the international situation was unfavourable to China, but the government took the initiative to open up a new strategic vision of 'neutral area in the bipolar system' and 'three worlds' externally, and established an independent and complete industry through a self-reliant system and a strong national defence force internally.

Opportunities are always given to those who are prepared, and the strategic self-reliant zone is also ready for the opening of a new strategic opportunity period.

When all three elements are present:

3.1 Strategic Opportunity Zone: The right time, place and people, the three elements are complete. This is the Tai (泰) hexagram of *Book of Changes*, 'When heaven and earth meet and all things are connected'. With the advantages of the heaven and the earth cooperating with each other, inner and outer strength working together, people will seize the opportunity, promoting a collective harmony.

The strategic opportunity period will also experience various states of birth, stay, change and death, including the opening, maintenance, changing and closing phases.

2. Review: Three periods of strategic opportunities since the founding of New China

A. *The first period of strategic opportunity (1949–1958)*

At the beginning of the founding of the People's Republic of China, the biggest challenge was the formation of the Cold War division between the United States and the Soviet Union. China's active intervention enabled the two camps to form a strategic balance in Asia, and the dividing line was drawn by the Korean War and the Indochina War.

It is precisely based on its profound insight into the general situation of the world that the new China adopted a 'one-sided' strategy. Mao Zedong said that the view that, China may gain a more independent position standing between the United States and the Soviet Union, is just an illusion. The United States and the United Kingdom will not help China. 'One-sided' is to be lined up with the Soviet Union, and in this China can be treated equally.[10]

Domestically, the strategy of 'one body and two wings' is promoted. Namely, socialist industrialisation is the main body, socialist transformation of agriculture and handicraft industries, and socialist reformation of capitalist industry and commerce are the two wings. Thus opened the first strategic opportunity period.

The first period of strategic opportunity won international recognition and security for the new China. The Soviet Union was the first country to establish diplomatic relations with the People's Republic of China, and the first eleven countries to establish diplomatic relations with the People's Republic of China were all socialist countries.[11]

At the same time, it also won foreign aid for China's construction of socialist industrialisation. The construction of 156 industrial projects aided by the Soviet Union constituted the backbone of the 'First Five-Year Plan'.[12] The 'First Five-Year Plan' established the initial foundation of the country's socialist industrialisation, making new China gain a firm foothold.

The first period of strategic opportunity was short-lived and closed gradually in the late 1950s. The external reason is mainly that the Sino-Soviet relationship went south. The two countries started to alienate from each other with continued friction, and finally this turned to confrontation. The internal strategic mistake was abandoning the stable line of industrialisation, first implementing the 'Great Leap Forward' and then changing the judgment on the main domestic contradiction to 'taking class struggle as the primary principle'. This caused major setbacks in domestic economic construction, and at the same time China fell into unprecedented isolation internationally, becoming what the West sees as an 'angry isolated power'.

The closure of the first strategic opportunity period also promoted China's strategic adjustment. When Richard Nixon visited China in 1972, Sino-US relations began to ease. The U.S.–China reconciliation was called by Nixon the 'most dramatic geopolitical event' since World War Two.[13] And this prepares the conditions for the opening of the second strategic opportunity period.

B. The second period of strategic opportunity (1978–1989)

The second strategic opportunity period was created after the reform and opening up.

The most important world trend in this period is peace and development. Deng Xiaoping believed that the real big problems in the world at that time had global strategic issues, one was peace, the other was development. Peace refers to the East-West problem, development guides the North-South problem. The core of the north-south problem is that if the south does not develop, the north may have no way out.[14]

Compared with the early days of new China, the geographical conditions at this time were very different. China already had an independent and complete industrial system and national economic system, strong national defence strength, and abundant natural and human resources. At the same time, its per capita income was still very low, most people lived below the international poverty line, and economic and social aspects were still lagging behind.

National leaders such as Deng Xiaoping and the others reviewed the situation, went beyond ideological boundaries, adopted a more pragmatic 'independent foreign policy of peace', and developed diplomatic relations of equality and mutual benefit with all countries in the world. The formal establishment of diplomatic relations between China and the United States has been achieved, and the normalisation of Sino-Japanese, Sino-Indian, and Sino-Soviet relations has been realised, creating a favourable external environment for reform and opening up. Domestically, the focus was shifted from 'taking class struggle as the primary principle' to 'taking economic construction as the centre', and the implementation of reform and opening up officially opened the second period of strategic opportunity.

This strategic opportunity period had won a peaceful international environment for China, as well as a strategic opportunity to develop by integrating into the world, promoting opening up through reform. Vice versa, the reform was pushed by opening up. In this way, there generated the dividend of the policy, accelerating the speed of development.

The closure of the second strategic opportunity period is mainly due to the disintegration of the Soviet Union, the drastic changes in Eastern Europe and the collapse of the Cold War pattern. The United States no longer regarded China as a pawn to check and balance the Soviet Union. What Nixon called 'the common interest of both nations in containing the Soviet Union' no longer existed. At the same time, the ideological conflict between China and the Western world had become more prominent, and the United States and other Western countries had imposed sanctions on China.

C. The third period of strategic opportunity (1993–2016)

Facing the sudden change in the international situation, Chinese national leaders took stock of the situation and adopted the fundamental national policy of keeping a low profile and 'not taking the lead'. Deng Xiaoping when talking with Jiang Zemin, Li Peng and other comrades, said: 'There are some countries in the third world that want China to take the lead, but we must not take the lead. This is a fundamental national policy. We can't afford to take the lead, and our own strength is not enough. There is absolutely no benefit, and a lot of initiative will be lost if we took that position.'[15] At that time, China's economy was still small. As a developing country, 'Making a fortune in silence' was a wise strategic choice to focus on running the country's affairs well.

Domestically, the policy of reform and opening up was clarified and unswayable, and the 'Decision of the Central Committee of the Communist Party of China on Several Issues Concerning the Establishment of a Socialist Market Economic System' was passed at the third plenary meeting of the fourteenth Central Committee. After a short period of adjustment, a new period of strategic opportunity had been opened.

This period of strategic opportunity is fundamentally different from the second one. It occurred in the Post-Cold War international order. Since the United States had strong confidence in China's 'peaceful evolution' and believed that China would be the next domino after the Soviet Union and Eastern Europe. The 'engagement policy' was thought to enhance China's change from the outside, while the isolation policy will only make China return to the 'state of anger' that threatened the West in the past. In the 1991 US National Security Report, the George H. W. Bush administration stated that 'China is bound to change', and the centre of US policy toward China is 'dialogue and engagement.' The Clinton administration's China policy was carried out within the framework of a diplomatic strategy of engagement and expansion, with the basic goal of bringing China into the system of 'market democracy' through engagement.

At the same time, other strategic factors also made the United States unable to deal with China. After the '9/11' incident in 2001, the Bush administration regarded international terrorism and the so-called 'axis of evil' as its main threats. The Obama administration had made the prevention of nuclear proliferation and nuclear terrorism a primary goal of national security. The United States continued to pursue a policy of engagement with China, which

Table 1 Comparison of the four strategic opportunity periods since the founding of New China

	First	*Second*	*Third*	*Fourth*
Period	1949–1958	1978–1989	1993–2016	2013–
Right Time (International Environment)	The bipolar Cold War pattern between the US and the Soviet Union was formed, and the third industrial revolution was launched.	The loosening of the bipolar Cold War pattern; peace and development had become world themes; the third industrial revolution was advancing.	The end of the Cold War; the pattern of one superpower and multiple powers; the rapid development of the information revolution.	The pattern of two poles and multiple powers; the fourth industrial revolution; the rupture of the process of capitalist integration; the rise of southern countries.
Right Place (Domestic Condition)	The industrial level was extremely low, the people lived in extreme poverty, 80% of the population was illiterate, and a new socialist China was established.	Already had an independent and complete industrial system, with abundant human resources and natural resources, but most of the population still lived below the international poverty line, and the economy and society were still in a backward state.	Entered the middle-income stage; began to transform from a shortage economy to a buyer's market; becoming the second largest economy in the world.	In the transition from a middle-class society to a high-income society, the problem of insufficient effective demand has become prominent, and the economy has moved from the second largest economy to the largest economy.

	First	*Second*	*Third*	*Fourth*
Period	1949–1958	1978–1989	1993–2016	2013–
People's Support (Main strategy)	'One-sided' internationally, and domestically socialist industrialisation.	Reformed the planned economy, having a dual-track system; opened to the outside world, and actively introduce foreign capital.	Carried out market economic reforms; joined the World Trade Organisation; kept a low profile in the international arena.	Entering the stage of high-quality development, innovation leads dividends, promotes the "One Belt One Road" and a community with a shared future for mankind, and achieves an inclusive rise.
Dividend from Opportunities	Established industrial base, gained national security and international recognition.	Entered a stage of rapid development, and people's living standards had rapidly improved.	Accelerating reform and opening up, the economy grew rapidly and became the second largest economy in the world.	The process of China's great rejuvenation is irreversible, and China will become a new global power. Its comprehensive national strength will jump from the second to the first in the world.

also enabled China to continue the third period of strategic opportunity without making fundamental strategic adjustments.

Furthermore, during this period, the global information revolution developed rapidly. China promoted its rapid development by actively participating in the third industrial revolution and joining the WTO. The comparative advantage of China's abundant labour force had been brought into full play, and low-priced Chinese products had begun to be sold all over the world. China had started to appear on the world stage as the 'world's factory' and an 'economic power.'

3. Changes: The third strategic opportunity period closes

The changes in the international environment that China faces are the resource competition issues confronted by the new forces. Since the 1990s, China's influence has begun to rise, but it had not caused much shock or touched the existing world pattern. By the beginning of the 21st century, although small frictions continued between China and the United States or China and the West, there were no major problems. By the second decade of the 21st century, the hegemony of the United States had begun to be shaken, and the cheese of the Western world had been touched by China, which led to the closure of the third strategic opportunity period. This process began after the international financial crisis in 2008, and then began the process of de-globalisation. With Trump's coming to power, the third strategic opportunity period was officially closed. At the present, Sino-US economic and trade frictions have made it more explicit. Of course, the trade dispute will form some kind of compromise, but it does not mean that the deeper path disputes, system disputes, and interests disputes can be eliminated.

The fundamental reason for the closure is that the US-led neoliberal international order allows China to integrate with a ceiling, and China has gradually reached this ceiling.

This has led to three fundamental changes in Sino-US relations and the relationship between China and the West, in the eyes of some Western elites:

First, the economic complementarity turns into competition. The United States and other Western countries have occupied the high-end of the industrial chain, and then outsourced the low-end and middle-end parts to developing countries such as China by means of outsourcing and offshore operations. This model had worked well in the past 30 years. However, as China's scientific and technological strength increases and the industry moves towards the mid-to-high end, it has formed a profound competitive relationship with the Western world led by the United States. Recent reports from the United States and Europe have identified China as the main competitor in key technologies such as 5G and artificial intelligence.[16]

Second, the political absorption relationship is transformed into a check and balance relationship. Since the reform and opening up, the premise of the U.S.'s 'engagement strategy' with China is to absorb China into the global capitalist system dominated by the U.S. This has not changed, and the U.S. also believed that they have strategic confidence and patience, waiting for China's final change. But today, their confidence has been suddenly overturned. Not only is the Western system incapable of digesting the Chinese model, but it has also discovered that this model may have an increasing global impact and pose a challenge to the Western-dominated institutional model and order. The 2017 *U.S. National Security Strategy Report* states that: 'For decades, U.S. policy was rooted in the belief that support for China's rise and in its integration into the post-war international order would liberalize China. Contrary to our hopes, China expanded its power at the expense of the sovereignty of others.' Former U.S. Vice President Mike Pence stated in his speech in a manner of referring to the Cold War: China has begun to reassert its influence regionally and globally, contesting America's geographical advantages and trying in essence to change the international order in their favour.[17] In his 'New Iron Curtain' speech, Pence also emphasised that Nixon's policy focus at that time was to change China, and today this goal has not been achieved, with the fact that China will not change according to what the US expects.

Finally, China has transformed from a passive recipient of globalisation to an active contributor. Since China's reform and opening up, China has actively participated in the globalisation led by Western countries; and according to the strategic goal of the United States, it is to integrate China into a globalised system to realise the expansion of the order headed by the United States. But two major changes have taken place today. One is that the United States has doubts about the international order it has led and built, and hopes to reshuffle the cards. Second, China has changed from an acceptor to an exporter of the international order. On the one hand, it has become a new standard-bearer of advocating the multilateral international order. On the other hand, it has launched the concept of a 'community with a shared future for mankind' and the 'One Belt One Road' initiative, becoming an active promoter of a new globalisation.

This has led the West to re-examine their relationship with China, from the original view of the end of the Cold War to the so-called 'Cold War rematch', the outcome of this rematch may be that China wins and the West loses. On the cover of the November 2017 issue of *Time Magazine* (Asia version), the words 'China won' were written in both English and Chinese.

This outdated hegemonic mentality, Cold War attitude, and zero-sum game thinking have led some Western elites to lose calm in facing China's rise, believing that China's rise will bring about the decline of the West, weaken the technological and industrial advantages of the West, and at the same time destroy the Western foundation of the institutional model and way of life, which is the root of the so-called 'New China Threat Theory'.

The 2017 U.S. National Security Strategy report listed 'revisionist countries' represented by China and Russia as the first of the three challenging forces the U.S. was facing, which is a change from the formulation in the decades following the Cold War. The report also believes that 'China is seeking a strategy that can replace the US influence in the Asia-Pacific region, expanding the sphere of influence of its state-led economic model and rewriting the regional order in its favour.'

Correspondingly, the United States has also made fundamental adjustments to define China's strategic positioning, from 'responsible stakeholder' in the Bush administration, 'responsible leader' in the Obama administration[18] to 'strategic competitor' in the Trump administration. This marks the biggest transformation of the U.S. strategy towards China since the establishment of diplomatic relations between China and the U.S. Although the Biden administration will make major adjustments to its China policy, however fundamentally it will remain unchanged in its grand strategic competition with China. What has changed is the strategy of competition and suppression towards China.

'The green mountains can't cover, after all, it flows east.' Like it or not, the old days are going away. The Chinese people need the courage and wisdom that Comrade Mao Zedong had when he said: 'Farewell, John Leighton Stuart.'

4. The right time: The general trend of the world in the new era

A. *The rise of the fourth industrial revolution*

The industrial revolution will lead to the subversion and transformation of traditional industries, as well as the replacement of core industries and the reorganization of industrial chains, which will lead to revolutionary changes in the economic structure.

The key factor for the rise of world powers in history is to take leadership of the emerging industrial revolution. From the 1760s to the 1840s, Great Britain led the first industrial revolution and became the world's number one power at that time. In the 1860s and 1870s, Western developed countries such as Germany and the United States led the second industrial revolution and became world powers. Since the 1940s and 1950s, the United States has been the leading country in the third industrial revolution, which has cemented the United States unshakable position as the most powerful country in the world.

During the first and second industrial revolutions, China was in a marginalised position. After the founding of the People's Republic of China, on the one hand, it had to catch up, complete the first two industrial revolutions, and at the same time it became a follower and an active participant in the third industrial revolution.

The fourth industrial revolution, characterised by digitalisation, intelligence, biotech, quantum technology, and so forth, is blooming. This is the greatest and most profound economic and social transformation since the industrial revolution in the eighteenth century. Its speed, depth and breadth of the transformation may surpass the previous industrial revolutions.

The competition for the commanding heights of the fourth industrial revolution has become the focus of the game between major powers in the world. In February 2019, the White House Science and Technology Policy Committee released a new industry initiative, listing four major industries of artificial intelligence, high-end manufacturing, quantum information science and 5G as the key needed by United States to dominate the future industry. Subsequently the White House issued a statement that the United States will dominate the competition in the world's 5G industry. Germany's 'National Industrial Strategy 2030' clearly states that 'only countries that possess and master new technologies can always maintain a favourable position in the competition'.

Unlike the previous industrial revolutions, China has become one of the leaders of the fourth industrial revolution. In key fields such as digital economy, artificial intelligence, quantum computing, 5G, and so forth, China is in the leading position. This of course means vast opportunities, but it also huge risks, not only to face fierce market competition, but also the suppression and blockade of competitors.

B. The basic pattern of the world has shifted from 'one superpower, many strong powers' to 'two poles and many strong'

After the Cold War, the basic pattern of the world is 'one superpower, many strong powers'. Although global power has been dispersed to multiple centres, the United States is the only superpower. Since the beginning of the new era, this basic pattern has gradually transformed into 'two poles and multiple powers'.

This is mainly driven by two factors. The first is the decline of American hegemony. Perhaps it is too early to say that the decline of the United States is now, but the decline of American hegemony is an observable fact. As mentioned earlier, the decline of American hegemony is due to its inherent crisis, the separation of the real economic centre from the virtual economic centre, the mismatch between the investment and income of the global military system, and the global presence of the United States has exceeded its national carrying capacity. Secondly, the rise of China has made China gradually break away from the second group, and its strength has gradually approached that of the United States.

At the same time, other major powers in the world do not have the conditions to grow into global powers like China and the United States in terms of size of territory, total population, economic output, foreign trade, scientific, technological, and military strength. It is difficult to see them growing to be a 'pole' of the world. The changes in the basic pattern of the world are not 'multi-polarisation' but 'bipolarisation', changing from 'one superpower, many strong' to a 'two poles and many strong' pattern.

Of course, this does not mean that there will be a pattern of co-governance between China and the United States like the G2. Instead, China and the United States will compete with each other, check and balance each other, and carry out high-intensity games. Former US President Trump called it the 'global power race'. At the same time, the interdependent and complementary world governance system is similar to the global order of 'contact of two extremes' postulated by Karl Marx.

C. *The integration process of the global capitalist system is broken*

Since the Second World War, the rapid development of productive forces and the continuous improvement of living standards have led to the integration process of global capitalism. Domestically, the integration process is manifested as a great relaxation of class contradictions. The interests of the bourgeoisie are the 'universal interests' of the whole society. The rise of the middle class has become the backbone of society, and the poor have also received better welfare guarantees. Western society has emerged as a 'comfortable, stable, rational and democratic' one-dimensional society that Herbert Marcuse posited.[19] Among countries, the integration process is manifested as a win-win situation between developed countries and developing countries, and free capital investment and free trade in developed countries also promotes the prosperity of developing countries.

With the outbreak of the financial crisis, the process of integration of the global capitalist system since the end of the Cold War is breaking down. The middle class in western developed countries has increasingly become the 'misery class', the olive-shaped income distribution is changing to 'M-type', and an exclusive few occupy most of global wealth. According to Oxfam, the world's 26 richest people in 2018 were as wealthy as the 3.8 billion people who make up the poorer half of the world's population.[20] The intensification of confrontational contradictions between classes is manifested in politics, as populism and extreme right forces are on the rise, and the operation of political parties has changed from being neutralised to polarised. From the perspective of international relations, the rupture of the integration process is manifested by the shrinking of global foreign investment and trade, and the emergence of the trend of anti-globalisation, unilateralism, isolationism, separatism and trade protectionism.

The rupture of the global capitalist integration process means that the Western economy and society are undergoing a profound transformation, which will bring many uncertainties to the future development of the world, but also means many new possibilities. Correspondingly, with the rise of China, the new type of socialism will increasingly show vigour and vitality of universal significance in the twenty-first century.[21]

D. *World history from great divide to great flip*

Since the 'long sixteenth century' as historians call it, the world has seen a great divide between the West and the non-West, and the Western world has emerged as the dominant civilisation in the global system. Under the pressure of strong military superiority, material superiority and spiritual superiority displayed by the West, all differences between non-Western and Western civilisations in national conditions have been disciplined as the gap between pre-modern and modern, periphery and centre. The combination of Western-ness and modernity has transformed into a universality, and non-Western countries have actively joined or been coerced into this system.

China's rise will lead to a full-scale revival and collective rise of southern countries. From 1950 to 2015, the proportion of Western Europe and the United States' GDP in the world's total dropped from 53.6% to 32.7%, and this trend is still ongoing. It will change from big divergence and diversion to big convergence and reversal.[22]

The process of economic convergence is accompanied by a collective revival of non-Western civilisations, with non-Western countries transforming from recipients of the world system to co-builders. This is a process in which different civilisations in the world achieve true universality through equal communication and dialogue, rather than the universality that is disguised by Western standards. This is the process by which non-Western civilisations, countries, and people gain subjectivity in world history. Once this latent, repressed, and marginalised subjectivity is turned over, it will surely write a new epoch of human history.

The end of the 'American century' does not mean that a new hegemony will replace the United States to dominate the world. The 21st century is neither the 'American century', the 'Western century', nor the 'Chinese century', but the 'world century'.

5. Geographical advantage: domestic conditions in the new era

From a domestic perspective, China has entered a new era. Compared with the second and third strategic opportunity periods, the geographical conditions have undergone profound transformations in four aspects.

First, the comprehensive strength has changed from a regional to a global power. As mentioned earlier, China is the only major country in the world other than the United States that has comprehensive strategic resources. It is very different from what Comrade Deng Xiaoping said back then, when China lacked strength. This has given China the conditions and strength to grow into a global power.

Second, the main contradiction of economic development has changed from insufficient effective supply to insufficient effective demand. The uneven distribution of wealth in the market economy will lead to insufficient consumption. And the decline of average profit rate will lead to insufficient effective investment, which creates the problem of insufficient effective demand, after the economic development of each country reaches a certain level. China's economic development transformed from a shortage economy to a relative surplus stage, insufficient effective demand has become a fundamental challenge. Objectively, this also requires China to plan its own development on a larger global scale.

Third, China will transform from a middle-income society to a high-income society. In 2020, China's per capita income exceeded 10,000 US dollars. It is expected that during the '14th Five-Year Plan' period, China will cross the threshold of high income and transform into a society dominated by urban population and an economy dominated by service industries, with global competitiveness. It will shift from the factor cost advantage to the comprehensive advantage of innovation as the core. The needs of the people are more diversified, the contradiction between unbalanced economic and social development is further highlighted, the population is aging, the birthdate is declining, the population with chronic diseases is increasing, and 'developed diseases' such as 'small wealth is safe' are prominent.

Fourth, the modernisation engine has changed from the 'old five modernisations' to the 'new five modernisations'. The second and third strategic opportunity periods mainly relied on the 'five': industrialisation, urbanisation, internationalisation, informatisation and marketisation, which provide continuous impetus for China's development. In the new era, the driving factors of China's development have already changed and become the 'new five modernisations': modernisation of the industrial system, urban agglomeration and urban-rural integration, new globalisation, digitisation and intelligence, and modernisation of the governance system. Industrialisation has been transformed into the modernisation of the industrial system, which is to build a modern industrial system. Urbanisation is no longer mainly based on population and land. China's urbanisation rate has exceeded 60%. The period of rapid urbanisation is difficult to continue for a long time. The new round of urbanisation is mainly driven by the integration of the metropolises and rural areas. Internationalisation has also changed from opening to foreign countries to building a larger domestic market, from the recipient of globalisation to the exporter of globalisation. In the context of anti-globalisation, China has become one of the important leaders of a new type of globalisation. Informatisation has been further transformed into digitisation and artificial intelligence, leading the fourth industrial revolution by promoting high digital technologies. The driving force of marketisation is also weakening, and the marginal benefits that can be released by market-oriented reforms are getting smaller and smaller. The new driving force for institutional innovation comes from the modernisation of the national governance system.

6. Risks: New Age strategic traps

In the new epoch, China is also facing several strategic traps and strategic risks which it needs to avoid:

The first is to avoid the trap of a 'new cold war'. Although the Trump administration has launched a 'total war without borders' against China, this is not a new Cold War. Different from the Cold War, the interests of China and the United States are much more connected than that of between the United States and the Soviet Union, and it is difficult for China and the United States to completely decouple. It is also impossible to completely overturn the existing international order. The nations of the world will never be divided into two opposing blocs. The Biden administration's attempt to create an anti-China encirclement is also difficult to achieve.

When it comes Sino-US relations, it is needed to be vigilant to not fall into the trap of a 'new Cold War', which is to avoid the relations from heading to a comprehensive confrontation in economy, technology, and culture. Sino-US relations should not be a full-scale cold war, nor a relationship of competition-cooperation, but a relationship of struggle-cooperation over a long time. It is necessary to maintain a pattern of struggle and cooperation.

This requires stabilising and expanding the common interests of China and the United States, and strengthening exchanges with American local governments, enterprises and individuals who are willing to engage with China.

At the same time, it is necessary to implement balanced diplomacy, and make more mutually beneficial relationships with other countries to respond to the great alliance of the United States, hence to carry out grand strategic competition with the United States.

Finally, to be active and promising, China still needs to keep a low profile, and find strategic gaps, try its best to maintain the coordination and stability of Sino-US relations, and maintain the pattern of struggle while not breaking off entirely.

The second is to avoid the American-style 'contemporary aristocracy' trap. China will not repeat the mistakes of Japan, Germany and other countries that engage in military expansion after they become strong, but needs to be wary of being overwhelmed by the policy of strong only in appearance, like the US. The United States for maintaining 'the elegant status quo', has increased its national debt and brought the burden and risks on its people.

When Mao Zedong commented on the United States, he quoted Wang Xifeng's words from *Dream of the Red Chamber*, 'The big ones have big issues'.[23] After China becomes strong, it will encounter 'big issues'. Although China will not put its hands everywhere like the United States, it must be wary of having friends all over the world while taking burdens accordingly. In the process of advancing the global strategy, the U.S. has surpassed its own national strength, and has been overwhelmed by taking on too many responsibilities. China needs to put the whole world in its heart, yet at the same time, must regard domestic affairs as the priority. China would not meddle the leaves while hurting the root. Foreign aid and international responsibilities must be premised on not exceeding the country's development stage and national strength. The implementation of international cooperation strategies must be based on mutual benefit and win-win results.

The third is to avoid entering the 'high income trap'. Developed countries such as Japan have fallen into the high-income trap of close to zero growth for a long time, and China needs to take precautions to deal with the challenges of aging and 'low birth-rate'. In addition, if the problem of the huge gap between the rich and the poor cannot be solved, it will not only make economic growth lose momentum, but also may cause severe social unrest and conflict.

The fourth is to avoid the trap of de-industrialisation. Many developed countries have entered the post-industrial stage and have transferred their manufacturing industries to foreign countries. On the one hand, resources are allocated more effectively, but it has also caused the problem of de-industrialisation, which results in a decline in national competitiveness and a large amount of labour groups have lost employment opportunities. The United States, Germany and other countries have proposed the goal of re-industrialisation. For example, Germany proposed to increase the proportion of industry to 25% by 2030, and the European Union to 20%.[24] The lesson must be learnt, de-industrialisation is a strategic trap that needs to be avoided in the process of China's economic transformation and upgrading. At the same time, the manufacturing industry must maintain its advantages, not relying on traditional cost advantages, but relying on comprehensive advantages to achieve Made in China and Created in China.

7. Harmony among the people: grand strategy to create the fourth strategic opportunity period

Although the third strategic opportunity period officially ended when Trump came to power in early 2017, since 2013, China has taken the initiative to undertake a major strategic transformation. Internally, the most important thing is to change the policy from 'not taking the lead' to giving full play to global leadership, putting forward the 'One Belt One Road' initiative and the concept of building a community with a shared future for mankind. Domestically, the most significant task is to promote the transformation of the development model, and promote the transformation from high-speed development to high-quality development with innovation as the core. This series of 'first moves' has promoted the gradual opening of the fourth strategic opportunity period.

Here are three additional suggestions:

First, China must promote the second emancipation of the mind. Since the founding of the People's Republic of China, the opening of the three strategic opportunity periods had experienced great ideological discussions, and a consensus was formed to unite the people and look forward to the future. In particular, the opening of the second strategic opportunity period benefited from the great discussion on 'practice is the only criterion for testing truth', and the 'Resolution on Several Historical Issues of the Party since the founding of the People's Republic of China' was formed, thus breaking the dogmatism and forming the consensus on reform and opening up, created the conditions for the second strategic opportunity period in terms of ideology. Although the report of the Nineteenth National Congress of the CPC has clearly stated that China has entered a new era, social consensus has not yet been formed. Many people's bodies have entered a new era, but their minds are still stuck in the old one. They need a new emancipation of their minds to escape from the trap of new dogmatism, especially some 'foreign dogmas' which formed since the reform and opening up. It is necessary to systematically summarise not only the experience of reform and opening up, but also the lessons of reform and opening up, so as to create the appropriate ideological conditions for the fourth strategic opportunity period.

Second, China must realise the shift from the previous benefit of opening up to obtaining dividends led by innovation. The core strategy of the second and third strategic opportunity periods is reform and opening up, but the dividends of reform and opening up are already declining. The reform of institutional mechanisms is of course never-ending, but it is increasingly entering a stage where no clear model can be followed, which essentially requires institutional innovation rather than traditional reform. Internationally, the dividend of integrating into the world through openness has also been decreasing, and has increasingly turned into a leading dividend. Opening the dividend is to follow the global trend, while leading the dividend is to lead the world trend and provide Chinese products, solutions, standards and modes.

The core strategy of the fourth strategic opportunity period should be innovation and leadership, from obtaining the dividend of reform and opening up, to generating the dividend of innovation and leadership. In order to build China into an innovative society and an innovative country, an atmosphere of innovation and catching-up will be formed in all fields. Only by catching up with the frontiers in all fields can China gain new strategic opportunities and vitality to form leading advantages.

There are three new innovation systems: a new national system for major strategic needs, an efficient Research and Development application system with market-oriented enterprises as the main body, and a basic research system for cutting-edge technologies and cutting-edge theories. In the future, it is necessary to further improve these three, especially to strengthen the fundamental research system.

In addition, it is necessary to promote the innovation and leadership of products, and the transition from 'made in China' to 'created in China'. China has to actively promote institutional innovation and leadership, and create the most advanced institutional model in the world in terms of economic, political, and social systems. Finally, China needs more innovation and leadership of ideas, sharing good Chinese stories, solutions and wisdom.

The third is that China needs to realise the transition from peaceful rise to inclusive rise. We must fully understand the shock of China's rise to the world. There are concerns and misunderstandings that China must clarify. The first concern, is for developed countries, who are afraid that the rise of China will weaken their industries and put forward a challenge to the Western-dominated global order. The second is that geopolitical regional powers like India are afraid that as China becomes stronger, it will pose a geopolitical threat. The third is China's neighbouring countries, worried that the rise of China will cause the return of the 'tributary system'.

The idea of peaceful rise today is no longer sufficient in convincing those who believe in the so-called 'New China Threat Theory', therefore China is required to explain the concept of inclusive rise, derived from 'inclusive growth'.[25] Inclusive rise means that the rise of a great power is peaceful rather than aggressive; it is a win-win relationship rather than excluding participants; it improves the global order rather than destroying it; it brings opportunities rather than threats.

China's rise is a peaceful rise. It will not repeat the logic that a strong country must hegemonise, nor will it repeat the mistakes of other countries' territorial expansion, nor will it pursue geopolitical expansion. This is due to the characteristics of Chinese civilisation, system and national strategy. China will be a staunch defender of world peace, not a destroyer.

China's rise is a win-win situation, and its global influence is mainly reflected in providing a platform for the common development of the world. For developing countries, China's inclusive rise will bring real opportunities, and China's investment will become the driving force for development. The 'One Belt One Road' policy is the best gift from a rising China to the world.

For developed countries, China's inclusive rise does not pose a threat, but rather healthy competition. More than 200 years have passed since the Industrial Revolution, but only one billion people have entered the club of developed countries. The development of the world still has huge potential. The rise of China can make the cake bigger with other countries in the world, and nobody's cheese will be taken.

For neighbouring countries, a strong China will not repeat the logic that a strong country must gain hegemony, nor will it expand its territory. On the contrary, China's development will form a radiation effect of economic development, which will promote East Asia to become the second largest region after North America and Europe, forming the third largest developed economic circle.

The rise of China will not subvert the existing global order, but promote the improvement of it. China has integrated into the existing global system, and is a conservative force, not a subversive one. By building a community with a shared future for mankind, China will promote the development of the global order in a more just direction.

The rise of China is not exclusive, but inclusive. It will not bring threats to other countries in the world, but will bring opportunities from China to other countries, and bring peace, stability and prosperity to mankind in the 21st century.

---

1 Guiguzi [《鬼谷子•飞箝篇五》："将欲用之天下，必度权量，能见天时之盛衰，制地形之广狭，岨崄之难易，人民货财之多少，诸侯之交孰亲孰疎孰爱孰憎。"]
2 *Sun Bin's Art of War* [《孙膑兵法•月战》]
3 Harvard's 'Three Circles Theory' refers to 'values, capabilities, and support – analytical framework'. It is an analytical tool for leadership strategic management and decision-making proposed by the Harvard Kennedy School of Government. It is widely used in analysing public management teaching and strategy
4 *Book of Changes* [《易经》 泰卦的九三爻]
5 *Mencius* [《孟子•公孙丑》]
6 Luo Yin, *Choubiyi* [罗隐：《筹笔驿》]
7 *Mencius* [《孟子•公孙丑下》]
8 Sun Yat-sen, 2011, 'Strategies for the Founding of the People's Republic of China', *Selected Works of Sun Yat-sen*, Vol. 1, People's Publishing House. [孙中山：《建国方略》,《孙中山选集》（上卷），人民出版社 2011 年版]
9 *Book of Changes* [《易经》履卦六三: 眇能视，跛能履，履虎尾咥人，凶，武人为于大君。《象》曰：眇能视，不足以有明也，跛能履，不足以与行也，咥人之凶，位不当也，武人为于大君，志刚也]
10 Mao Zedong, 1994, 'Is "One-sided" correct?', *Selected Works of Mao Zedong's Diplomacy*, Central Literature Publishing House, pp. 278–279. [毛泽东：《"一边倒"对不对》,《毛泽东外交文选》，中央文献出版社1994年版，第278—279页]
11 Jin Chongji, 1998, *Biography of Zhou Enlai (1949–1976)*, Central Literature Publishing House, p. 33. [金冲及：《周恩来传(1949-1976)》，中央文献出版社 1998 年版，第 33 页]
12 The 'First Five-Year Plan' stipulates: the construction of 156 industrial units with the aid of the Soviet Union, 145 projects will start construction during the 'First Five-Year Plan' period, and 11 projects will be constructed during the 'Second Five-Year Plan' period, out of 156 projects, 150 projects were actually implemented, mainly heavy industry projects, including 44 projects in the national defense industry, 20 in the metallurgical industry, 52 in the energy industry, 24 in the institutional industry, 7 in the chemical industry, and 3 in the light industry. The Office of the Finance and Economics Committee of the National People's Congress, et al., 2008, *Compilation of Important Documents on the Five-Year Plan for National Economic and Social Development since the founding of the People's Republic of China*, China Democracy and Legal System Press, p. 623. Liu Guoguang et al., 2006, Research Report on China's Ten Five-Year Plans, pp. 76-78. [全国人大财经委办公室等：《建国以来国 民经济和社会发展五年计划重要文件汇编》，中国民主法制出版社 2008 年版，第 623 页。刘国光等：《中国十个五年计划研究报告》，2006 年，第 76—78 页]
13 Richard Nixon, 1997, *1999: Victory Without War*, Translated and published by World Knowledge Press, p. 284, Originally published in 1988, Simon & Schuster. [尼克松：《1999: 不战而胜》，世界知识出版社 1997 年版，第 284 页]

14 Deng Xiaoping, 1993, 'Peace and Development are the two major issues in the contemporary world', *Selected Works of Deng Xiaoping*, Vol. 3, Renmin Press, pp. 105-106. Originally the article was published in 1985. [邓小平：《和平和发展史当代世界的两大问题》，《邓小平文选》（第3卷），人民出版社1993年，第105–106页]

15 *Selected Works of Deng Xiaoping*, 1993, Vol. 3, People's Publishing House, p. 363. [《邓小平文选》（第 3 卷），人民出版社 1993 年版，第 363页]

16 On 12 March, 2019, the European Union released the report *EU-China: A Strategic Outlook*: 'China can no longer be regarded as a developing country, it is a key global actor and leading technological power.'

17 <https://www.whitehouse.gov/briefings-statements/remarks-vice-president-pence-administrations-policy-toward-china>, [4 May 2021]

18 The 2015 'US National Security Strategy Report' pointed out: The United States welcomes the rise of a stable, peaceful, and prosperous China. We seek to develop a constructive relationship with China that delivers benefits for our two peoples and promotes security and prosperity in Asia and around the world. We seek cooperation on shared regional and global challenges such as climate change, public health, economic growth, and the denuclearisation of the Korean Peninsula

19 Herbert Marcuse, 2008, *One-Dimensional Man: Studies in the Ideology of Advanced Industrial Society*, translated and published by Shanghai Century Publishing Group, Originally published in 1964, Beacon Press. [马尔库塞：《单向度的人——发达工业社会意识形态研究》，上海世纪出版集团 2008 年版]

20 <http:// finance.sina.com.cn/stock/usstock/c/2019-01-22/doc-ihqfskcn9227915.shtml>, [4 May 2021].

21 Yan Yilong et al., 2018, *The world is for the public: Chinese socialism and the long 21st century*, Renmin University Press. [鄢一龙等：《天下为公：中国社会主义与漫长的 21 世纪》，中国人民大学出版社 2018 年版]

22 Hu Angang, Yan Yilong, Wei Xing, 2013, *2030 China: Towards Common Prosperity*, Renmin University Press. [胡鞍钢、鄢一龙、魏星：《2030 中国：迈向共同富裕》，中国人民大学出版社 2013 年版]

23 *The Chronicle of Mao Zedong (1949–1976)*, Vol. 5, 2013, Central Literature Publishing House, p. 262. [《毛泽东年谱(1949—1976)》第 5 卷，中央文献出版社 2013 年版，第262页]

24 Made in Germany: Industrial Strategy 2030

25 The concept of 'inclusive growth' was first proposed by the Asian Development Bank in 2007, and its original meaning is that 'effective inclusive growth strategies need to focus on high growth that can create productive jobs and ensure equal opportunities. social inclusion and social safety nets that reduce risk and provide buffers for the most vulnerable'

CHAPTER 13
Communitism: A New Paradigm for International Relations in the 21st Century*

[* The first draft of this article is the author's speech at the 29th Wanshou Forum on the theme of 'The Great Change in the World and Xi Jinping's Diplomatic Thought' held in Beijing on 25 June, 2019. It was published in the September 2019 issue of Economic Tribune, when it was included in this book, the author made revisions, and the author thanks Wang Xiangsui and others for their comments.]

Since entering the second decade of the 21st century, the world seems to have entered an era of unprecedented anxiety. The optimism about globalisation since the Cold War is disappearing, and anti-globalisation, nationalism, populism, and unilateralism have resurged. Conflicts of nations and clashes of civilisations are rampant. Mankind is at a crossroad full of uncertainty.

Today, the liberal international order appears to be in unprecedented trouble, with Russian President Vladimir Putin proclaiming that liberalism is outdated.[1] American international relations scholar John Mearsheimer believes that 'the politics of the liberal international order formed after the Cold War is on the verge of collapse in 2019'.[2] So is international politics going to return to the law of the jungle? Former US President Donald Trump is a politician with a high degree of Realism, but the dilemma of Trump's international strategy also reflects the complex dilemma of realist theory dealing with international relations in the 21st century.

The participants in the 29th Wanshou Forum represented 20 countries, and according to their speeches, a common voice could be heard. Since the old world order represented by the United States is declining, where will the world go? Many have turned their eyes to the East, hoping to find answers about the new world order in China.

The concept of building a community with a shared future for mankind proposed by President Xi Jinping and the practice of China alongside other countries in the world in recent years, have realised a new paradigm for international relations in the 21st century that is different from Realism and Liberalism – communitism (共同主义).

The premise of Realist theory is the anarchy of international politics and the relentless pursuit of power by states (especially great powers). However, we must see that the anarchy of international politics is by no means putting the world in the law of the jungle, it has formed a set of concepts, rule systems, and multilateral international institutions that are commonly accepted by everyone. What we need to do is to reform and upgrade, instead of abandoning it.

As emphasised by the liberal theoretical paradigm, globalisation has formed a high degree of interdependence among countries. The interdependence between countries is not only tight, but also mutual. Any complete 'decoupling' is unimaginable, and any unilateral act of containment will encounter corresponding opposing forces.

Neither of these two theoretical paradigms can effectively respond to the two realities of international politics in the 21st century. The first is that the biggest issue of globalisation lies in its imbalance and inequality. The second is the continuous expansion of the global public field. This makes the narrow nationalist thinking of Realism increasingly lag behind the needs of the times. Furthermore the inequality makes the international order advocated by 'liberalism' unstable and fragile, and it is weak in dealing with complex international challenges.

Communitism not only conforms to the reality of international politics but also responds to the challenges of international politics in the 21st century; meanwhile it is idealistic, reflecting Chinese tradition, Chinese solutions and Chinese wisdom. Compared with Realism and Liberalism, it mainly has the following characteristics:

1. Universal security concept versus the balance of power security concept, collective security concept

Neither the realistic idea of balance of power security nor the liberal concept of collective security can solve the security dilemma of international politics. The realistic international theory emphasises the formation of a strategic balance of power. The strategic balance of power cannot solve the common security problems of all countries, instead it can lead to national power competition, arms competition, and confrontation between different alliances. All parties involved are trying to expand their strategic advantages, and hegemonic countries are also trying to pre-emptively occupy absolute strategic advantages and pursue military advantages over their competitors. The strategic balance of power is often unstable. The rise and fall of the national power of various countries will cause the adjustment of the security pattern under the original strategic balance of power, and this adjustment is often achieved through war, or even a world war.

After the two World Wars, the international community realised that it is difficult to maintain world peace only by force. The United States took the lead in proposing a collective security mechanism, and on this basis established a collective security mechanism centred on the United Nations Security Council. It has played an important and positive role in maintaining peace in the Post-War world. However, under the condition of unequal power, the collective security maintenance mechanism has often become a tool for hegemonic countries to sanction their opponents by 'using what is right, or discarding it if they are not.' Maintaining the world order, unfortunately it often creates new enemies.

The communalist security concept is a universal idea, which transcends the balance of power security concept and the collective security concept. It connotes comprehensive, cooperative and sustainable security concepts posited by President Xi Jinping.[3]

The universal security concept is a common security concept that coordinates the concerns of all parties. In a modern world of interdependence and diversity, no country should pursue absolute security. Security should be common and mutual, and all countries have equal rights to participate in security affairs and assume corresponding responsibilities. Every country and nation has the right to survival and development. History has repeatedly warned us that neither global nor regional hegemony should use power to oppress other countries and pursue the absolute security concept of suppressing strategic opponents. In the long run, all kinds of hegemony are sowing the seeds of hatred and confrontation. For example, the deterioration of the Iranian nuclear issue is largely caused by hegemonic countries' pursuit of unilateral absolute security and their insistence on adopting unilateralism.

The security concept of the 21st century is recommended to adopt the idea of a community with a shared future for mankind. While pursuing one's security, it must also consider the security concerns of the other parties, and gradually establish strategic mutual trust in security. China has a long land border, and at the same time, the historical situation is complicated. In the spirit of good-neighbourly friendship and taking into account common security concerns, China has demarcated the land borders of 12 of the 14 land neighbours except India and Bhutan, laying the foundation of the legal basis for peace in the surrounding area. In dealing with the border issue with India, China has always responded to border frictions with restraint. After China's national strength has become stronger, it will not believe in 'strength and despise morality', invading neighbours, like Japan did. Following the jingoist way, certain strategic benefits may be obtained in the short term, and in the long run, the repayment will only be doubled.

The universal security concept is a cooperative security concept that coordinates various mechanisms. On the one hand, it firmly upholds the authority of the UN Security Council and other multilateral security mechanisms; on the other hand, we must oppose the wilful use of force intimidation, unilateral sanctions and other means, which will not help solve problems, but will create new issues. Now the world needs to seek security through cooperation and promote common security through consultation and dialogue. For example, in the process of denuclearisation of the Korean Peninsula, unilateral sanctions and extreme pressure cannot solve the problem. While it is possible to achieve a bright future, through equal consultation and coordinated progress, taking into account the concerns of all parties.

The status quo is that the United States tends to sanction other countries. Although the sanctions have caused difficulties for these countries for a certain period of time, they have not made them act according to the intention of the United States, but have aroused anti-US sentiments. Sanctions are essentially an unequal international relationship. Hegemonic countries designate unsatisfactory countries as 'rogue countries' and treat them with the attitude of police to prisoners. This approach will become increasingly unsuitable for contemporary situations, the most recent example being the August 14, 2020 US Security Council meeting that the arms embargo on Iran must be extended. The resolution requires nine out of the fifteen members of the Security Council to vote in favour, and no veto from permanent members. As a result, only the United States and Dominica voted in favour, while Russia and China both gave vetoes. Even the United Kingdom, France, Germany, Belgium and other countries all abstained from voting, which is equivalent to de facto opposition to the U.S. proposal.[4]

The universal security concept is a comprehensive security concept that takes into account traditional and non-traditional areas. The urgency of global challenges such as climate change makes it difficult for us to distinguish the so-called 'high politics' and 'low politics' issues, which need to be dealt with comprehensively, instead of ignoring non-traditional security challenges facing mankind such as climate change from the self-interest of a country like the U.S. under the Trump administration. The reason why non-traditional security is becoming more and more important is precisely because people in the world are increasingly becoming an inseparable community with a shared future. The crisis of the COVID-19 epidemic is one of the biggest lessons. The epidemic once again reminds us that mankind is a community with a shared future. No country can stay out of it. Cooperation and mutual assistance are the only correct choices.

In the midst of the global COVID-19 pandemic crisis, the Trump administration not only did not take the initiative to help global anti-pandemic cooperation, but instead politicised the issue, constantly attacking China and the World Health Organisation (WHO), even announcing its withdrawal from WHO. This self-prioritising behaviour of the United States undermines global leadership, global anti-pandemic cooperation, and exacerbates the crisis in its own country at a time when the world needs leadership and cooperation most. In the process of fighting the pandemic, China has responded to this non-traditional security crisis with the mind of a community with a shared future for mankind, empathising with the suffering in other countries in the world. It helped the other countries when it was still struggling. China dispatched medical experts to assist with anti-pandemic materials and experience. At the same time, the Chinese government actively promoted the construction of a healthy 'One Belt One Road', wishing to strengthen mutual assistance, implement joint prevention and control around the world, and promised to provide vaccines as global public goods. China's aid has provided warm and powerful support for the global fight against the pandemic. China's supply chain has provided the world with the most resourceful anti-pandemic materials, a guarantee of the world peace.

Universal security concept is a sustainable security concept that coordinates security and development. 'Development is the greatest security'.[5] Security without development is unsustainable, and the road to development leads not only to prosperity, but also to sustained peace and stability. As the most belligerent country in the world, the United States has been waging wars all over the world, destroying the foundation of local development, and causing some originally prosperous regions and countries to fall into turmoil and depression. The stagnation of development creates a vicious circle of crisis.

We live in an era of general peace, but also an era of ever-increasing security risks. The security challenges we confront are getting more and more complex. The universal security concept of communitism provides a new way for mankind to solve the security dilemma.

2. The concept of common development versus zero-sum game, the concept of free development

At the 29th Wanshou Forum, an African representative asked: Europeans, Americans, and Japanese have all been in Africa before. We used to be full of expectations, but apart from the plundered resources, Africa has gained nothing. Today, the Chinese people came. So how can we trust you that we will not be hurt again?

In dealing with this problem, there is no solution under the old thinking framework of Realism and Liberalism. The concept of communal development is a development idea that surpasses Realism and Liberalism. It provides a new path for mankind to solve the development dilemma.

For the pragmatists, development is a zero-sum game of competition for resources, markets, and control, while the concept of communal development believes that development is not a zero-sum game but a win-win situation. Make the cake bigger and fairly divide the cake.

Liberalism believes that as long as free trade, free investment, and free competition are maintained, the government should do nothing else. However the liberal development concept has also failed to solve the dilemma of unequal and unbalanced development in the world.

The communal concept is the concept of mutual development, which goes beyond the concept of zero-sum and free development. It believes that the old way of taking developing countries as the target of resource plunder done by the West, should not be followed, but to help the host country to enhance its indigenous development capability. The construction of 'One Belt One Road' is different from the neoliberal international development order, instead it is under the framework of free investment and free trade, providing a development support platform with all elements, including capital, infrastructure, technology, talented people, market, equipment, and so forth.

The communal development requires closer cooperation among countries, and the coordinated development of different countries through direct connection in strategy, policy, and project realisation. By coordinating fiscal, financial, investment and other policies, the coordinated development of different countries can be achieved.

The communal development requires the provision of public goods for global development, and 'One Belt and One Road' is the world's largest public good. For example, by connecting facilities in different countries, logistic costs can be greatly reduced, making the previously expensive international trade routes profitable.

Rwanda is still remembered by many as the tragic and failed country that experienced the genocide of millions of people in the 1990s. In fact, today's Rwanda has undergone earth-shaking changes. It has achieved the miracle of rapid economic growth, and has become the star of African development, showing a vibrant and prosperous scene. Of course, this is first of all due to domestic political stability and good policies. At the same time, a very important condition is to catch the fast train of China's rise, and seize the once-in-a-lifetime opportunity that China's rise brings. Rwanda not only adopts a friendly policy towards China, but also imitates the Chinese model in many aspects, keeping up with the pace of China's development. China has become Rwanda's largest trading partner and project contractor. The roads built by Chinese companies account for 70% of the total mileage of Rwanda's national roads.[6] China not only assisted Rwanda in building gymnasiums, diplomatic buildings, various factories and enterprises, but also helped Rwanda develop agriculture, digging wells, and relieving their drinking water difficulties. The Chinese factor has really driven the development of Rwanda. After the COVID-19 outbreak, China's live streaming business flourished, and Rwanda also followed China's pace, selling out 1.5 tons of Rwandan coffee in one second on China's live streaming platform, which is equivalent to their sales volume in the past year. Rwandan students have studied the live stream business model in China, hoping to set up similar business back in their country.

3. Views on the theory of blending of civilisations versus theory on clash of civilisations in multiculturalism

At present, multiculturalism is facing unprecedented difficulties in both domestic and international politics in the Western world, and some American politicians are again advocating the theory of clash of civilisations. For example, Kiron Skinner, director of the Policy Planning at the U.S. State Department's Office, sees China-U.S. competition as the first clash of civilisations that the U.S. has faced with a non-Western rival.[7] The theories of clash of civilisations and multiculturalism are twins, both of which are artificially strengthening the identity boundaries between people, eventually leading to division and conflict.

The communalist view of civilisation is the view of the blending of civilisations, which transcends the theory of 'clash of civilisations and multiculturalism'. The idea is to blur the boundaries of artificial division and strengthen the idea that we belong to a community. At the same time, we place great emphasis on diversity, and diversity is for connecting all. Traditional Chinese culture emphasises tolerance and integration between cultures. During the process of Buddhism being introduced into China, there was also large-scale anti-Buddhist movements, as Buddhism was not tolerated by Confucian orthodoxy. But eventually, Buddhism, Confucianism, and Daoism merged into one after many collisions. Since the Ming and Qing dynasties, most national leaders advocated the unity of the three religions. Zhu Jianshen, Emperor Xianzong of the Ming dynasty, created a painting *A Mass of Harmony* (一团和气) in which the faces of three figures were fused together. On the left is the profile of an old man wearing a Daoist crown, on the right is the profile of a scholar wearing a Confucian square scarf, and in the middle is a monk with a disc-like face. In the postscript on the painting, he wrote: 'Three religions unify as One Body; Nine trends are from One Source, Hundred Schools follow One Principle, and Thousand Laws render in One Rule'. The spiritual world of the ancient Chinese people also follows the pattern of 'one-to-three and three-to-one' as depicted in the picture. Buddha cultivates the mind, Daoism cultivates one's body, and Confucianism cultivates the world. The three schools, Confucianism, Buddhism and Daoism, play a role of blending and complementing in people's lives.

The concept of civilisation integration believes that different cultures are equal, there is no difference between superior and inferior, and there is no difference between the centre and the edge, and no one civilisation can replace the other. Civilisations would not conflict, but can learn from each other. Diversity of civilisations does not mean that 'people who are not my race must have different hearts', namely artificially strengthening the boundaries of different groups. It can be achieved through cultural exchange, and we can find a common ground. In May 2019, the Conference on Dialogue of Asian Civilisations held in China was a grand gathering that not only respects cultural diversity, but also seeks the integration of civilisations. The concept of civilisation integration does not advocate 'universal values', but common values; does not export development models, but contributes to the solutions and wisdom of various countries.

4. Partnership versus alliance

Alignment is an ancient state behaviour that reached its peak during the Cold War, when different states were divided into 'Eastern and Western' blocs. However, in a world where interests are highly intertwined, while winning allies, the alliance strategy also creates enemies and confronts different alliance groups. The Non-Aligned Movement, which began in the 20th century, asserts the basic principles of independence, autonomy, non-alignment, and non-grouping. In the 1990s, China became an observer state of the Non-Aligned Movement, and clearly stated that it 'will not form an alliance with any country or group of countries, and will not participate in any military group'.[8] Of course, the Non-Aligned Movement is only a passive principle for handling state-to-state relations. Since the 1990s, China has promoted the building of more active partnerships between states.

At present, mankind has increasingly become a community with a shared future, the relationship between countries has become difficult to define in terms of alliances or hostility, and the world can no longer be divided into two opposing groups. The intertwined interests of countries are nothing more than a close and distant relationship that is differentiated according to the closeness of the community. The 'communalist' state relationship is a partnership that transcends alliance and non-alignment.

Communitism emphasises on engaging in partnership rather than alliance, and constantly expands the 'circle of friends', but does not engage in exclusive small circles. In bilateral relations, a partnership of 'mutual respect, seeking common ground while reserving differences, and win-win cooperation' should be established. This kind of partnership is a voluntary and equal cooperative relationship. China has established cooperative relationships at different levels with more than 70 countries and groups of countries, and with the deepening of friendship, the level of cooperation has been continuously improved. For example, recently, Sino-Russian relations have been upgraded to a comprehensive strategic partnership of coordination in the new era. (see Table 1).

Table 1 Countries and groups of countries partnering with China

Partnership	Countries/Groups	Quantity
Comprehensive strategic partnership of coordination for a new era	Russia	1
All-weather strategic partnership	Pakistan	1
Comprehensive strategic partnership of coordination	Vietnam, Cambodia, Myanmar, Laos, Thailand, Sierre Leone, Mozambique, Zimbabwe Namibia, Egypt, Argentina	11
Strategic partnership	The Republic of Korea, India, Sri Lanka, Turkey, Afghanistan	5
All-round strategic partnership	Germany	1
Comprehensive strategic partnership	United Kingdom, France. Brazil, Denmark, Spain, Italy, Portugal, Kazakhstan, Mexico, South Africa, Greece, Belarus, Indonesia, Peru, Venezuela, Malaysia, Australia, Algeria, New Zealand, Mongolia, Egypt (EU)	22 (2+1)
Strategic cooperation partnership	United Arab Emirates, Angola, Uzbekistan, Poland, Tajikistan, Turkmenistan, Nigeria, Canada, Serbia, Chile, Ukraine, Qatar, Kyrgyzstan, (ASEAN), (AU)	15 (13+2)

Partnership	Countries/Groups	Quantity
Mutually beneficial strategic partnership	Ireland	1
Strategic partnership	Turkey, Saudi Arabia, Philippines, Brunei, (Arab League)	5 (4+1)
All-round friendly partnership	Belgium	1
All-round partnership of coordination	Singapore	1
All-round friendly partnership	Romania, Bulgaria, Maldives	3
Comprehensive partnership	Republic of Congo, Croatia, Nepal, Tanzania, Bangladesh, Ethiopia, Netherlands, Timor-Leste, (CELAC)	9 (8+1)
Friendly partnership of coordination	Hungary	1
Important partnership	Fiji	1
Friendly partnership	Jamaica	1
		79 (74+5)

Source: Men Honghua, Liu Xiaoyang, 2015, 'China Partnership Strategy Evaluation and Prospect', *World Economics and Politics*, No. 2, revised by the author.

As Marx and Engels once said: 'In the conditions of a true community each person obtains his own freedom in and through his union.'[9] Realism and Liberalism are 'seeing the world through a small state', namely short-sighted. Meanwhile Communitism is 'viewing the world from the perspective of the world', with a grand perspective of generosity and appropriate measures. On the one hand, the community with a shared future for mankind is a real community that highly respects the independence and equality of its members, which makes it different from the false community that requires the transfer of sovereignty, and in reality the strong bully the weak. On the other hand, through equal and free association, the members will better themselves with the help of the common interests and common strength formed by the association.

Communitism is a new paradigm of international relations proposed in response to the global development trends and challenges faced by global governance in the 21st century. It incorporates and integrates the advanced achievements of previous international relations theories and transcends the two dominant paradigms of international relations—Realism and Liberalism (see Table 2). A community with a shared future for mankind is an upgrade of the international order, promoting its development in a more just, inclusive and sound direction, rather than replacing it and starting over.

Table 2 Comparison of three paradigms of international relations

	Realism	*Liberalism*	*Communism*
Basic premise	Anarchy in international politics; competition for state power	The link between individual freedom and the world political order; the interdependence of globalisation	The interdependence of globalisation; the unbalanced nature of globilisation; the expansion of the global public sphere
Representation theory	Classical Realism, Neorealism, Offensive Realism, Defensive Realism	Idealism; Institutionalism	The Theory of Community of Shared Future for Mankind
Security concept	Balance of power security	Collective security	Universal security
Developing view	Zero-sum game	Free development	Co-development
Civilisation view	Clash of Civilisations	Multiculturalism	Blend of civilisation
State relations	Allied or Hostile		Partnerships
Geographical relationship	Geopolitics	Economic geography	Political Economy of Geo-development

'In a peaceful world, everyone feels the same weather.' Communitism represents the mighty world trend of the 21st century. Examining today's world, the liberal order has declined sharply, and the 'realism' international strategy represented by 'America First' has cast a huge shadow on the prospects of mankind and caused great division and opposition in the world. Nevertheless, the concept of world progress represented by a 'community with a shared future for mankind' has brought bright hope to mankind, provided a new engine for a new type of globalisation, and will lead the human world to develop great cooperation.

---

1 <http://www.ftchinese.com/story/001083409?dailypop&archive>, [4 May 2021]
2 <https://www.mitpressjournals.org/doi/full/10.1162/isec_a_00342>, [4 May 2021]
3 Xi Jinping, 2014, 'Actively Establishing an Asian Security Concept to Create a New Situation for Security Cooperation—Speech at the Fourth Summit of the Conference on Interaction and Confidence Measures in Asia', *Xinhuanet*, 21 May. [习近平：《积极树立亚洲安全观 共创安全合作新局面———在亚洲相互协作与信 任措施会议第四次峰会上的讲话》，新华网 2014 年 5 月 21 日]
4 Xinhua News Agency, United Nations, 14 Aug, 2020
5 Xi Jinping, 2014, 'Actively Establishing an Asian Security Concept to Create a New Situation for Security Cooperation – Speech at the Fourth Summit of the Conference on Interaction and Confidence Measures in Asia', *Xinhuanet*, 21st May. [习近平：《积极树立亚洲安全观 共创安全合作新局面——在亚洲相互协作与信任措施会议第四次峰会上的讲话》，新华网2014年5月21日]
6 Xi Jinping, 2018, 'China-Luxembourg friendship is higher than a mountain', *People's Daily*, 22 July, p. 1. [习近平： 《中卢友谊情比山高》，《人民日报》 2018 年 7 月 22 日第 1 版]
7 <https://www.newsweek.com/china-threat-state-department-race-caucasian-1413202>, [4 May 2021]
8 Jiang Zemin, 1992, 'Accelerating the pace of reform, opening up and modernization, and striving for greater victory in the cause of socialism with Chinese characteristics – Report at the 14th National Congress of the Communist Party of China', 12 October. [江泽民：《加快改革开放和现代化建设步伐，夺取有中国特色社会主义事业的更大胜利——在中国共产党第十四次全国代表大会上的报告》，1992年10月12日]
9 *Selected Works of Marx and Engels*, 2012, Vol. 1, People's Publishing House, p. 199. [《马克思恩格斯选集》(第 1 卷)，人民出版社 2012 年版，第199页]

CHAPTER 14

'One Belt One Road' and Geo-Development `Political Economy Exploration*

[* Yan Yilong, 2019, 'The Belt and Road Initiative is not a geopolitical expansion', Frontline, No.2. Significant revisions were made when it was included in this book.]

In the eight years since the joint construction of the 'One Belt One Road' initiative (BRI), great achievements have been made and widely recognised by the international community. At the same time, some people in the West are keen to use traditional geopolitical theories to explain China's BRI practice, believing that China is pursuing geopolitical expansion. For example, the Heritage Foundation's *2019 U.S. Military Power Index* listed China as one of the top six global threats alongside Russia, the Democratic People's Republic of Korea (DPRK), Iran, Middle Eastern terrorism and Afghanistan-Pakistan terrorism. One of the important reasons is that China's BRI has promoted the geopolitical expansion of Eurasia and the Indian Ocean, touching the global interests of the United States.[1]

The smearing of the 'One Belt One Road' by the United States is not only out of its strategic goal of suppressing China, but also reflects the inherent geopolitical thinking of Westerners. Western geopolitics looks at geography from the perspective of geo-war and geo-strife. Regardless of 'land power theory' and 'sea power theory', they all consider how to occupy key areas, gain geographical advantages by controlling key resources, and win geopolitical war for controlling the world. On land they heard the neighing of war horses, on the sea they heard the roar of naval guns, and their ears were filled with the sound of scramble and slaughter. Halford Mackinder, the originator of the Land Power theory, regarded horses and camels as the most important mobile forces for land supremacy, and ships as the most important mobile forces for maritime supremacy. BRI looks at geography from the perspective of geo-development and geo-cooperation. What Chinese people hear from the land Silk Road are the camel bells of business and travel, and from the Maritime Silk Road comes the sound of the boats of maritime trade. All ears are filled with the sound of friendly exchanges and win-win cooperation. It is based on this kind of thinking that China proposed the 'One Belt One Road' initiative—the most ambitious geo-development initiative in the 21st century.

We need to explore new academic theories to explain the BRI practice and provide the necessary theoretical resources for further promoting it. It is a new model of common development, international cooperation and cultural exchange. It has many new practices and new ideas, and provides the possibility to explore the 'political economy of geo-development'.

1. Building a big platform for geopolitical development

The two dominant paradigms of Western international relations theory—Realism and Liberalism—focus on traditional security. Realism is the most influential paradigm in international theory. Although there are different variants such as Classical Realism, New Realism, Offensive Realism and Defensive Realism, they all emphasise that in an anarchic international system, countries need to achieve national security through international power games. Among them, Offensive Realism further believes that powerful countries will actively pursue their own security interests and maximise their power, so conflicts between powerful countries are inevitable. The Liberalism paradigm also focuses on security, and the theory of Institutional Transnationalism, constructs a collective security strategy based on the Liberalistic international order. Although Liberal Institutionalism emphasises economic integration and leads to interdependence among countries, it still articulates that this interdependence helps ensure international security.

A security-focused state-to-state relationship is essentially a competition for power, a zero-sum game. A security-centric geopolitical strategy requires control over key geopolitical, political, and economic geographies to dominate the world. Mackinder summed up the key to his global geopolitics as control over the 'Heartland/Pivot Area'.[2] While Alfred Mahan's Sea Power theory emphasises controlling the world by controlling the ocean.[3] The key to Nicholas Spykman's 'Rimland' argument is the control of the Eurasian coast.

This serves as a theoretical background for some people in the West to interpret the 'One Belt One Road' initiative proposed by China, as expanding international power and advancing the security agenda. Stephen Bannon, Trump's former chief strategist and senior adviser, claimed that China's 'One Belt One Road' is a new practice that mixes three geopolitical theories: World Island theory, Land Power theory and Sea Power theory.

Bannon's view is that 'with the heart of the villain, to measure the great heart of the gentleman'; in fact, it is the United States, not China, that uses a mixture of different geopolitical theories to achieve and maintain global hegemony. The United States is keen to control the sea, and Mahan, who proposed the 'sea power theory', was a U.S. naval strategist. The United States established a powerful navy, tried to control the ocean to gain world dominance, and successively gained many islands in the Pacific Ocean to establish maritime hegemony. During the Reagan administration in the 1980s, the U.S. Navy announced that it would control the world's 16 pivot points, which are not only the military hubs at sea, but also the throats of the world's maritime trade routes.[4] During the Cold War, the core of the competition between the US-led North Atlantic Treaty Organisation (NATO) and the Soviet-led Warsaw Pact, between the two military blocs lied the central area of the world island. After the Cold War, NATO continued to expand eastward, trying to suppress Russia in the struggle for the central area; this is the practice of the Land Power theory. The Americans further believe that in order to ensure the security of the United States and global hegemony, it is necessary to control the marginal areas of the world island, and then put forward the Rimland theory. During World War Two, the United States allied with the United Kingdom, using Britain as a base to attack the European continent. During the Cold War, it tried to control the Korean Peninsula and Vietnam, and at the same time formed alliances with Japan, the Republic of Korea, and China's Taiwan to fight against the great powers in the Asian continent. All are the practice of Rimland theory.[5] Today, the U.S. geopolitical goal is to occupy the global sea, air, land and cyber domains.

Unlike the United States, BRI is not centred on traditional security, but on development. China has no intention of replacing the United States as a hegemonic country in any sense. BRI is not promoting geopolitical expansion, but building a political and economic platform for the common development of all countries in the world.

Contrary to the expectations of 'geopolitical theory', BRI focuses on the geopolitical economy centred on development. It aims to reshape the political and economic geography of the world, build a platform for the common development, and achieve mutual benefit between China and other countries. It does not try to compete for world dominance by controlling key geographies. Geopolitical control embodies the zero-sum thinking of limited resources in the 20th century, competing with each other, dominating others but not being dominated by others, causing violent conflicts leading to world wars. The geo-developmental political and economic platform embodies the win-win thinking of resource expansion in the 21st century, builds a development platform, realises common development, benefits others and then oneself, creates mutual benefit and win-win results, and promotes world harmony.

Referring to the framework proposed by the World Bank's 2009 World Development Report 'Reshaping the World Economic Geography', BRI is a political and economic platform for international geo-development that shapes points, lines, dimensions and trends, and promotes the agglomeration of international development accordingly.

Point agglomerated – to increase economic density: Increasing economic density refers to increasing economic and population agglomeration in urban and economic zones, and developing agglomeration economies. The construction of BRI promotes economic development through industrial layout, park construction, port construction, and so forth, forming agglomeration effects and increasing the density of economic development. As of 2018, Chinese enterprises had built 82 overseas economic and trade cooperation zones in countries along the route, with a cumulative investment of 28.9 billion USD and 3,995 enterprises in these zones, promoting the aggregation of local economic development factors.[6]

For example, the 'China-Belarus Industrial Park' also known as the 'great stone industrial park' is a benchmark project for cooperation between China and Belarus under the framework of BRI. China Merchants Group played an important role in the implementation of this project and is also the main Chinese shareholder. China Merchants Group is a state-owned enterprise with rich experience in the development and operation of parks. When we went to investigate in the summer of 2018, we learned that China Merchants Group began to participate in the project in 2015. A major concern is the inconvenience of Belarus as a landlocked country exporting goods. Later, they decided to participate in the construction after they learned that the port of Klaipeda in Lithuania, which is nearly 500 kilometres away from the industrial park, is the estuary to the Baltic Sea. At the end of 2018, the author participated in an international seminar in Minsk, the capital of Belarus, to commemorate the 40th anniversary of China's reform and opening up. At the meeting, both government officials and scholars were discussing the 'China-Belarus Industrial Park', and they were full of hope and longing for it. It was like a ray of light over the grey sky of Minsk. After the meeting, when we visited the 'China-Belarus Industrial Park', which is 25 kilometres away from Minsk, the snow-swept 'China-Belarus Industrial Park' still seemed deserted, but some modern buildings had been erected, and many mechanical equipment still remained running. From the interviews, we learned that much of China's experience in park construction had been utilised here. They set up development companies to develop parks and build modern industrial parks that integrate both industry and city.

The construction of the park insisted on planning first, carrying out industrial positioning, division of functional areas, staged development, land levelling and hardening, water, electricity, ventilation, access, network and other construction. It can be referred to as 'seven connections and one levelling'. To attract enterprises to settle in, they used the method of tax reduction: the profit tax for the first 10 years of the settled enterprises is fully exempted, and the tax is halved from the 20th to the 50th year. According to reports, by July 2020, the first batch of factories have started operation, and 22 of the 62 settled enterprises have built factories there. Driverless cars and 5G technology have been put into testing, an emerging industrial park is on the rise and will undoubtedly become an agglomeration highlight for the modern economy of Belarus.[7]

Line unblocked – shortening economic distance: Economic distance is not physical distance, but refers to the time economic cost of the movement of goods and people. The efficiency of economic activities can be improved by shortening the economic distance. BRI vigorously promotes infrastructure construction, and promoting facility connectivity will also shorten the economic distance between different development points. China has proposed the 'six corridors and six roads, multiple countries and multiple ports' to promote the main framework of BRI construction. Among them, the 'six corridors' refer to the six major international economic cooperation corridors, namely the New

Eurasian Continental Bridge, China-Mongolia-Russia, China-Central Asia-West Asia, China-Indochina Peninsula, China-Pakistan and Bangladesh-China-India-Myanmar. 'Six-roads' refer to the integrated information network of railways, highways, shipping, aviation, pipelines and space, and is the main content of infrastructure interconnection. 'Multiple countries' refers to the group of early cooperation countries. 'Multiple ports' refer to a number of cooperative ports that ensure the safety and smoothness of major maritime transport channels.[3] Infrastructure construction has greatly promoted the connectivity between countries along the route and shortened the economic distance between different countries.

Most Central Asian countries are landlocked countries and are in a disadvantageous position in the maritime-dominated trade process; the construction of the land-based Silk Road has brought new development opportunities for their development. The ancient Silk Road was a passage connecting East Asia and Europe. Central Asia once acted as the trade hub of the Silk Road and prospered. Central Asian countries have memories of the glory of the country during the ancient Silk Road period. Today's BRI can help them have better access to global markets and better connectivity with other countries. The opening of Trans-Eurasia Logistics has strengthened the trade of countries along the route. By 2019, the cumulative number of China-Europe Railway Express routes has exceeded 20,000, with rapid development. In 2019, there were 8,225 trains, reaching 74 cities in 21 European countries. The opening of new seaports and land passages connecting to the seaports has also brought new convenience to the trade for landlocked countries. For example, the construction of the China-Pakistan Economic Corridor and the Gwadar Sea Port will not only facilitate the maritime trade between China and Pakistan, but also facilitate the maritime trade of neighbouring countries.

Demension connectivity – Eliminate circulation barriers: Eliminating circulation barriers can improve the efficiency of economic activities. China has adopted a large number of trade connectivity and policy communication measures to reduce the cost of trade customs clearance and capital circulation, promoting the flow of goods, personnel, information and capital. By the end of 2019, China had signed or upgraded 5 free trade agreements with 13 countries along the route, and was making negotiations on 12 free trade areas. At the same time, China actively promotes the formation of capital financing mechanisms, and has formed a capital financing platform with the Asian Infrastructure Investment Bank, the New Development Bank of BRICS, and the Silk Road Fund as the main carriers. For the majority of developing countries, an important challenge to paving the way for development is the investment shortage. BRI provides great financing opportunities for the economic construction of various countries. It does not have much advantage in terms of interest rates compared with the development assistance projects of the World Bank and other institutions; nevertheless it has become the most important source of external funds for many countries due to the large scale of funds that can be provided and more flexible repayment methods. This is a relief, not a 'debt trap'. For example, the Kenya Mombasa-Nairobi Railway, which opened in 2017, is the first railway built since Kenya's independence. It not only helps the Kenyan people realise the dream of a new railway channel, but also takes a solid step to connect East African countries by railway. Localised management has been preliminarily realised through technology transfer and training. The low-interest loans from the Export-Import Bank made up for the key investment gap in Kenya. At the same time, due to the construction of the railway, local economic growth was boosted, the value of assets such as land was increased, and the Kenyan government's ability to repay the loan was enhanced.[9] As of the end of May 2020, the Mombasa-Nairobi Railway has transported 4.32 million passengers and 830,000 twenty-foot equivalent units of goods, driving economic growth in East Africa.[10]

Trend in style – the point-axis development model: Economic geography emphasises the point-and-axis development model, whether it is gradient transfer or the so-called 'geese flying model', it is the infiltration of industrial transfer and economic development along the main transportation line. BRI is a development initiative that connects points into lines. The land-based Silk Economic Belt and the 21st-Century Maritime Silk Road are not only trade lines, but also extensions of foreign investment and industrial development. Moreover, this point-axis model is connected to domestic and international routes. BRI is in line with the layout of the 'four horizontal and four vertical' urban agglomerations model in China, with the layout of the main transportation lines following this. The design of the 'six economic corridors' also promotes opening up the main road of economic geography at home and abroad.

The construction of BRI will make major changes in the geopolitical development pattern. In the future, there will be three major developed economic circles in the world. The first is the developed economic circle in North America, the second is the developed economic circle in Europe, and the third is the emerging economic circle in East Asia. China's development will also radiate and drive the development of neighbouring countries, and form a pattern of mutual benefit and common development with them. The radiation effect can be achieved by increasing the opening of border areas, creating inland open highlands, building nodes for the Maritime Silk Road, and promoting China's development to Southeast Asia, the Indian Ocean, the South Pacific and other regions. At the same time, a new Eurasian Continental Bridge that connects the East Asian Economic Circle and the European Economic Circle will be formed to smooth the channels for cooperation and exchange between countries. The middle area between the two developed economic circles connecting the two ends of the Eurasian Continental Bridge can be regarded as a geographical hub.

Of course, when we say that BRI is focused on development, it does not mean that it cannot promote security. For example, in terms of energy security, BRI improves energy through the connection of oil and gas pipelines with neighbouring countries, hence enhancing security of resources. At the same time, participating in the construction of Pakistan's Gwadar Sea Port and Myanmar's Kyaukpyu Port has also added two more ports on the Indian Ocean for China, thus breaking the shipping bottleneck that China's energy resources imports and cargo imports having to pass through the Strait of Malacca for a long time. The security of energy resources and trade has been further guaranteed. This kind of security is not the traditional military security concerned in international politics. It is a non-traditional security. It is a defensive security that enhances national autonomy. It does not pose a threat to any country, nor does it reduce the security interests of any country, unless those, obsessed with regional or global hegemony will consider this a threat, because they usually would not allow other countries to have the right to independent development.

2. Building a new order of geopolitical development

From an explicit perspective, the Liberalistic international order is manifested in the value norms, interaction norms and system arrangements that are commonly accepted by members of the international community. Politically it confirms the sovereign equality of states, national self-determination and other principles. Economically, the principles of free trade and multilateralism have a progressive side.

However, in the long run, the Liberalistic international order is inherently unequal. Economically such inequality manifests as unbalanced globalisation, that is, trade liberalisation is based on the premise of not harming the industrial interests of developed countries. Technology diffusion is based on the premise of not disturbing the technological leadership of developed countries. The industrial division of labour system with global participation is based on the premise that the developed countries occupy the high end of the global value chain. Politically manifested as unequal international relations, that is, common value norms are the transformation of Western values into 'universal values'. Formal equality of states presupposes substantial inequality, and the multilateral international system presupposes the control of hegemonic states.

Since the second decade of the new century, the break in the process of integration of the global capitalist system has had a huge impact on the 'liberal' international system. The Trump administration's unilateralism and the Covid-19 epidemic have caused a huge impact on the 'liberal' international order and are in a precarious state. For a hegemonic country, the liberal international order is a façade to decorate and expand its power, and it can be completely reshaped if it does not conform to its interests. For developing countries, the globalisation that the liberal international order allows them to participate in has a ceiling set by hegemonic countries. Once this ceiling is reached, one cannot develop their own window of opportunity by integrating into the global system dominated by hegemonic countries. Because the window will be closed.

As the practice of the concept of a community with a shared future for mankind, BRI has broken through the liberal international political and economic order, not only creating a new window of strategic opportunity for China's development, but also the start of a new and better political and economic order for the world.

The new model of common development shifts from unbalanced globalisation to a more balanced one. Globalisation under the liberal international order is a centre-periphery one, dominated by capital. Its essence is an unbalanced globalisation that projects capital and labour-employment relations onto the relations of deprivation between countries. BRI goes beyond simply emphasising on maximising national interests, and has a certain degree of internationalism. As President Xi Jinping pointed out, 'Everything we do is to seek happiness for the people, rejuvenation for the nation, and great harmony for the world.'[11] BRI is a community of mutual benefits, focusing on win-win development, thus transcending the liberal globalisation model. It is embodied in the following aspects: it promotes the development of countries along the route. From 2013 to 2019, China's direct investment in countries along BRI exceeded 114 billion USD.[12] In particular, the investment in large-scale infrastructure has made up for the most important investment shortage in the local area and played a major role in promoting the economic take-off of various countries. As of 2018, the accumulated trade value in goods with countries along the route has exceeded 5 trillion USD, and the total investment in the overseas economic and trade cooperation zones established in countries along the route has exceeded 20 billion USD, creating hundreds of thousands of jobs and generating billions of USD in local tax revenue.[13] BRI, by improving the global industrial supply chain, enables developing countries to better participate in the global division of labour, and at the same time obtain a more favourable position in the value chain, and enhances the ability of host countries to participate in the international division of labour. BRI is a development initiative with developing countries as the main body. It transcends the centre-periphery pattern and will vigorously promote the all-round rise of developing countries. State-owned capital is the main force in China's promotion of BRI. It goes beyond simple profit maximisation and has a stronger political orientation, promoting many national collaborative projects with high risks, long cycles and small profit margins.

 The construction of BRI has truly improved the endogenous development capacity of the host countries. There are a large number of newly constructed roads, ports, energy facilities, water conservancy facilities, parks, factories, buildings, and so forth. They have become the real national wealth and an important step on the way to the peak of development for the host countries. Take Kyrgyzstan for example. It does not have abundant oil and natural gas resources. Although it has abundant hydropower resources, they not been well developed for a long time. The water conservancy resource centre is far away from the electricity centre. Electricity transmission needs to pass through the neighbouring Uzbekistan, where it is necessary to pay 'tolls', with also a loss of power. Every winter, the government needs to make a lot of financial subsidies for heating and electricity, and achieving energy independence is an important strategic goal. China helped Kyrgyzstan develop water conservancy and hydropower facilities, building a high-voltage power transmission pipeline network, which enabled the rich water resources in the south to be transported to the power centre in the north. In this way, Kyrgyzstan achieved energy independence.[14]

A new model of international cooperation is formed, shifting from strategic competition to strategic collaboration. The traditional intergovernmental development cooperation model is mainly carried out in the form of international trade and development assistance, and still faces the problems of global development failure and global market failure. BRI is a new model of cooperation between countries. The governments of various countries coordinate and link development to promote policy communication, facility connectivity, unimpeded trade, financial integration, and people-to-people bonds. China and the countries along the BRI will coordinate their strategies and plans, and build development partnerships. As of January 2021, 140 countries and 31 international organisations have signed 205 'Belt and Road' cooperation agreements with China. BRI and its core concepts have been written into relevant documents of the United Nations, G20, APEC, Shanghai Cooperation Organisation, Asia-Europe Meeting, and other regional organisations and multilateral platforms. BRI has achieved strategic alignment with many countries, such as Russia's 'Eurasian Economic Union', Kazakhstan's 'Bright Road' plan, Mongolia's 'Steppe Road' plan, the European Union's 'Juncker Plan', and Indonesia's 'Global Ocean Pivot' concept. BRI and the initiatives of these countries not only do not conflict, but form complementarity and connectivity, injecting new impetus into the realisation of these national initiatives.

International initiatives between different countries from the perspective of *geopolitics* try to divide the sphere of influence of geostrategic forces, which will lead to competition and conflict between countries. International initiatives between different countries from the perspective of *geo-development* can connect and help each other. For example, Russia, Belarus, Kazakhstan, Armenia, Kyrgyzstan and other countries advocate the 'Eurasian Economic Union' to promote the free flow of goods, services, capital and labour among member states, achieving regional economic integration. The ultimate goal is to build an economic union similar to the

EU. The member states of the Eurasian Economic Union are fundamentally countries along the 'One Belt One Road'. BRI not only achieves a good connection with the Eurasian Economic Union, but also injects new impetus into the construction of the Eurasian Economic Union. The 'Belt and Road' has invested a large number of projects in these countries, which has promoted the development of these regions and further expanded their market demand, at the same time, the interconnection of infrastructure has made the mutual trade between the Commonwealth of Independent States more convenient. Of course, achieving strategic alignment is premised on mutual strategic trust between countries. With strategic mutual trust, some conflicts can also be resolved through negotiation. India has huge doubts in BRI, because it still holds the perspective of traditional geopolitical conflicts, believing that it will weaken India's dominant position in South Asia.

A new model of international communication, shifting from inequality to equal political order. A true community is one in which members participate equally. BRI is a community of equal consultation, participation and sharing. China is the initiator, but it emphasises extensive consultation, joint contribution and shared benefits. Through the implementation of the 'Silk Road' scholarship program and the establishment of overseas educational institutions, China has cultivated talented persons of technical and management skills for the countries along the route. In 2017, China trained more than 300,000 international students from countries along the route, and sent more than 60,000 students to those countries.[15] China advocates common values instead of 'universal values', conducts exchanges and dialogues among civilisations without exporting ideology, and provides Chinese solutions without exporting Chinese models. 'A just cause attracts much support while an unjust cause finds little.' BRI has become a multilateral international cooperation framework that has a significant impact on world development. It has not only been widely welcomed by many countries and international institutions, but also written into the resolution of the 71st United Nations General Assembly.

BRI is not a geopolitical expansion, but a political and economic platform for geo-development. Practice is an inexhaustible source of theoretical innovation. The great practice of the 'Belt and Road' calls us to carry out theoretical innovation in the 'political economy of geo-development', and theoretical innovation will further guide practical innovation. Of course, in regards to China's geopolitical thinking, this does not necessarily mean that China does not have geopolitical thinking, just that it is different from the aggressive and predatory geopolitical thinking of the West. China's geopolitical thinking represents self-defence and counterattack. 'When Taiwan was not guarded, north China was invaded, so many traitors lurked around, the central land was rugged. We have served the country, fighting hard for many years, preparing for adventure and danger. Not until Xiongnu is defeated, could we have a place called home.'[16] Mao Zedong's poem *At the Mausoleum of the Yellow Emperor* embodies China's geopolitical struggle mentality with strong mountains and rivers, self-defence and counterattack. In the face of incoming enemies, China will firmly defend its own sovereignty and development interests. China's rise is not only a peaceful rise, but also an inclusive rise. Not only will it not repeat the wars, bloodshed and conflicts that the rise of world powers did in history, but it will also create huge opportunities for the world to develop together. The rise of China is the best gift to the world in the 21st century. Whether it is a developing country or a developed country, China is willing to be a sincere friend of all countries in the world. However, if some countries must force China into an opponent, China will become a formidable opponent, and if they must force China into an enemy, China will definitely become their invincible enemy. As Nixon predicted, if the United States does not know how to accept China's goodwill, the United States 'will one day to be confronted with the most formidable enemy that has ever existed in the history of the world.'[17]

---

1 <https://www.heritage.org/military-strength/download-the-2019-index>, [4 May 2021].
2 Halford Mackinder, 2010, *The Geographical Pivot of History*, Translated and published by the Commercial Press. [参见麦金德：《历史的地理枢纽》，商务印书馆 2010 年版]
3 Alfred Mahan, 2012, *The Influence of Sea Power upon History Series*, Translated and published by Tongxin Press. [参见马汉：《海权论》，同心出版社 2012 年版]
4 'The United States announces control of the throats of sixteen waterways', 1986, *World Knowledge*, 1 April. [《美国宣布要控制十六个航道咽喉》，《世界知识》1986年4月1日]
5 Nicholas Spykman, 2014, *The Theory of Rimland*, translated and published by Petroleum Industry Press. [斯皮克曼：《边缘地带论》，石油工业出版社 2014 年版]
6 'The State Council Information Office held a press conference on the five-year progress and prospect of the joint construction of the Belt and Road Initiative', People's Daily Online: <http://tv.people.com.cn/n1/2018/0827/c43911-30253152.html>, [4 May 2021]
7 'How about the biggest Belt and Road project in Belarus, China-Belarus Industrial Park?', 2020, *China Belt and Road Network*, 29 July. [《"一带一路"在白俄的最大项目，中白工业园怎么样了?》，中国一带一路网，2020 年 7 月 29 日]

8 Office of the Leading Group for Promoting the Construction of the Belt and Road Initiative: Jointly Building the Belt and Road Initiative: Concept, Practice and China's Contributions, China Belt and Road website: <https://www.yidaiyilu.gov.cn/zchj/qwfb/12658.htm>, [4 May 2021]
9 Zhao Yining, 2018, *China and Africa in the 21st Century*, CITIC Publishing Group, pp. 285–386. [赵忆宁：《21世纪的中国与非洲》，中信出版集团 2018 年版, 第 285–386 页]
10 *Promoting the high-quality development of the Belt and Road Initiative*, 2020, China Planning Press, p. 116. [《推动共建"一带一路"高质量发展》, 中国计划出版社 2020 年版, 第116页]
11 'Xi Jinping Meets with UN Secretary-General António Guterres', 2018, *People's Daily*, 9 April. [《习近平会见联合国秘书长古特雷斯》, 《人民日报》2018年4月9日第1版]
12 *Promoting the high-quality development of the Belt and Road Initiative*, 2020, China Planning Press, pp. 96–98.[《推进共建"一带一路"高质量发展》, 中国计划出版社 2020 年版]
13 'The State Council Information Office held a press conference on the five-year progress and prospect of the joint construction of the Belt and Road Initiative', People's Daily Online: <http://tv.people.com.cn/n1/2018/0827/c43911-30253152.html>, [4 May 2021]
14 Zhao Yining, 2015, *Grand Strategy: Five Country Visits under the Belt and Road Initiative*, Zhejiang People's Publishing House, pp. 2–50. [赵忆宁：《大战略："一带一路"五国探访》, 浙江人民出版社 2015 年版]
15 'The State Council Information Office held a press conference on the five-year progress and prospect of the joint construction of the Belt and Road Initiative', People's Daily Online: <http://tv.people.com.cn/n1/2018/0827/c43911-30253152.html>, [4 May 2021]
16 Mao Zedong, 1937, *Four-character Poems at the Mausoleum of the Yellow Emperor*, 5 April. [琉台不守，三韩为墟，辽海燕冀，汉奸何多……万里崎岖，为国效命，频年苦斗，备历险夷，匈奴未灭，何以家为]
17 Richard Nixon, 2019, *The Memoirs of Richard Nixon*, translated and published by Tiandi Press, p. 608, Originally published in 1978, Warner Books [《尼克松回忆录: 时代的破冰者》, 天地出版社 2019 年版, 第608页]

Postscript

This book is the author's phased achievement in exploring the Chinese philosophy of governance from different perspectives in the past ten years, trying to conceptualise with new interpretations and expressions of the Chinese Path.

The term Chinese Path has three interpretations: one is the theoretical interpretation and expression of the Chinese Path, the second is the principle of the right way, and the third is the principle of the middle way, the principle of 'listen to both sides and choose the middle course (执两用中)'.

Research and writing is an academic ascetic as well as an intellectual tour and adventure. 'Why do I like to argue? I have no choice'. When the draft is completed, I call it 'new account' (新语). What does this new account mean? It is not simply to make up new words to show off. First, there are new explorations in practice, and then there are 'new accounts' in theory. Each new account is just the fruit of a young thought, and it will undoubtedly require more effort to mature. I might be arrogant to say it, and please bear with me and listen. I also regard personal academic exploration and thought experiment as a kind of 'generating' process, and always maintain a spirit of awe and openness to the ever-changing practice.

I would like to thank the Institute of National Conditions of Tsinghua University and the Institute of National and Global Governance of Tsinghua University for their support in the research and writing of this book. I want to thank Professor Hu Angang and Professor Wang Shaoguang from the School of Public Administration of Tsinghua University for their comments. Thanks to editors such as Liu Yancai of China Fangzheng Press for their hard work. Each chapter of this book has been reported in different forums, seminars, and so forth, and I have been inspired by the valuable opinions of many scholars. Their names have been mentioned and credited in the chapters.

Thanks to my mother Yan Chunxiang, my wife Huang Yixuan and our child Xiao Long Bao, your silent support is my inexhaustible source of strength. Thanks to my late father Yan Zaoli, he was an ordinary and great father, and I hope to live up to his expectations.

I have been writing this book for several years with great anxiety, which can be expressed in this poem:

The academic life is sentimental;
The body and visage have decayed;
One is lamented about what is beautiful;
While thinking about new account that is wishful.

One idea bolted in mind like thunder;
Books melted into an iceberg;
The Great Way has no glory to fight for;
Only knows and punishes me making this book.

Fei Dun Zhai, Tsinghua Garden

---

1 *Mencius* [《孟子·滕文公下》]